SINGAPORE
AN ILLUSTRATED HISTORY
1941~1984

SINGAPORE
AN ILLUSTRATED HISTORY
1941~1984

Published by the Information Division, Ministry of Culture, Singapore

Editors:
Daljit Singh   V T Arasu

Text:
Daljit Singh   V T Arasu
Sulosana Karthigesu   Pang Cheng Lian

Research:
Mohd Ali Baksh   K Ismail Sudderuddin
S B Balachandrer   Chng Soh Koon
Veronica Chee May Lan   Choong Ket Che

Review Committee:
Cheng Tong Fatt   Chan Heng Chee
Pang Cheng Lian   S Chandra Mohan

First Published December 1984
Second Impression February 1985
Third Impression April 1985

Copyright © 1984 Information Division, Ministry of Culture, Singapore.

Published by the Information Division, Ministry of Culture, City Hall,
St Andrew's Road, Singapore 0617, Republic of Singapore.

ISBN 9971-75-029-5 (Softcover)

ISBN 9971-75-030-5 (Hardcover)

Design and Production: Singapore News and Publications Ltd (Book Publications Dept)
Colour Separation: Pica Colour Separation Pte Ltd
Printed by Toppan Printing Co (S) Pte Ltd

PREFACE

This book presents the history of Singapore from 1941 to 1984 in pictures and a short accompanying narrative. It is aimed at the general reader rather than the scholar. The narrative preceding the pictures in each chapter describes the main events and explains why things happened the way they did. Where photographs to illustrate an event were not available, newspaper clippings have been used.

A brief introduction sketches developments from 1819 onwards that are relevant to understanding the story. The story itself begins in 1941, for events since then have been decisive in shaping the Singapore of today. These include the Japanese invasion and occupation of Singapore; the communist united front activities and insurgency in the 1940s and 1950s; constitutional developments leading to self-government; merger with Malaysia, and then separation and independence; the partnership and the struggle for power between the communists and the PAP; the communal conflicts of the 1960s; the Indonesian Confrontation. Singapore's political evolution was also influenced by regional and international events, and the most important of these have been given their due place in the book.

The last two chapters deal with the formidable problems that confronted an independent Singapore after 1965 and how these were overcome. By the early 1980s Singapore had undergone an economic and social transformation. A new generation of political leaders were taking over the reins of government and facing a new generation of voters with new expectations and attitudes. But certain fundamentals had not changed over the years, and the last chapter seeks to draw attention to what they imply for the years ahead.

This book was prepared by Information Officers of the Ministry of Culture who did the research, gathered and selected the pictures, and wrote the captions and the narrative. However, a number of other persons made valuable contributions. Under the chairmanship of Mr Cheng Tong Fatt, a Review Committee painstakingly went through the text with the editors and provided many useful comments. Special acknowledgement also goes to Mr Dennis Bloodworth who went through the final draft and made improvements, and the staff of the History Department of the National University of Singapore who also checked the text for accuracy of facts.

1 October 1984

CONTENTS

INTRODUCTION   8

1 WAR COMES TO SINGAPORE   14

2 THE STRUGGLE TO LIVE   50

3 EARLY POLITICAL STIRRINGS   86

4 COMMUNISTS LAY THE GROUNDWORK   118

5 TURBULENT YEARS   150

6 TOWARDS NATIONHOOD   186

7 BATTLE FOR MERGER   220

8 STORMY YEARS IN MALAYSIA   266

9 THE MAKING OF A NATION   292

10 NEW HORIZONS   334

INDEX   392

PHOTO CREDITS   396

ACKNOWLEDGEMENTS   397

The Padang, 1851

INTRODUCTION

Singapore's modern history began in 1819 when Sir Stamford Raffles, agent of the East India Company, set up a British trading post on the island after signing an agreement with the Sultan of Johor and his Temenggong (Justice Minister). Raffles, who was then the Lieutenant-Governor of Bencoolen, had seen the need for a new outpost to secure Britain's trade route to China through the Straits of Malacca and to expand British commercial interests in the Malayan archipelago. In 1824, a treaty with the Sultan and the Temenggong of Johor gave the British possession of Singapore.

Soon after the founding of Singapore, Raffles laid down as his objective the development of "a great commercial emporium" and "free port" in Singapore which would become the "pride of the East". The other ports in the region which were controlled by the Dutch, imposed levies and restrictions on trade. Singapore's strategic location and free trade policy made it the natural choice for a port of call for trading vessels from the Indonesian archipelago, China, Vietnam, Cambodia, India, the Arab countries, and Europe.

Sir Stamford Raffles

Raffles spent only nine months in Singapore between 1819 and 1823, but the principles and plans he laid down led to Singapore's rapid growth. When he first landed, Singapore had less than a thousand inhabitants. Within two years, it had a multi-racial population of around 5,000. Nearly 3,000 of these early immigrants were indigenous to the neighbouring Indonesian islands and the Malay Peninsula – they included Malays, Javanese, Boyanese, Bugis and others. More than 1,000 Chinese came from Malacca, Rhio and other places in the region. The first immigrant Indians came mainly from Penang. Among the others who came were Arabs and Europeans.

In subsequent years more immigrants came from China and India. The Chinese, who came mostly from Guangdong and Fujian provinces in southeast China belonged to four main dialect groups: Hokkien, Teochew, Cantonese and Hakka. Some came as traders while others came as labourers, artisans or refugees escaping hunger and civil war in China. Many of the Indians came as garrison troops, police, and labourers. Some came as convicts who provided cheap labour for the construction of public works. The majority of the Indian immigrants were South Indians, but there were also Punjabis, Gujaratis and Bengalis. By 1860 the population of the island had risen to 82,000, the majority of whom were Chinese.

The rapid growth of Singapore after 1860 was due to a number of factors. There was an expansion of trade between the European powers and China and Japan as both these countries were forced to open their ports. With the development of the American West, there was more trade across the Pacific. The French occupied Indochina and the Dutch liberalised trade with their

Chinese immigrants arriving at
Boat Quay in the 1850s.

empire in the East Indies. The arrival of the steamship and the opening of the Suez Canal in 1869 gave new impetus to international trade and to Singapore's role in it.

A more crucial development for Singapore was the British intervention in the Malay Peninsula from 1874, leading to the expansion of the tin industry and, later, to the establishment of the rubber industry. Singapore soon became the distribution centre for tin and rubber besides providing the financial and promotional infrastructure for trade in these commodities. By 1903 it was the world's seventh largest port in tonnage of shipping.

The Esplanade, 1905

Throughout its pre-World War II history, Singapore had close connections with the Malay Peninsula. It was part of the Straits Settlements, which also included Penang and Malacca. Until 1858 the Straits Settlements were under the control of the British East India Company, while from 1858 to 1867 they were ruled directly from London. Even when the Malay states, beginning in 1874, came progressively under British control, the Straits Settlements remained jurisdically distinct. However from the late 19th century there were increasingly close links in trade, travel and administration between the Straits Settlements and the Malay states. The Governor of the Straits Settlements was also the High Commissioner for the Federated States of the Peninsula.

Immigration, especially of Chinese, continued to increase. In 1901 Singapore's population had grown to 227,000 of which 72 percent were Chinese. Singapore had a marked cosmopolitan character: apart from the Chinese there were Malays, Javanese, Bugis, Boyanese, Tamils, Punjabis, Gujaratis, Bengalis, Ceylonese, Arabs, Jews, Eurasians and Europeans.

British rule in Singapore was generally *laissez-faire*. As far as possible the different ethnic communities were left alone to manage their own affairs. Education had made a slow start in the 19th century. The colonial government spent public money only for a few English- and Malay-medium schools; it was indifferent to Chinese education. The Chinese community, however, began building schools on its own or with help from China. Especially after 1911, China began sending teachers, textbooks and funds to help run Chinese schools in Singapore and Malaya, with a view to keeping the overseas Chinese under its influence. The colonial education policy thus sowed the seeds of some of the political problems and divisions which were to plague the post-World War II administrators of Singapore: the alienation of the Chinese-educated, and the division between the English- and Chinese-educated.

After World War I (1914 to 1918), which had little impact on Singapore, immigrants continued to come in ever-increasing numbers. The first communist agents came in 1925. In 1928, a Nanyang (South Seas) Communist Party, supported mainly by the poorer sections of the Hainanese community, was formed in Singapore. It attempted to infiltrate Chinese schools and trade unions, but was not as successful in this as the Kuomintang (KMT). The Malayan Communist Party (MCP)* was founded in 1930 at a meeting held in Kuala Pilah, Negri Sembilan. However, its early success with Chinese school teachers and students was short-lived as police arrested the key figures of the party.

Singapore was hard hit by the Great Depression of 1929 to 1933 as international trade, including trade in Malayan tin and rubber, declined. There was widespread unemployment and poverty on the island. The colonial government imposed immigration restrictions on unskilled male Chinese and repatriated large numbers of Chinese and Indian workers. The immigration of women was, however, left uncontrolled in an effort to balance the sex ratio.

The people of Singapore were not unaffected by the major events in Asia during the first 40 years of the 20th century — the humiliations of the decaying Chinese empire at the hands of the European imperialists, the Chinese revolution of 1911, the struggles between the Chinese Communist Party (CCP) and the Kuomintang, the Indian independence movement and, finally, the Japanese invasion of Manchuria in 1931 and the outbreak of the Sino-Japanese War in 1937. These events aroused the immigrant population of Singapore along ethnic lines and caused, in effect, stirrings of Chinese or Indian nationalism among a people who identified themselves with their countries of origin. They had no feeling of belonging to Singapore. Colonial rule was taken

Empress Place, 1930

for granted and generally regarded as unshakeable. In the 1930s the Chinese population, both pro-KMT and pro-CCP groups, became increasingly pre-occupied with the Sino-Japanese conflict. Anti-Japanese feelings grew.

The Malayan Communist Party which remained closely linked to the Chinese Communist Party which in turn generally followed the Comintern line, could operate only clandestinely in the 1930s. It tried to infiltrate other political groups and workers' organisations and to exploit the anti-Japanese feelings among the Chinese population. It made considerable headway with the anti-Japanese movement.

The changing strategic alignments in Asia after World War I led Britain to develop a naval base in Singapore and to build up the island's seaward defences. Japan, a British ally in Asia since 1902, was developing a large navy and ambitions of its own. Though first proposed in 1919, the construction of the Naval Base got underway only in the 1930s and the King George VI dry dock was completed in 1938. New airfields were also constructed at Tengah and Sembawang, and at Changi, heavy artillery and anti-aircraft defences covering the eastern approaches to the Naval Base were installed. Anti-ship guns and fortifications were also built on the southern coast line.

War broke out in Asia in July 1937 when Japan attacked China, while in Europe it broke out in September 1939 when Germany invaded Poland. In 1940/1941 Britain was fighting for its survival, its resources stretched to the limit. In 1940 the Germany-Italy-Japan Axis was formed, and in June 1941 Hitler invaded the Soviet Union. Moscow instructed communist parties worldwide to cooperate with the Western colonial powers against the Axis powers.

*Throughout this book, the term
Malayan Communist Party (MCP)
is used, although the organisation
later came to be referred to as the
Communist Party of Malaya (CPM).

1

WAR
COMES TO SINGAPORE

1
One of the five 15-inch guns facing the sea.

These guns, together with six 9.2-inch and 18 six-inch guns, formed part of the island's seaward defences. They proved to be irrelevant when the Japanese marched down the Peninsula and invaded Singapore from Johor.

1941~1942

China and Japan had been at war since July 1937, and Europe since September 1939. Yet, through much of 1941 it was generally thought that there was no immediate threat of war in Southeast Asia.

Singapore was regarded as an "impregnable fortress". The general feeling was that the thick, impenetrable jungles of the Malay Peninsula and the armed forces of the British Empire would deter any landward invasion. There was confidence that the seaward defences of Singapore, which included heavy 15-inch guns, would defeat any attack from the sea. The arrival of more Indian, British and Australian troops in early 1941 strengthened this sense of security among the authorities as well as the local population. The colonial administration remained pre-occupied with producing rubber and tin in Malaya to support Britain's war effort in Europe.

The responsibility for the defence of Singapore was in the hands of the British. The local people were content with this situation as they had confidence in the ability of the mighty British Empire to protect them. The only local military units were four battalions of the Straits Settlements Volunteer Corps, led by British officers. There was also a small civil defence force which had been formed in 1939 as part of the "Passive Defence Services". The volunteers of this force were grouped into units of air-raid wardens and medical, fire, transport, demolition and debris squads, as well as burial squads.

By October 1941 the possibility of a Japanese attack was real. The Japanese had already occupied bases in southern Indochina, and Singapore was now within range of the aircraft they had based there. By late November the Japanese were making naval movements towards Indochina and landing craft were being moved south from China, while more aircraft had arrived in southern Indochina. On 1 December 1941 a state of emergency was declared in Singapore, which, in practical terms, largely meant the call-up of the few battalions of volunteer forces.

Even at this late hour the people of Singapore did not believe that they could be attacked and conquered. The troop reinforcements, the pronouncements of the authorities that all was well, and finally the arrival of the battleship the *Prince of Wales* and the battle-cruiser the *Repulse* on 2 December reinforced this confidence.

When the first Japanese air raid took place in the early hours of 8 December 1941, Singapore was caught off-guard. Bombs fell on Raffles Place and at the Seletar and Tengah airfields; 60 people were killed and over 700 injured. The raid had been carried out by 17 Japanese planes from bases in Indochina.

This dawn raid on Singapore was part of an audacious Japanese military offensive. On the previous day, 7 December, the Japanese had destroyed the American fleet at Pearl Harbour, invaded Hongkong and the Philippines, and landed forces in Singora (Songkhla) and Patani in southern Thailand as well as Kota Baru in northern Malaya. By the evening of 8 December, the Kota Baru airfield was in Japanese hands. Within 40 hours the Japanese had been able to gain mastery of the air over the battle zone.

Japanese mastery of the sea was now only a matter of days away. It came on 10 December when Japanese torpedo bombers sank the *Prince of Wales* and the *Repulse*, two of Britain's modern warships, off Kuantan in the South China Sea. The ships had left Singapore

two days earlier in the hope of intercepting the invading Japanese forces; but without air cover they proved sitting ducks for Japanese bombers. Their destruction was a severe blow to British morale and pride.

Once the Japanese had gained undisputed control of the air, it was difficult to stop the advance of their army down the Peninsula. The task of conquering Malaya and Singapore had been given to the Japanese 25th Army comprising the 5th, 18th and the Imperial Guards Divisions. For the Malayan campaign total Japanese combat strength was about 67,000, supported by 150 tanks and 560 aircraft.

Lieutenant-General Percival, the General-Officer-Commanding Malaya, had over 80,000 troops under his command, but no tanks. At the start of the war he had over 150 aircraft as well, but these were inferior in performance to the Japanese aircraft. The British troops were dispersed over the Peninsula to guard airfields and other strategic points.

From 10 December there was a continuous British retreat down the Peninsula. The main Japanese thrust was down the west coast with subsidiary or diversionary thrusts through the centre, from Patani to Kroh and Grik in central Perak, and on the east coast from Kota Baru. Where the British tried to make a stand, their defences were overcome by Japanese tanks and artillery or by infantry flanking movements which threatened to cut lines of supply and retreat. Thus efforts to halt the Japanese advance at Jitra in Kedah and at Kampar and Slim River in Perak failed. At Slim River the British suffered a major defeat, losing 4,000 men and a considerable amount of equipment.

Penang had fallen without a fight on 18 December 1941 and Ipoh on 26 December. After the disaster at Slim River, Kuala Lumpur was abandoned and taken by the Japanese on 11 January 1942. The British then attempted to put up a fight in Johor along the Muar River, but the Japanese swiftly overcame these defences, and by 25 January they had taken Air Hitam and Kluang in central Johor. Nothing now stood between them and the Causeway.

The Japanese invasion of Malaya brought about a change in the outlook of the Chinese in Singapore. Until then they had been split into three camps — the Straits-born, the pro-Kuomintang and the pro-communist. The English-educated Straits-born Chinese were generally pro-British and not particularly interested in events in China. The other two groups, however, had been pre-occupied with the problems of China, and had supported the two warring factions during the Chinese civil war.

As the Japanese advanced down the Peninsula, word spread to Singapore that they were indiscriminately killing Chinese in the towns they captured. This threat from a common enemy, the Japanese, led the pro-communist and the pro-Kuomintang factions to forget their differences, and together they sent a deputation of Chinese leaders to the Governor to offer their help in the war. The British accepted their offer and on 31 December 1941 the Chung Kuo Council (China National Council) was formed under the leadership of Tan Kah Kee, a prominent busi-

nessman. Local Chinese from all sectors of society responded enthusiastically to the Council's call for assistance in the defence of Singapore.

The Council mobilised a labour force to man the essential services and to construct defence works. It also urged the government to arm a Chinese military force. With some misgivings, the British agreed to form a Singapore Chinese Anti-Japanese Volunteer Battalion, known as Dalforce, under the command of Lieutenant-Colonel John Dalley. Dalley gave the force a 10-day crash training course and equipped the men with uniforms and elementary weapons.

The British also released communists from jail and reached an agreement with Lai Teck, secretary-general of the Malayan Communist Party, to organise and train communists for guerilla warfare in Japanese-occupied territory. One hundred and sixty-five men trained in special guerilla schools under this scheme formed the nucleus of the Malayan People's Anti-Japanese Army.

By late January, Singapore was under intense air attacks which caused heavy civilian casualties. The streets were overflowing with refugees fleeing from Malaya. The population had in fact swelled to one million, nearly double the peace-time size.

Meanwhile, the Japanese kept up their advance in Johor. On the morning of 31 January, the British blew a 55-metre-wide gap in the Causeway and withdrew to Singapore for the final showdown. Barely nine hours

later, Japanese troops moved into Johor Baru and the Japanese commander, Lieutenant-General Tomoyuki Yamashita, established his headquarters at the Bukit Serene Palace of the Sultan of Johor.

Troop reinforcements – British, Indian and Australian – had continued to arrive in Singapore even in January. However, with the Johor coastline in Japanese hands and Japanese control of the air, the defence of Singapore had become a difficult task. While on the east and south coasts the beaches were strongly defended with pill-boxes, anti-tank obstacles, barbed wire and heavy anti-naval guns, the entire northern shore was without defence works. The troops who had retreated from Malaya, weary and demoralised, had to set to work under Japanese air and artillery attacks to construct last-ditch defences facing the Straits of Johor.

Yamashita realised that he must begin the invasion of Singapore quickly before the British recovered their strength and acquired more reinforcements. Unknown to the British, he did not have enough supplies to last out a long-drawn siege of Singapore. With the same meticulous planning that had gone into their Malayan campaign, the Japanese, working in the dead of night, established a beach-head in

the Lim Chu Kang area on the northwest coast of Singapore on 8 February. By the evening of 9 February, Tengah airfield was in their hands. Within a few days, after repairing the Causeway, the rest of Yamashita's army marched into Singapore.

The morale of the British forces had reached rock-bottom, but they were under orders from the British Prime Minister Winston Churchill "to fight to the bitter end", and they put up a valiant struggle in the last days. Some of the most bitter fighting took place in Bukit Timah, MacRitchie and Pasir Panjang, resulting in heavy casualties on both sides. Members of Dalforce and other Chinese volunteers fought ferociously in the Bukit Timah area, while the Malay Regiment put up a heroic fight trying to defend the Pasir Panjang Ridge.

The water mains were destroyed during the air and artillery attacks and, except for some wells, Singapore was almost totally without water. The air became filled with the stench of filth and death, and the danger of an epidemic outbreak was very real. To Lieutenant-General Arthur Percival, who was in command of all the Allied forces in Singapore, the situation looked hopeless. To avoid the destruction and loss of life that prolonged fighting would entail, he requested the permission of the Far East Supreme Commander, General Archibald Wavell, to surrender.

Permission was granted on 14 February. On Sunday, 15 February, the first day of the Lunar New Year, Percival met Yamashita at the makeshift Japanese headquarters in the Ford Factory at Bukit Timah to discuss surrender terms. The Japanese insisted on immediate and unconditional surrender. Their only concession was the agreement not to enter the city until the following morning. By 8.30 on the evening of 15 February all gunfire and fighting ceased and an uneasy calm settled over the city.

The unthinkable had happened. The island of Singapore, hailed as Britain's impregnable fortress, the bastion of her eastern empire, had fallen. Yama-

shita raised Japan's flag on Singapore soil 70 days after his initial landing at Kota Baru, 30 days earlier than he had expected to complete the Malayan campaign.

The British had been defeated even though their troops outnumbered the Japanese. The Japanese 25th Army was superior in training, experience, leadership and morale. Japanese control of the air and the sea from almost the outset of the Malayan campaign was also an important factor in the British defeat. But underlying these factors was also the failure, in the years before 1941, to provide for adequate defences, with good air support, against both a seaward attack and a landward attack down the Peninsula.

Singapore now lay in grim apprehension of the occupying forces, whose reputation as fierce fighters was matched by their notoriety as cruel and savage victors.

Singapore 1941

2
An aerial view of Singapore,
1941.

3
South Bridge Road with Elgin
Bridge in the background. Life
is relaxed and unhurried as
people go about their daily
work in pre-war Singapore.

To Meet the Threat

4

4/5
(Above) A mortar crew of the
Malay Regiment assembling
weapons and (right) Malay,
Chinese and Indian recruits of
the Straits Settlements
Volunteer Corps during
training.

5

6

7

8

6/7/8
Troop reinforcements arriving
from England (top); India
(left); and Australia
(above) in 1941.

9
In Singapore, local men respond to a call for volunteers from the colonial government.

The volunteers served in the Volunteer Corps as well as in civil defence ("passive defence") units.

10
In an air-raid shelter during a drill.

11
Key British and Australian officials meet in Singapore on 29 September 1941 to review the security situation.

This was after Japan had acquired military bases in southern Indochina. (Left to right): Air Chief Marshal Sir Robert Brooke-Popham, Commander-in-Chief Far East; The Rt Hon Sir Alfred Duff Cooper, Churchill's special envoy; Sir Earl Page, special Australian envoy to the British War Cabinet; Sir Archibald Clark-Kerr, British Ambassador, China; Sir Shenton Thomas, Governor of the Straits Settlements; Vice-Admiral Sir Geoffrey Layton, Commander-in-Chief China Station.

12
In November 1941, General Archibald Wavell (extreme left), Commander-in-Chief India, visits Singapore to inspect the Indian troops.

In January 1942, Wavell became the Commander-in-Chief Far East, with his headquarters in Java.

13/14
The arrival on 2 December 1941 of the battle-cruiser *Repulse* (below) and the battleship *Prince of Wales* (bottom) boosts the island's confidence.

13

15
The Japanese residents in pre-war Singapore, who numbered about 1,300, worked as photographers, dentists, journalists, barbers, and businessmen.

The Singapore Herald (right), an English daily started in 1939, was Japanese-owned. The editor of the paper, T Fujii, was interned by the British when hostilities broke out.

When the Japanese occupied Singapore, he became the editor of *The Straits Times* which the Japanese renamed *Syonan Shimbun*.

16
(Extreme right) A week before Singapore is hit by Japanese bombs, Governor Sir Shenton Thomas, declares a state of emergency and calls up the volunteer force.

14

The Singapore Herald

SINGAPORE, TUESDAY, SEPTEMBER 30, 1941.

Vol. 3. No. 148.

Much Diplomatic Activity In Tokyo

'VERY IMPORTANT QUESTIONS' DISC
BY ENVOY GREW, MINISTER TOY

U.S. Said Favouring Monroe Status For Japan On Terms

IMPORTANT diplomatic movements are taking place in Tokyo.

After the exclusive announcement in yesterday's Singapore Herald that Sir Robert Craigie, British Ambassador, had postponed his departure on leave, it is revealed that Mr. Joseph Grew, U.S. Ambassador, has discussed "very important questions" with Admiral Toyoda, Japanese Foreign Minister. Sir Robert Craigie's postponement of leave is said to be due to his Chancellor's illness but he also has had talks recently with the Japanese Foreign Minister.

Some despondency about the slow progress of the U.S.-Japan talks is evident in Washington, but American diplomats have not abandoned hope of a solution. It is said that America does not object to Japan being in a position of leadership in the Far East provided the open door is maintained and conquest and exploitation are avoided.

A gradual relaxation of Japanese freezing regulations is reported from Tientsin.

Sir Robert Craigie, the British Ambassador in Tokyo, had indefinitely postponed his leave, announced a Bri-

at present. Barring future difficulties he may leave later, but his departure is considered to have no political significance.— Reuter.

The exploratory talks between the United States and Japan may taper off into an unproductive effort because of Japan's failure or inability to give definite guarantees regarding her future actions, it was reliably learned in Washington.

American diplomats have not abandoned all hope of a solution, but it is understood that before the conference can be prevented from bogging down the Japanese must give evidence they have no intention of depriving Americans of what they consider their rights in China. It was said

Despite weeks of intensive activity, these conversations have not reached a point where they could be converted into formal negotiations and the Americans have become discouraged over prospects which seemed hopeful when Prince Konoye sent his letter to President Roosevelt on August 28.

The main difficulty for Japan is to guarantee United States rights in China, either due to the traditional independence of

THE MALAYA TRIBUNE, TUESDAY, DECEMBER 2, 1941.

STATE OF EMERGENCY DECLARED IN COLONY

Volunteer Forces Called Out

Singapore, Monday.

A STATE of emergency was proclaimed in the Colony of the Straits Settlements to-day, by a proclamation by H.E. the Governor, Sir Shenton Thomas, issued under the name of Mr. S. W. Jones, Colonial Secretary. It reads:—

"Whereas it is enacted by Section 23 of the Volunteer Force Ordinance (Chapter 99) and by Section 21 of the Royal Naval Volunteer Reserve Ordinance (Chapter 100), and by Section 20 of the Volunteer Air Force Ordinance (Chapter 101) that the Governor shall have power to declare that a state of emergency exists in the Colony or any part of it.

"And whereas the said sections also empower the Governor to call

from mobilisation, will hold themselves in readiness to report for duty in accordance with instructions which they will receive from their Unit Commanders.

"Those away from their usual place of residence, but still in Malaya, will return at once, reporting their arrival to their Unit Commander.

"Any changes of address or telephone number not already recorded will be reported immediate ly to Unit Commander.

HONG KONG GETS READY

Hong Kong, Dec. 1

FOLLOWING two days of intense defence exercises in which 20,000 civil and defence workers were given their first realistic taste of war-time conditions in the Colony, all troops were called back to the barracks and all naval personnel were ordered to stand by for immediate notice.

The Orders came as a complete surprise, and were conveyed by means of messages flashed in cinemas, and notices posted in hotels and elsewhere, while pickets were stationed at ferries and street corners ordering

15   16

THE MALAYA TRIBUNE, WEDNESDAY, DECEMBER 3, 1941.

JAPAN'S HOPELESS TASK IN PACIFIC WAR

By Major Fielding Eliot

● The arrival of an Eastern Fleet at Singapore, headed by the Prince of Wales, has changed the whole complexion of the Far Eastern situation. This article tells just how hopeless Japan's chances will now be should she decide to go to war with the A.B.C.D. bloc.

SPELLS TROUBLES

WITH the completion of the King George V and Prince of Wales, Britain had sixteen capital ships. Three more were in stages of advanced construction; all may now have been completed, so that Britain's total battleship strength may now be nineteen.

Four modern aircraft carriers and two older ones are known to be in commission, and three others may be finished by this time, a possible total of nine. [This article was written before the news of the sinking of the Ark Royal.]

At a rough guess, it might be possible for Britain to send to the Far East a force of six battleships and two or three carriers, with a certain number of cruisers and a few destroyers (the latter being very much needed everywhere).

This would still leave three battleships and a carrier for each end

of the Mediterranean, and from four to seven battleships and from one to four carriers for the Atlantic.

A Far Eastern detachment of the size suggested would not be able to seek out the Japanese Navy in Japanese waters and force it to battle, but neither would the Japanese Navy dare venture into the South China Sea to seek out and bring to battle such a British force, in the presence of British and Dutch shore based aircraft and submarines, reinforced by American light forces from Manila and with the prospect of being cut off from the base by the American Pacific Fleet.

★

IN fact, the arrival of some British battleships at Singapore would render the Japanese naval problem in the Pacific quite hopeless

17
However, the Japanese are still not considered to be a serious threat. As late as 3 December, *The Malaya Tribune* writes: "…the Japanese are caught in a trap of their own making … neither by land nor sea nor in the air do they have even a glimmer of a chance of victory …"

The cartoon characterises the Japanese as "short-sighted, buck-toothed, little men" who do not appreciate the strength of the combined forces of the Allied powers.

Japanese Invasion

18/19
Rescue workers clearing wreckage in Raffles Place. Japan dropped its first bombs on Singapore at 4.00 am on 8 December 1941, hitting Raffles Place, Seletar and Tengah airfields, and leaving 60 dead and over 700 injured.

18

20
One of the Japanese bombers used during the war.

20

Latest Type Of Bomber In Malaya

Latest Bristol Beaufort Bomber of the type being used by an Australian Squadron which arrived in Malaya last week.

THE STRAITS TIMES, MONDAY, DECEMBER 8, 1941

ENEMY CRAFT ARE NOW RETIRING
Official Communique On Malayan Operations

THE following communique was issued by General Headquarters at 7 a.m. to-day :

A landing was made by the enemy at Kemassin. This led to an infiltration towards Kota Bahru.

Large concentrations of ships were observed off Kemassin.

A Hudson aircraft secured a direct hit on the leading ship leaving her on fire. Another direct hit was made on the second ship.

A landing was effected at Sabak and contact was made by both our aircraft and land forces, fighting taking place on the beach.

Another Hudson secured a direct hit on a barge full of troops in the Kelantan River.

A few bombs were dropped on Singapore Island and the aerodrome at Kelantan. There were no casualties at the aerodrome. No bombs were dropped on the Naval Base.

It appears that these two raids approached over Tanjong Datok (the south eastern corner of Johore). The first raid consisted of six bombers, the second of five. Their estimated height was 17,000 feet.

It is unofficially reported, but not confirmed, that mustard gas bombs had been dropped.

At 7.40 it was officially stated:

All surface craft are retiring at high speed. The few troops left on the beach are being heavily machine-gunned.

ALL JAPANESE ROUNDED UP

THE rounding up of all Japanese nationals in Malaya began early to-day. In Singapore, Japanese women and children surrendered to the Immigration and Police authorities, while the men were rounded up at about 5 a.m.

It is expected that 1,300 Japanese in Singapore will have been rounded up by time of going to press. About 400 were at the Immigration depot this morning.

Brought into the Immigration depot by the rear entrance, the Singapore Japanese were examined, labelled and numbered, then checked on the records and then put into an apartment where they awaited the military authorities to transport them to an unknown destination.

In Singapore

THE first most people in Singapore knew of the existence of a state of war with Japan was when the air raid sirens sounded at about 4 15 a.m. Many people thought it was a test.

A.R.P. wardens were immediately on duty and though most of them had no advance warning. They acted with great initiative and enterprise.

The street lights of Singapore were not extinguished when the air raid sirens sounded.

Bombs were heard falling in several districts. It was officially stated subsequently that slight damage was done and there were a few casualties.

Singapore radio was on the air at 6 a.m. broadcasting the official communique.

This communique was issued by the Services Public Relations Organisation shortly after 4 15 a.m.

There is no news yet from Hong Kong and Thailand (8 a.m.).

News bulletins will be broadcast at every hour.

The air raid on Singapore took place in bright moonlight and a cloudy sky. The raiders, it is believed, flew over the clouds and were subjected to heavy anti-aircraft fire.

The Passive Defence Services who rushed to their posts on the first intimation of the air raid did excellent work in clearing debris and conveying the casualties to hospital.

The passive defence services of the Harbour Board sped to their stations within the minute of the alarm ready to go into action.

Rudely awakened, residents of Tiong Bahru jumped out of bed and started putting the lights in their flats as the sirens sounded. But no sooner had the lights appeared than the shrill whistles of the wardens of the Tanjong Pagar A.R.P. district ordered the lights out. They were put out.

Communique

The following communique was issued this morning at 4.20 a.m.

The first attempted landing was made shortly after 0100 hours and was repulsed by small arms fire and air action.

Enemy troops succeeded in landing on the beach near Padang Sabak and were last reported infiltrating towards Kota Bahru aerodrome.

They are being engaged by our land forces and our aircraft are attacking enemy ships and also enemy troops which have landed.

Ten ships are reported off Bachok.

Padang Sabak is slightly south of Kota Bahru. Bachok is 15 miles south.

Scenes After To-day's Air Attack

MEMBERS of the M.A.S.—both men and women—were on the streets in their uniforms, reporting for duty at their various posts soon after the sirens sounded this morning. Some of them attended their first real casualties soon after arriving at their posts.

Skeleton staffs will be on duty at all the first aid posts to-day, with full numbers on to-night.

Office workers coming through one of Singapore's shopping centres this morning had to step their way over the glass and debris scattered in great piles over pavement and roadway.

Governor On The War
60 Dead In Air Raid

THE Governor, Sir Shenton Thomas, speaking at a meeting of the Legislative Council this morning, stated that at an early hour to-day the Japanese attempted a landing off Kota Bahru.

The enemy force consisted of one cruiser, four destroyers, an armed merchantman and one transport.

They were engaged by our forces and at a later hour it was reported that their surface craft were retiring and cruising north.

A certain number of Japanese on the beaches have collected and these are making off in boats. They are being machine-gunned.

The main landing is taking place at Singora, in south Thailand. Malaya and Thailand are therefore being attacked without provocation.

At 4 a.m. this morning Singapore was subjected to an enemy air raid.

There were sixty fatal casualties and 133 are in hospital while a certain number are treated in hospital and returned home.

The Inspector General of Police reports that the behaviour of the civilian population under this sudden attack was exemplary. (Cheers).

There is only one thing for us to do and that is to show ourselves worthy, concluded Sir Shenton.

19

MALAYA HITS BA[CK]

JAPANESE RETREAT AFTER KELANTAN

BENRIMO
OPTICAL CO.
QUALIFIED OPTICIANS.
165, NORTH BRIDGE RD.

The Malaya Tribune

Net Sales Exceed 18,100 Daily

FIVE CENTS.

SINGAPORE, MONDAY, DECEMBER 8, 1941.

Enem[y]
From
Co[n]

FIGHT[

A LA[
a
tion towa[
communi[
ing).

Large[
off Kem[
direct h[
fire. Ar[
second [

A [
made by [
taking p[

A[
full of [

A
and the [
ties at [
Naval [

(the s[
of six [
was l[

gas l[

spee[
mac[

TH[
SU[
FI[
Pre[
tia[
th[

**Our New
Battle
Front**

NEI Declares War On Japs

THE Netherlands East Indies has declared war against Japan, according to the National Broadcasting Company.

Wake Island in the Pacific has been occupied by the Japanese, according to Columbia Broadcasting System.

JAP AIRCRAFT CARRIER, FOUR SUBMARINES SUNK

OUTSTANDING HIGHLIGHT OF THIS MORNING'S NEWS IS THE SINKING OF A JAPANESE AIRCRAFT CARRIER OFF HONOLULU (ACCORDING TO RADIO REPORTS), WHERE A NAVAL ENGAGEMENT IS NOW IN PROGRESS, AND WHERE IT IS REPORTED "AT LEAST ONE ENEMY AIRCRAFT CARRIER ENGAGED THE PEARL HARBOUR DEFENCES." A NEW YORK REPORT, QUOTING A RADIO MESSAGE, SAYS THAT THE U.S. FLEET HAS STEAMED OUT OF PEARL HARBOUR.

According to Japanese reports, the Imperial headquarters in Tokio have announced that a naval battle is in progress in the Western Pacific between Japanese and British and American units.

Dramatic events are foreshadowed following the Japanese air and land attack on Malaya and the declaration of war from Tokio on the United States and Britain this morning. The Japanese announced that they were at war with Britain and the U.S. from dawn to-day, but long before that they had made their first attack.

Japs Gun Honolulu Civilians

Honolulu, Dec. 7.

THE Japanese planes sprayed bullets in the streets of Wahiawa, a town of 3,000 souls, 25 miles north-west of Honolulu.

The first reports show that ten or more persons were injured.

The attack was aimed at points in the Island of Oahu and the heavily-fortified Pearl Harbour Naval Base.

The attack ended at about 9.25 a.m. (local time). At least 50 planes participated in the first attack, which started, according to Army officials, at 8.10 a.m. (local time).

President Roosevelt's secretary, was unable to confirm the reported naval engagement off Honolulu. Mr. Stephen Early said that he After conferring with the War and Navy Departments, President Roosevelt began dictating a special message to Congress.—Reuter.

New York, Dec. 8.

Telephone messages from Honolulu say that there is much commotion going on with sirens. In the air and anti-aircraft fire. Officials of Honolulu have been warning the streets by military and told residents to remain by civilian columns and [...] carrying arms. Many citizens took to the hills to watch the [...] and get a general view of the action.—Reuter.

MALAYA SUFFERED THE FIRST BLOW AT KELANTAN SHORTLY AFTER ONE O'CLOCK THIS MORNING, WHERE JAPANESE ATTEMPTED A LANDING AND AFTER BEING BEATEN BACK SUCCEEDED IN ESTABLISHING A FOOTHOLD. AN AIR RAID ON SINGAPORE RESULTED IN DAMAGE TO CIVILIAN PROPERTY, AND CASUALTIES, SOME FATAL.

A stirring Order of the Day has been issued by The Commander-in-Chief, Far East, (Sir Robert Brooke-Popham) and Vice-Admiral Sir Geoffrey Layton (Commander-in-Chief, China Station), in which stress is laid on our preparedness and strength. "We are ready, confident," it says. It calls on the civilian population to be calm.

THE WHOLE FORCES OF THE EMPIRE HAVE MOVED INTO ACTION, AND PRESIDENT ROOSEVELT HAS ALSO ORDERED THE SERVICES OF THE U.S. TO "CARRY OUT UNDISCLOSED ORDERS."

Japanese attacks have been made on Hawaii where the naval base was damaged, the Philippines (Manila) and Malaya. Bachok, where the Japanese landed, is 18 miles south of the Thai border on the Kelantan coast.

"A second wave of Japanese planes is just coming over Honolulu," Governor Poindexter of Hawaii told President Roosevelt by telephone.

Mr. Poindexter reported that there was already heavy damage and loss of life in Honolulu.

Honolulu—Several fires were started in the city area of Honolulu which were immediately controlled. The Governor has proclaimed emergency defence measures with immediate effect. Two Japanese [...] dead in the city

[...] formation yet available about damage or loss of life in Manila.

London, Dec. 8.
Official papers were being burnt at the Japanese Embassy in London last night, Mr. Matsui, the
(Continued on page 9)

Stirring Order Of The Day To Malayan Population

The following is the Order of the Day issued by the C-in-C Far East:

Japan's action to-day gives the signal for the Empire Naval, Army and Air Forces, and those of their Allies to go into action with a common aim and common ideals.

We are ready.

We have had plenty of warning and our preparations are made and tested.

We do not forget at this moment the years of patience and forbearance in which we have borne with dignity and discipline the petty insults and insolence inflicted on us by the Japanese in the Far East.

We know that those things were only done because Japan thought she could take advantage of our supposed weakness.

Now when Japan herself has decided to put the matter to a sterner test she will find that she has made a grievous mistake.

We are confident.

Our defences are strong and our weapons efficient.

Whatever our race and wherever we are now in our native land, have come thousands of miles to defend these shores, to destroy such of our enemies as may set foot on our soil, and then from firm bases to cripple the power of the enemy to endanger our ideals, our possessions and our peace. We shall, before long, [...]

Honolulu Attack:
Vivid Description

New York, Dec. 8.
Hawaii [...]

CK! ANDING

Ships Hit

The Air: t Made

G ON BEACH

was made by the Japanese
sin. This led to an infiltra-
a Bahru (states an official
ed in Singapore this morn-

cations of ships were observed
A Hudson aircraft secured a
e leading ship leaving her on
irect hit was made on the

s effected at Sabak and contact was
r aircraft and land forces, fighting
e beach.
dson secured a direct hit on a barge
he Kelantan River.
bs were dropped on Singapore Island
ne at Kelantan. There were no casual-
rome. No bombs were dropped on the

at two raids approached over Tanjong Datok
corner of Johore). The first raid consisted
the second of five. Their estimated height

ially reported, but not confirmed, that mustard
een dropped.
All Japanese surface craft are retiring at high
w troops left on the beach are being heavily

MESSAGE, QU
FIGHTING IN K

ING TO-NIGH
in Singapore
ve all three-watchers
Director of Air R
to-day, un
tomorrow morning
OUT ORDER
ers are now in
a until further n

NNY
SE

OUND
EOLIS

21/22
Overnight, the people of
Malaya and Singapore
awake to the fact that they
are at war.

23
Blenheim bombers over
Malaya, May 1941. The British
Command had only 158 first-
line aircraft in Malaya against
the 560 of the invading

Japanese forces. Inadequate
air cover was to be one of the
decisive factors in the fall of
Malaya and Singapore to the
Japanese.

23

THE STRAITS TIMES, MONDAY, DECEMBER 8, 1941   7

JAPAN STRIKES AGAINST BRITAIN & U.S.

War Declaration After Attacks

LANDING ATTEMPT IN NORTH MALAYA

JAPAN declared war on Great Britain and the United States
as from dawn to-day. Before the declaration Japanese air attacks
were carried out on Singapore Island and Honolulu and elsewhere.
Japanese troops attempted to land in North Malaya near Kota Bahru.
They were repulsed with small arms fire and aircraft attacks.
Some troops landed and were reported early to-day infiltrating towards
Kota Bahru aerodrome.

Air raid sirens sounded in Singapore shortly after 4 a.m. An
air attack on the island developed immediately. Several bombs
were dropped. Slight damage was done and there were a few
casualties, it is officially reported.

Other developments reported so far to-day, in
Reuter and United Press flashes are as follows:
THE JAPANESE HAVE OCCUPIED THE
WATERFRONT OF THE INTERNATIONAL
SETTLEMENT AT SHANGHAI.

JAPAN HAS DECLARED WAR
ON GREAT BRITAIN AND
THE UNITED STATES RE-
PORTS REUTER FROM TOKIO
THIS MORNING.
WASHINGTON. Mr. Roosevelt
has ordered the Army and
Navy to carry out undisclosed
orders to prepare for the de-
fence of the United States.
WASHINGTON. The War
Department has ordered all
military personnel in the Unit-
ed States to mobilise.—Reuter.
HONOLULU—At least five

Island and another at Pearl
Harbour, setting oil tanks on
fire, according to first reports.
American antiaircraft opened
up and the sky was filled with
American warplanes.—Reuter.

Japanese Act In Shanghai

Shanghai, Dec. 8.
The Japanese flag is now flying
over the American gunboat U.S.S.
Wake, the British gunboat Petrel
having been blown up in harbour.
An eyewitness said that two
Japanese gunboats drew alongside the British gunboat Petrel
and ordered her to surrender.
When she failed to comply, they
gave her a full broadside immediately. The casualties are at
present unknown.
Naval authorities believe that
the Japanese have probably sunk
or seized the President Harrison
somewhere off the mouth of the
Yangtze en route to Chinwangtao,
where she was due to pick up
American Marines from Tientsin
on Wednesday. It is believed
that the Japanese will probably
intern or disarm the 203
U.S. Marines from Peiping and
Tientsin.
United States naval men
aboard the U.S.S. Wake—now
seized by the Japanese—wer
mostly reserves who were recently called up for duty in this ship

PETREL OPENED FIRE

Captain Polkinghorne, aged 62 of
the Royal Naval Reserve, a former
Tientsin river pilot commanding the
Petrel is believed to have been drowned
with his ship, which was armed with
only two machine-guns, which opened
up fire when the ship was commanded
to surrender. Only half the crew were
manning the Petrel when she was sunk
The Japanese destroyer which took
over the U.S.S. Wake later pulled up
at the Customs Jetty and trained her
guns on the British Embassy. Later
she steamed down river while Japanese speedboats patrolled the Whang-
poo.
It is understood that there were no
casualties aboard the Wake which the
Japanese occupied without assault.

Wake Island Taken By Japanese

WAKE Island in the Pacific
has been occupied by the
Japanese, according to the
Columbia Broadcasting System.
—Reuter.

NAVAL BATTLE OFF PEARL HARBOUR

A NAVAL engagement is reported off Pearl Harbour, Hawaii. Subsequently it was disclosed
that the United States fleet had steamed out of
Pearl Harbour.
A Japanese aircraft-carrier has been sunk off Honolulu,
according to a radio report from New York.

The United States warships in
Pearl Harbour were attacked by
Japanese bombers, and the
battleship Oklahoma (20,000 ton)
with ten 14-inch guns) is said to
have been set on fire.
A heavy anti-aircraft barrage
drove off unidentified enemy
bombers, which made an
attempt at a surprise blast of the
whole island, starting at 3 a.m.
The Army authorities officially
declared that an attack was under way. All emergency organisations were immediately mobilised and citizens were ordered
off the streets.

PEOPLE WATCH ATTACK

Roy Witousek, a private pilot
who was in the air over the
municipal airport, told United
Press that he was machin-
gunned and was lucky to land
alive. He said that about 25
dive-bombers swung over Pearl
Harbour in the first wave and
then over Ford Island and the
Middle naval base.
Witousek said he saw about 20
big four-motored bombers sweep
towards Honolulu but they we
driven off. Several outlying districts he said, were black with
smoke.
The entire side of the two-
storey residence of J. S. Perry was
blown out in a direct hit. Mrs
Perry and her 12-year-old son

field—No statement has yet been made
by the Navy. The Army has issued
orders for all people to remain off the
streets.
The first raiders carried torpedoes
and did considerable damage to shipping in Pearl Harbour and off Honolulu—United Press and Reuter.

Hawaii Attack Repulsed

Honolulu, Dec. 7.
JAPANESE planes sprayed bullets in the streets of Waihia-
wai, a town of 3,000 souls, 25
miles north-west of Honolulu.
The first reports show that ten
or more persons were injured.
The Press attack was aimed at
points on the island of Oahu and
the heavily-fortified Pearl Harbour naval base.
The National Broadcasting
Corporation in a late broadcast
from Honolulu declares:
"There has been severe fighting
going on in the air and on sea.
It has been a very severe attack.
The Army and Navy, it appears,
now have the air and sea under
control."—Reuter

Japanese Consul's Story Of 'Mutiny'

San Francisco, Dec

22

25

24/25
Sailors leaping from the sinking *Prince of Wales*.
The sinking of *Prince of Wales* and the *Repulse* by Japanese torpedo bombers on 10 December 1941 struck a severe blow to British morale. The ships had left Singapore on 8 December to carry out operations against the Japanese invasion force in northern Malaya, but with no air cover and only four destroyers as escorts, the ships were easy targets. The Commander-in-Chief of Eastern Fleet, Sir Thomas Philips, and more than 800 of his men went down with the ships.

26
Map shows air bases in Indochina from where Japan made its first air raids on Thailand and Malaya, and the route taken by the ill-fated *Repulse* and *Prince of Wales*.

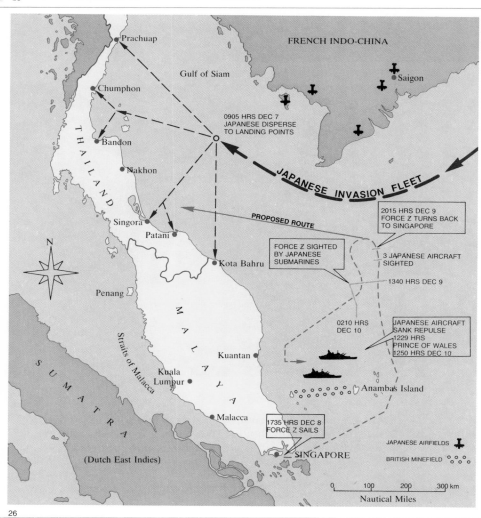

26

27

28

29

27
Japanese troops advancing down the Malay Peninsula on bicycles. Bicycles were an important factor behind the quick advance of the Japanese forces through Malaya. The three divisions of the Japanese Army engaged in the campaign were equipped with about 18,000 bicycles.

28
Japanese soldiers prepare to cross a river using improvised boats made of light steel and *kapok* wood.

29
Bicycles strapped on their shoulders, these soldiers are using logs to cross a river.

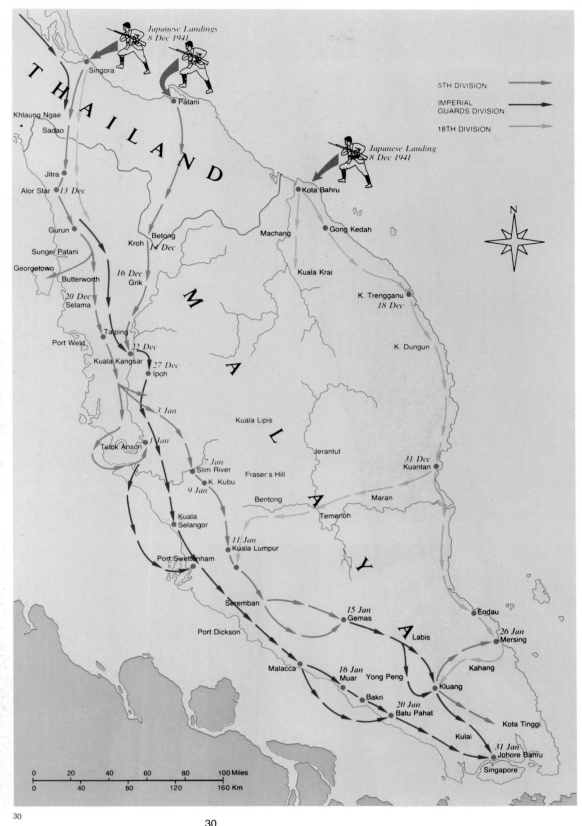

Japanese Landings
8 Dec 1941

5TH DIVISION

IMPERIAL
GUARDS DIVISION

18TH DIVISION

THAILAND

Singora

Patani

Khlaung Ngae

Sadao

Jitra

Alor Star *13 Dec*

Gurun

Betong
Kroh *14 Dec*

Sungei Patani

Georgetown

Butterworth

16 Dec
Grik

20 Dec
Selama

Taiping

Port Weld

Kuala Kangsar

22 Dec

27 Dec
Ipoh

3 Jan

Telok Anson

1 Jan

7 Jan
Slim River

K. Kubu

9 Jan

Kuala
Selangor

Port Swettenham

11 Jan
Kuala Lumpur

Seremban

Port Dickson

Malacca

16 Jan
Muar

Bakri

15 Jan
Gemas

20 Jan
Batu Pahat

Yong Peng

Labis

Kluang

Kulai

Kahang

31 Jan
Johore Bahru

Singapore

Kota Tinggi

26 Jan
Mersing

Endau

Japanese Landing
8 Dec 1941

Kota Bahru

Machang

Gong Kedah

Kuala Krai

K. Trengganu
18 Dec

K. Dungun

Kuala Lipis

Jerantut

Fraser's Hill

Bentong

Maran

Temerloh

31 Dec
Kuantan

M A L A Y A

N

| 0 | 20 | 40 | 60 | 80 | 100 Miles |
| 0 | 40 | 80 | 120 | 160 Km |

30

30
The Japanese entered Johor
Baru on 31 January 1942, 55
days after the start of their
invasion. This map shows how
the Japanese advanced through
Malaya to Singapore from their
first landings at Singora, Patani
and Kota Baru.

Ravages of War

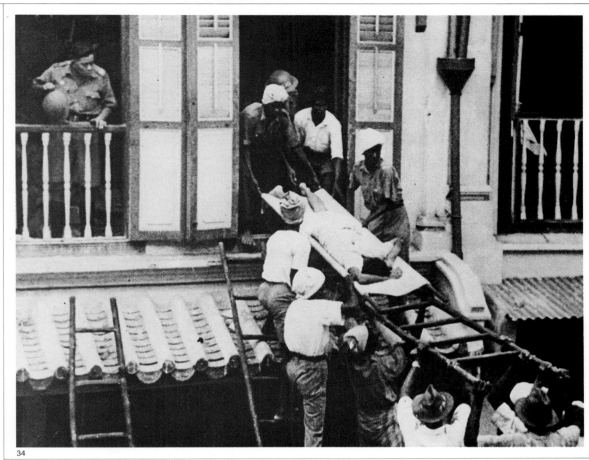

34

31/32/33
An estimated 150 to 200 people died each day in the intense air attacks on Singapore in late January and early February 1942. The bombing destroyed many buildings and started many fires.

34
Air-raid workers remove an injured person from a bombed building.

35
Using handkerchiefs as masks against the sting of explosion gases, this couple rush out of a bombed building; one of them clutches a baby.

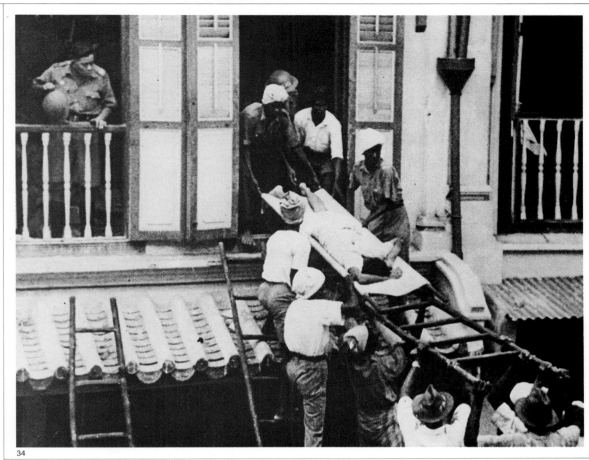

35

36

36/37
Chinatown, overflowing with
refugees from Malaya, was the
worst affected. Often entire
families were wiped out by
Japanese bombing.

37

38

40

39

41

38
The *Queen Mary* at the graving dock of the Naval Base in pre-war days.

With the Japanese just across the Causeway, the British military command ordered the destruction of installations and property that could help the Japanese war effort. The Naval Base, built at a cost of £60 million, was partially destroyed and abandoned.

39/40
Oil tanks in flames at the Naval Base after the British set them on fire.

The pall of black smoke from oil dumps at the Base hung over the island for days.

41
British soldiers push a car into the harbour as part of the plan to destroy property that would prove useful to the Japanese.

42
Despite the official policy against evacuation, many Europeans begin evacuating their families.

Many wealthy Asian residents also caught the first available boat to escape the war. Towards the end of January 1942, exit permits were refused to European and Asian men of military age, but some managed to buy their way out in the last few days before Singapore's fall. Many perished at sea under Japanese attack.

43
Though war was so near, the island's hotels, clubs and cabarets, among them Raffles Hotel and the New World Amusement Park, remained open past midnight.

42

43

44

45

44

As the Japanese advanced down Malaya, some local men came forward to mobilise the people for the war effort. One such man was Lim Bo Seng.

He came to Singapore from China at the age of 16 and studied at Raffles Institution. Later he became a wealthy trader. As head of the Labour Services Corps, Lim provided the British Government with thousands of labourers for the war effort during the Japanese invasion.

Just before Singapore fell to the Japanese he escaped and later joined Force 136. This was a special operations force formed by the British and the Chinese governments in June 1942 to support resistance groups behind enemy lines and to coordinate guerilla operations in support of the eventual British invasion of Malaya.

Members of Force 136 entered Malaya from 1943 by submarine and established contact with the communist-controlled Malayan People's Anti-Japanese Army. It was during one such infiltration trip, in March 1944, that Lim was captured by the Japanese. He died in Batu Gajah jail on 29 June 1944 after being tortured. He was 34 years old.

45

Tan Kah Kee, another prominent local Chinese leader, also played a significant part in the anti-Japanese movement in Singapore. He came to Singapore at the age of 17 as a penniless immigrant and later became a millionaire. A philanthropist, he spent most of his money opening schools in China. Later, in 1919, he raised money to open the first Chinese middle school in Singapore, the Nanyang Hua Chiao Middle School.

When the Japanese invaded Malaya, Tan Kah Kee formed the Chung Kuo Council for general mobilisation to fight the Japanese. Eleven days before Singapore's fall, he fled to Sumatra and then to Java. He remained in hiding there till his return to Singapore at the end of the war. When China became communist he openly supported the new regime. The British banned him from returning to Singapore when he visited China in 1950.

Japanese Capture Singapore

46

47

46
On 31 January, the British blasted a 55-metre gap in the Causeway, hoping to keep the Japanese at bay.

The gap is visible below the tower of Bukit Serene Palace of the Sultan of Johor which was used as an observation post by the Japanese before their assault on Singapore.

47
A party of Japanese troops land on Singapore.

On the night of 8 February, the Japanese began their landings on the northwest coast of the island between Tanjong Buloh and Tanjong Murai in the Lim Chu Kang area.

48
Having repaired the breach in the Causeway, the Imperial Guards Division of the Japanese 25th Army crosses into Singapore.

49
Japanese forces fighting their way through Singapore streets.

THE SUNDAY TIMES

"Singapore Must Stand; It SHALL Stand"—H.E. the Governor

SUNDAY, FEBRUARY 15, 1942.

STRONG JAP PRESSURE

Defence Stubbornly Maintained

VOLUNTEERS IN ACTION

BRITISH, Australian, Indian and Malay troops, and including now men of the Straits Settlements Volunteer Force, are disputing every attempt, by the Japanese to advance further towards the heart of Singapore town.

THERE was a strange diminution of activity during last night, with little shelling and no bombing of the city area. Reasons for this were still unapparent when we went to Press at 7 a.m. British guns had been heard again from 6 a.m. and after a while there was another lull

The official communique issued at 5.30 p.m. yesterday (Saturday) stated:

"During yesterday afternoon enemy attacks developed in the Paya Lebar area and in the West. Both were in considerable strength.

"To-day the enemy has maintained his pressure, supporting his attacks with a number of high level bombing raids by large formation of aircraft, continual shelling by his artillery, and low dive-bombing attacks. His artillery have also shelled the town intermittently throughout the night and this morning

"Our troops—British, Australian, Indian and Malay—are disputing every attempt to advance further towards the heart of Singapore town.

"In the town itself, the civil defence services are making every effort to deal with the damage and civil casualties caused by hostile shelling and bombing."

It is understood that our artillery engaged some of the enemy forces with considerable success inflicting about 100 casualties.

Lord Moyne's Message To Singapore

THE following telegram has been received by His Excellency from the Secretary of State for the Colonies to all those who are so gallantly and doggedly helping in the defence of Singapore

"You are going through a great trial but I knew you are doing everything you can and are resolved to continue to do so. I send to all of you my grateful thanks for your devoted assistance

FIRST V'C' WON IN MALAYA

THE first Victoria Cross to be awarded for fighting in Malaya, goes to Lieut.-Col. Wright Anderson of the Australian Imperial Forces, says the B.B.C.

JAPANESE CLAIMS MORE SUBDUED

THE Australian Army Minister, Mr Forde, said at 6 a.m. yesterday that he was expecting a cable from Lieut.-Gen. Percival, G.O.C. in Singapore, but the absence of this cable did not necessarily mean that the news was bad

The Japanese have almost ceased to broadcast claims of striking successes. The Domei Agency could only say, for instance, that the British continued to counter-attack yesterday, with an intense British bombardment from Elakan Mati and elsewhere.

A London view is that the Japanese have met a far more determined resistance than they expected.

Tokyo radio last night admitted that the Japanese forces have to "evade a rain of enemy bullets, and grudgingly declared : "It appears to be the British plan to defend the fortress to the last" It also stated that the Singapore causeway has been destroyed a second time."

More Chinese Troops In Burma

FROM Burma, there is news of the arrival of more Chinese reinforcements. These troops are veterans of Gen. Chiang Kai-shek's armies and old campaigners against the Japanese. They are among the best troops China is able to put into the field.

NEWS IN BRIEF

Reuter Radio Service

REUTER news in brief (specially broadcast to Singapore last night from London), excluding items given elsewhere

Heavy fighting is going on in the Paan area in Burma. The situation is rather obscure. It is not clear that the Japanese have succeeded in crossing the Salween River at Paan

When he visited the Khyber Pass, Gen. Chiang Kai-shek met Afridi tribesmen, who assured him of support for the democracies

Batavia : A Japanese parachute attack took place at Palembang in Sumatra. No details are available There have been enemy reconnaissance flights over several parts of the Outer Provinces, with attacks here and there

Australian units are apparently still holding out in scattered strong points in the island of Ambonia The attacking Japanese force comprised 13 transports and several warships, and landings were made at three points.

FILL YOUR BATHS

Residents of Singapore are advised to conserve water very carefully and to use every receptacle possible—bottles, baths, etc—to keep water to combat fire or for other emergencies.

AMERICAN ARMY IN JAVA

THE New York Times reported yesterday morning that American troops had arrived in Java, and are stationed there alongside British and Australian forces.—By Radio

LADY • THOMAS

We are happy to be able to state that Lady Thomas, who became ill several days ago, is now much better

(Printed and published by the Straits Times Press, Ltd., Cecil Street, Singapore)

PASS THIS PAPER ON TO YOUR NEIGHBOURS

50

The one-page issue of *The Sunday Times* of 15 February 1942, issued a few hours before the fall of Singapore, carries under its masthead Governor Sir Shenton Thomas' statement: "Singapore must stand; it shall stand."

Barely five days earlier, British Prime Minister Winston Churchill had sent a terse message to General Wavell: "There must be no thought of saving the troops or sparing the population. The battle must be fought to the bitter end at all costs … Commanders and senior officers should die with their troops …"

But permission to surrender was given on 14 February when it seemed clear that continued resistance would fail and would result in enormous destruction of civilian life and property.

The colonial government took over *The Straits Times* on the evening of 11 February and brought out the last four issues of the paper. After a break of four days *The Straits Times* was published again by the Japanese under a new title.

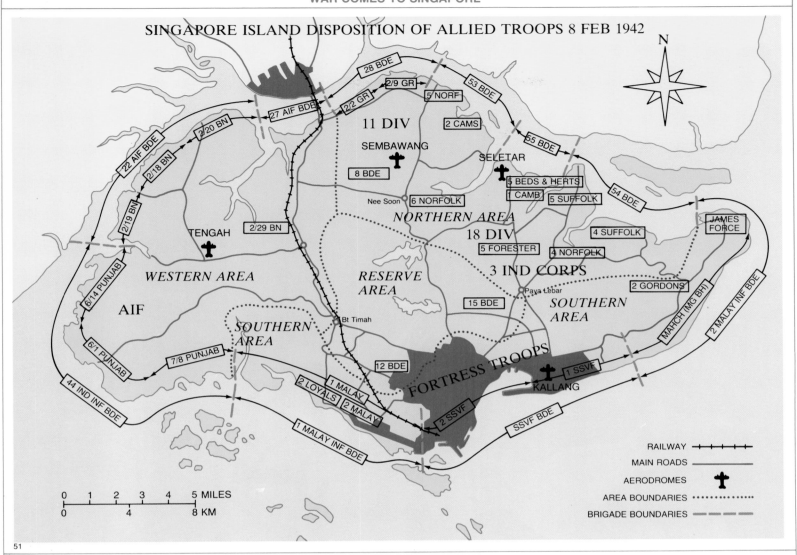

SINGAPORE ISLAND DISPOSITION OF ALLIED TROOPS 8 FEB 1942

28 BDE
2/9 GR
5 NORF
53 BDE
27 AIF BDE
2/2 GR
2 CAMS
55 BDE
22 AIF BDE
2/20 BN
11 DIV
SEMBAWANG
SELETAR
2/18 BN
8 BDE
5 BEDS & HERTS
54 BDE
2/19 BN
Nee Soon
6 NORFOLK
CAMB
5 SUFFOLK
2/29 BN
NORTHERN AREA
4 SUFFOLK
JAMES FORCE
TENGAH
18 DIV
5 FORESTER
4 NORFOLK
WESTERN AREA
RESERVE AREA
3 IND CORPS
Paya Lebar
6/14 PUNJAB
AIF
SOUTHERN AREA
15 BDE
SOUTHERN AREA
2 GORDONS
MAHCH (MG BH)
2 MALAY INF BDE
6/1 PUNJAB
7/8 PUNJAB
Bt Timah
12 BDE
FORTRESS TROOPS
KALLANG
1 SSVF
44 IND INF BDE
2 LOYALS
1 MALAY
2 MALAY
2 SSVF
SSVF BDE
1 MALAY INF BDE

RAILWAY	—+—+—+—
MAIN ROADS	——————
AERODROMES	✝
AREA BOUNDARIES	··········
BRIGADE BOUNDARIES	— — — —

0 1 2 3 4 5 MILES
0   4   8 KM

51

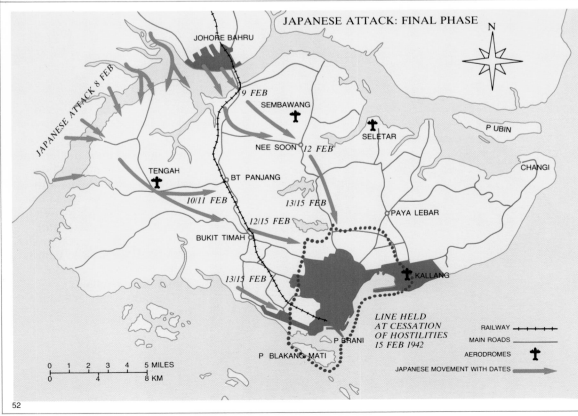

JAPANESE ATTACK: FINAL PHASE

JOHORE BAHRU
JAPANESE ATTACK 8 FEB
9 FEB
SEMBAWANG
SELETAR
P UBIN
NEE SOON
12 FEB
TENGAH
CHANGI
BT PANJANG
10/11 FEB
13/15 FEB
PAYA LEBAR
12/15 FEB
BUKIT TIMAH
13/15 FEB
KALLANG
13/15 FEB
LINE HELD AT CESSATION OF HOSTILITIES 15 FEB 1942
P BRANI
P BLAKANG MATI

RAILWAY	—+—+—+—
MAIN ROADS	——————
AERODROMES	✝
JAPANESE MOVEMENT WITH DATES	➤

0 1 2 3 4 5 MILES
0   4   8 KM

52

51
The disposition of Allied troops on Singapore island on 8 February 1942.

52
The lines of advance of the Japanese 25th Army, comprising the Imperial Guards (Konoe) Division and the 5th and 18th Divisions, as they moved towards the city. Note the positions held at the cessation of hostilities on 15 February 1942.

53

54

53/54
Lt Gen A E Percival, General-Officer-Commanding Malaya (above, extreme right) with Brigadier Torrens, Brigadier Newbigging and Major Wild, being led by Japanese Staff Officer Sugita to negotiate the surrender terms on 15 February at the Ford Factory in Bukit Timah Road (left).

The talks began at about 5.00 pm.

55

55

At the negotiating table, Lt Gen Yamashita acted tough and demanded from Lt Gen Percival the immediate and unconditional surrender of his troops.

An excerpt of the dialogue between the commanders:

YAMASHITA: I want to hear whether you want to surrender or not. If you want to surrender I insist on its being unconditional. What is your answer? Yes or no?

PERCIVAL: Will you give me until tomorrow morning?

YAMASHITA: Tomorrow? I cannot wait and the Japanese forces will have to attack tonight.

PERCIVAL: How about waiting until 11.30 pm Tokyo time?

YAMASHITA: If that is to be the case, the Japanese forces will have to resume attacks until then. Will you say yes or no?

PERCIVAL: (made no reply).

YAMASHITA: I want to hear a decisive answer and I insist on an unconditional surrender. What do you say?

PERCIVAL: Yes.

YAMASHITA: All right, then. The order to cease fire must be issued at exactly 10.00 pm. I will immediately send one thousand Japanese troops into the city area to maintain peace

and order. You agree to that?

PERCIVAL: Yes.

YAMASHITA: If you violate these terms, the Japanese troops will lose no time in launching a general and final offensive against Singapore City.

Percival, however, succeeded in getting Yamashita to agree not to enter the city till the following morning, 16 February. The surrender terms were signed at 6.10 pm on 15 February 1942.

Yamashita wrote later: "My attack on Singapore was a bluff – a bluff that worked. I had 30,000 men and was outnumbered more than three

to one. I knew that if I had to fight long for Singapore, I would be beaten. That is why the surrender had to be at once. I was very frightened all the time that the British would discover our numerical weakness and lack of supplies and force me into disastrous street fighting."

56

56
The British delegation with the Japanese delegation after signing the surrender terms. Lt Gen Percival and Lt Gen Yamashita are second and fourth respectively from the right.

57
"The Tiger of Malaya", Lt Gen Tomoyuki Yamashita (top right) on an inspection tour of Singapore on 23 February 1942.

Son of a village doctor, Yamashita was 56 years old when he was summoned from a military assignment in Manchuria to command the attack on Malaya/Singapore.

After his victory, he was posted back to Manchuria in July 1942. He remained there till he was recalled to Southeast Asia in October 1944 to resist the American invasion of the Philippines. When the Japanese surrendered in September

57

1945, Yamashita was the first Japanese general to be tried by the Americans for war crimes. He was hanged in February 1946.

58

Lt Gen A E Percival, General-Officer-Commanding Malaya from April 1941 to the end of the war.

Percival, who had fought with distinction in World War I, returned to Britain after the Japanese surrender, carrying with him the major blame for the fall of Singapore.

Ironically, in a study prepared for the UK War Office in 1937, Percival had predicted with uncanny foresight the landing points and lines of advance of the Japanese army in its invasion of Malaya/Singapore.

58

59/60
The vanquished (below) and
the jubilant victors (right).

59

60

48

2

THE STRUGGLE TO LIVE

61

61
Japanese troops marching down Battery Road towards Collyer Quay on 16 February 1942.

The buildings in the background have now been replaced, on the left by the new Hongkong and Shanghai Bank building and the Straits Trading building, and on the right by the Chartered Bank building.

1942~1945

The Japanese proclaimed themselves the "liberators" of Singapore when they took control on 16 February 1942. Yamashita set up his military headquarters at Raffles College. Singapore was renamed Syonan ("Light of the South") and clocks were put forward by 1½ hours in line with Tokyo time.

The major newspapers resumed publication within a week, but now under the control of the Japanese. Radio broadcasts were started in March, but these consisted mainly of Japanese propaganda and cultural programmes. The Japanese language was introduced in schools and the British currency was replaced with Japanese currency.

The military takeover had been orderly. But the initial order and calm belied the violence, horror and repression which the people of Singapore and the prisoners of war (POWs) were soon to experience.

The Europeans were the first to experience Japanese brutality. On the morning of 17 February, the entire European population including women and children was assembled on the Padang for inspection and questioning. The military personnel among them were forced to march to Selarang barracks 22 kilometres away, and the civilians to Katong. Then, after being herded together for two weeks without  enough food or basic conveniences, the 2,300 civilians began their long march from Katong to Changi Prison.

With the Asian troops, the Japanese took a different approach. Assembling the Indian and Malay POWs at Farrer Park on 17 February, the Japanese urged them to transfer their loyalty to Japan. Eight Malay officers who refused were executed, together with 100 of their men.

The Indians were urged to join the Indian National Army (INA), which had been formed to fight the British for India's independence. Many remained steadfastly loyal to the British despite pressures from the Japanese and other Indians. However, about half the Indian military personnel finally joined the INA, believing that it provided them with an opportunity to fight for India's independence. Those who refused were imprisoned at Selarang; some were later executed.

Treatment of POWs was harsh. Punishment for breaking the stringent prison rules was swift and severe, and prisoners were often tortured. Nearly all prisoners were forced to do manual labour at construction sites and at the harbour, and by the time the war ended in 1945, a new military runway had been completed at Changi with forced POW labour. Thousands of men were sent to work on the infamous Burma-Siam (Thailand) Railway from where few returned.

Life was little better for the civilian population of Singapore. The Japanese seized private homes for their use. Food was scarce, and rationing became a fact of life. The scarcity of goods soon sent prices sky-rocketing and a flourishing black-market sprang up.

In many instances, ordinary people were subjected to appalling torture or summary execution on mere suspicion, or for disrespect to Japanese authority. Lawlessness, especially looting, was effectively and swiftly stopped when the *Kempeitai* (Japanese Military Police) summarily decapitated those caught stealing, and displayed their heads in public. Often these offenders were people driven by hunger to steal food from shops. The brutality of the *Kempeitai* kept the people in a perpetual state of tension and fear.

It was the Singapore Chinese, however, who suffered most under Japanese rule. Japanese hostility towards the Chinese was a carry-over from the Sino-Japanese War. The local Chinese had shown sympathy to China in that war, and had been involved in acts such as the boycotting of Japanese goods. Most of the survivors of Dalforce, aware that the Japanese would show no mercy to them, had already fled to the Malayan jungles to join an anti-Japanese guerilla campaign under the Malayan People's Anti-Japanese Army (MPAJA).

The MPAJA was under the control of the Malayan Communist Party. Its guerilla campaign was assisted by the British, who air-dropped arms and provided advisers.

Some of the wealthy and several key figures of the other anti-Japanese organisations had also escaped from the island just before the British surrender to avoid Japanese reprisals. The vast majority of the populace, however, had no place to go or hide. Many were to be the victims of Japanese repression and atrocities.

Soon after taking control of Singapore, the *Kempeitai* began a purge of the Chinese community. On 18 February, many Chinese were driven from their homes and assembled at five major "registration camps" to be screened under Operation *Sook Ching*, which translated literally, means "to purge" or "eliminate". *Sook Ching*, in fact, amounted to a massacre of the Chinese. Many were dragged out of their homes at bayonet point. No standard procedure was followed at the centres. In some centres women and children were released while the men, and in some instances even boys, were herded into trucks and driven away never to be seen again. In other centres the *Kempeitai* condemned people at will, sometimes sending away entire families to their death. The lucky ones who passed this arbitrary screening were issued with identification passes, with the word "Examined" rubber-stamped on them in Chinese. However, many who had been cleared were re-arrested at the slightest excuse, and then executed. The estimates of those who perished in the *Sook Ching* vary from the *Kempeitai's* official record of 6,000 to unofficial figures which range from 25,000 to 50,000.

When Japan instructed the military authorities in Singapore and Malaya to raise their own revenue, they seized this opportunity to punish the Malayan Chinese further by extracting a $50-million "gift" from them. The task of raising $10 million, Singapore's share of the $50 million, fell on the Overseas Chinese Association. This Association had been formed, under a Japanese directive, to serve as a vehicle for conveying Japanese orders to the Singapore Chinese. The leaders of the Association included 72-year-old Dr Lim Boon Keng, who had with great reluctance agreed to its formation.

As the war dragged on, Singapore faced severe hardships. Basic foodstuffs, especially rice, became extremely scarce. In an attempt to solve this problem the Japanese administrators launched a "Grow More Food" campaign. When exhortations did not work, the Japanese ordered the people of Singapore to plant food crops on every available piece of land. Tapioca became a favourite, as it did not need much effort to cultivate. However, the campaign failed to solve the food shortage.

In August 1943, the Overseas Chinese Association was asked to create a new farming village – New Syonan – in Endau in northeast Johor. The Japanese authorities intended that the creation of New Syonan should help relieve Singapore's population pressure as the plan was to re-settle 30,000 people there under a voluntary migration programme. In the end, however, only about 12,000 people went to Endau. The Eurasians were ordered to create Fuji Village at Bahau in Negri Sembilan. This project, however, failed.

Life in Singapore became more difficult with each passing day, with overcrowding, food shortages and other deprivations. Many were not sure if they would survive the Occupation as the Japanese became more harsh, cruel and erratic in their administration. However, the Japanese had been suffering military setbacks in the war. Slowly, news of Allied victories in the Pacific and in Burma reached the people of Singapore. Some heard this news on secret wireless sets, and it swiftly spread throughout the population. America's first air raid on Singapore harbour in November 1944 confirmed these reports, and from then on Allied planes were frequently sighted.

The Japanese, however, were not prepared to relinquish Singapore without a fight. By early 1945 it became evident that the battle for Singapore was approaching. Expecting a long drawn-out siege of the island, the Japanese rounded up 6,000 prisoners for defence work in Singapore and Johor, and from May 1945 civilians were subjected to military training on the Padang.

In Europe the war had ended in May 1945, and the end of the war in the Pacific was only a question of time. The end came suddenly, surprising even most of the Japanese officials, as they had not been told of the dropping of atomic bombs on Hiroshima and Nagasaki on 6 and 9 August 1945 respectively.

Japan formally surrendered on 15 August 1945. This was announced in Singapore only on 17 August, and local newspapers did not carry the news till 21 August. The Japanese prepared an internment camp for themselves in Jurong and retreated there, leaving a few officers to hand over the island to the incoming British. Several bands of Japanese soldiers blew themselves up with hand grenades rather than surrender to the British.

Meanwhile, there was widespread panic in the city as the various pro-Japanese organisations disbanded for fear of retribution from the population, and people rushed to get rid of their useless Japanese currency. With no one effectively in charge, communist-controlled elements, including the MPAJA, seized the opportunity to assert themselves. Bands of youths carrying communist flags sought out alleged collaborators, and executed them after holding "people's trials".

When British warships and Commonwealth troops finally arrived three weeks later on 5 September, they received a tumultuous welcome from the people who lined the five-kilometre route from the port to the Cathay Building at Dhobi Ghaut. A week later, on 12 September, at the Municipal Building (now City Hall) the Japanese military leaders formally surrendered all their forces in Southeast Asia to Admiral Lord Louis Mountbatten, Supreme Allied Commander for the region.

The people of Singapore were relieved that the Japanese Occupation was over, and they genuinely welcomed the British back. But they were a different people from the population of pre-war Singapore. After the war and 3½ years of Japanese Occupation they no longer regarded the British as invincible, infallible or superior. The sight of demoralised and defeated British soldiers in 1942, and of British POWs doing menial tasks under the orders of Japanese prison guards had drastically changed perceptions of British power, pomp and superiority. Also, for the duration of the Occupation, the local people had helped to run the country for the Japanese military administration. They had seen that their alien rulers, whether British or Japanese, enjoyed a higher status and a better life, not because they were intrinsically superior, but because they had the military might. They would no longer give the same unquestioning obedience to British authority as they had done before the war.

Horrors of Occupation

62
The Japanese assembled all the prisoners of war (POWs) at the Padang for questioning on 17 February 1942. European POWs and civilians, including women and children, were eventually interned at either Selarang Barracks or Changi Prison.

62

63

63
The Indian and Malay soldiers were assembled at Farrer Park and urged to transfer their allegiance to Japan. Most remained steadfastly loyal to the British. Those who refused to join the Indian National Army (INA) were either interned or later executed. Many who were cajoled into joining the INA did so in the belief that Japan would help liberate India from the British.

64
Lt Gen Yamashita paying homage to Japanese soldiers killed in action in Malaya and Singapore.

According to Japanese sources, the total number of Japanese killed, from the landing at Singora to the surrender of Singapore, was 3,507 of whom 1,714 died during the battle for Singapore. The number of Allied soldiers killed was around 9,000.

65
Some of the private vehicles requisitioned by the Japanese military administration soon after it assumed control of Singapore.

Houses, schools and private buildings like the Cathay Building and Raffles Hotel were also taken over.

66/67
(Below) One of the interrogation centres for *Sook Ching* or operation clean-up in North Bridge Road at the entrance of Kandahar Street.

(Bottom left) Chinese males wait their turn to register at another interrogation centre.

In the early days of the Occupation, the Chinese were assembled at five different points in the city. They were herded together and kept under the hot sun for hours without food and water until the interrogation was over. Some were issued with identification passes while others were imprisoned or executed. Thousands of local Chinese perished as a result of *Sook Ching*.

66

67

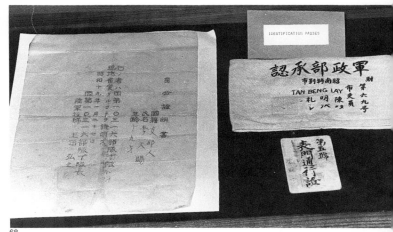

68

68/69
On many occasions, those who passed the "screening" were rubber-stamped "Examined" on their arms or clothes. Those whose clothes were stamped could cut out and carry the stamped portion like an identification card. But those who were stamped on their arms had the problem of ensuring that these "tattoos" were not washed away.

70

The first issue of *Shonan Times* (formerly *The Straits Times*) dated 20 February 1942.

Later renamed *Syonan Shimbun*, it was published in both English and Japanese. Several other newspapers were taken over by the Japanese and reappeared under different names. For instance, in place of the Chinese dailies *Sin Chew Jit Poh* and *Nanyang Siang Pau*, *Syonan Jit Poh* was published.

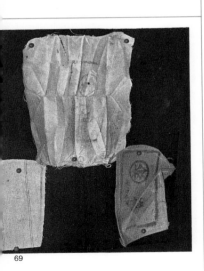

69

THE SHONAN TIMES

No. 1.   FEBRUARY 20,   SHOWA 17.   5 cents.

JAPAN'S POSITION IMPREGNABLE

Effect Of Fall Of Singapore

Gen. Shunroku Hata Issues Verbal Statement

GEN. Shunroku Hata, Commander-in-Chief, Japanese Forces in China, in a verbal statement at 3.30 p.m. Wednesday, said that with the fall of Singapore, Japan is now strongly established in an impregnable position to conduct the current war. Both Britain and the United States can no longer wage an offensive war against Japan in the South-west Pacific.

British Reverses In Malaya

Political Blunder In Colonies

Stockholm.

THE series of British reverses in Malaya is due to a British political blunder in her colonies, comments the London Times Wednesday. The Times declares that the British Government listened only to the opinions of Britishers in Malaya, and the Asiatic population remained only as spectators of the war. A correspondent reveals that the fall of Singapore is another indication of British bureaucracy. The natives in Malaya have always had an intense anti-British feeling.

British Aircraft Carrier Damaged

Lisbon.

A BRITISH aircraft carrier limped into the Gulf of Gibraltar for repairs yesterday, according to information received here.

Five ships have been torpedoed by Axis submarines in the Dutch West Indies, says a report from London on Wednesday.

AMERICANS' DARK DAYS

Buenos Aires.

Senator Tom Connolly, chairman of the Senate Foreign Relations Committee, told the Upper House that the Americans were having dark days in East Asia, and warned that there were still darker days ahead. He asked the nations to be prepared to meet hardships, adding that the nature of the war in East Asia demanded close co-operation between the U.S. Army and Navy commands but not necessarily with the Unified Command.

BATAVIA APPEALS TO AUSTRALIA

Berne, Switzerland.

WITH the Japanese attack on the Dutch East Indies increasing from the land, sea and air, Batavia has appealed to Australia for immediate aid, a United Press dispatch from Sydney reveals. The Australian Parliament was to-day summoned to discuss ways and means to satisfy the Batavia request, the report adds.

Joint action by Britain, America, Australia, India, China, and the Dutch East Indies has now collapsed to its very foundations. The Chungking regime, which has so far continued its resistance in concert with the Anglo-American powers, has been deprived of important bases and can no longer be able to keep up its resistance. By sending its troops into Burma, the Chungking regime shows it attaches much importance to the Burma Road, but this road is destined to be completely cut off in the near future. It is now high time for Chungking to cease its meaningless resistance. If this resistance continues, the Chungking regime will be completely wiped out.

Japanese operations in central Shantung Province in China, which is aimed at the annihilation of the remnants of the Chinese troops there, have reached its climax. After capturing Yuchuan, Japanese units are steadily tightening their cordon around the enemy.

Following the fall of Singapore, Japanese forces have captured two small surrounding islands—Batam and Samboe. Oil tanks have been seized by the Japanese. Japanese naval air forces are busy over the approaches to Shonan Island. Large formations of naval bombers and pursuit planes conducted incessant reconnaissance for enemy vessels.

REDS SMASHED BY GERMANS

Berlin.

AS a result of the thrust by German forces in the central sector of the Eastern Front, another powerful corps of the Red forces has been smashed with heavy losses. The Germans captured many prisoners and much war materials.

PUBLIC NOTICE

The Nippon Authority of Pulau Shonan desires the following persons to report for duty.

1. Workers and Engineers of Gas, Electric, Water-works and those connected with Broadcasting. They should report for duty at the Nippon Army Administration Office at the Municipal Building, Singapore, immediately.
2. The civilians are requested to clean the streets and compounds near their houses.
3. Blackout will be observed as usual.

THE ADMINISTRATION BRANCH.
JAPANESE IMPERIAL FORCES.

Australia Further Isolated

Saigon.

AUSTRALIA will be further isolated from the United States. Canberra announced to-day the suspension of radio telephone service with these countries with effect from Feb. 21. The Department of the Post Master-General says that the step has been decided upon by the War Cabinet for reasons of security. It is pointed out that the Australian radio telephone service to other countries has already been suspended.

Enemy Destroyer Sunk Yesterday

A FEW enemy destroyers were sighted to the south of Shonan Island. One was sunk while a second received several hits. Two enemy transports were also sighted, of which one was sunk.

Meanwhile, it is reported that Japanese airmen accounted for 32 enemy planes over Java Sea during the past nine days from Feb. 9 to Feb. 17.

Japanese naval units have escorted a fleet of Japanese armed transports up the river to the recently occupied city of Palembang.

The British Broadcasting Corporation, quoting a Batavia communique, states that Japanese warplanes raided Koepang Wednesday.

ENEMY HANGARS DESTROYED

Vichy.

THE United States War Department disclosed that the air attack on American positions in the Bataan Peninsula was gaining in ferocity.

From the Bataan front, it is reported that despite a furious barrage of the enemy's anti-aircraft guns, Japanese dive bombers swooped down and seriously damaged the airfield there. The Japanese destroyed one enemy plane and the hangars, it was revealed Wednesday.

U.S. NATIONALS FLEEING DUTCH EAST INDIES

A BATAVIA report says that large numbers of American nationals have been evacuated from the Dutch East Indies, making a total of 15,500 during the past few weeks.

Only 100 Americans remain in the Dutch East Indies, says a Saigon report.

THE SHONAN TIMES
FEBRUARY 20, SHOWA 17.

OUR FIRST ISSUE

To Our Friends—The People Of Malaya

In this fortress of Singapore (Shonan) and the Peninsula of Malaya, all arms and military objectives are under the control of the Nippon troops.

The Press, which is the most powerful organ for the expression of views, comes under the domination of the Nippon troops. By the wish of the Chief Nippon Commander, we are issuing the Shonan Times.

It is the wish of the Commander that the civilization of the people here shall be preserved, and that they shall enjoy good fortune and happiness with the restoration of peaceful conditions.

The policy of injustice, unrighteousness and cunning shall disappear automatically, just as the smoke of the burning Fortress is fast disappearing, and there shall arise in its place the germ of the New Order which will manifest itself. This must be believed by the people who should take all steps to cultivate an understanding of this New Order.

Those who believe in rumour or gossip from the enemy are hindering the growth of the New Order. The enemy who withdrew from here is wandering around the seas in the vicinity of the Malay Peninsula and the fortress of Singapore (Shonan). The people, therefore, should be on their guard.

We shall pray for and offer thanks to the souls of those of the Nippon Army and Navy who have lost their lives in battle. They have sacrificed their lives in laying the foundations of the New Order in East Asia.

ADVERTISEMENTS

Personal or business advertisements will be accepted at the office of The Shonan Times in Cecil Street.

Mrs. Irene Ferron last seen on Tuesday 10-2-42 together with Mr. and Mrs. J C. Mathieu in a blue "Citroen" saloon (Malacca registration). Anyone knowing of her whereabouts please contact Roy Ferroa c/o "Shonan Times," Cecil Street.

Will Chong Hup Kee last heard of in Ipoh or any one knowing of his whereabouts please communicate with Chong Tak Ngit, c/o The Shonan Times.

Will Miss Pak Yeung or anyone knowing of her whereabouts please communicate with N. Siebel, The Shonan Times, or 53, Lloyd Road.

Will Mr. Brett of Namly Avenue or anyone knowing his whereabouts please communicate with P. K. Jones, c/o "Shonan Times," Shonan.

Leembruggens would like to contact the Koelmeyers of Kuala Lumpur. Address 276a Orchard Road.

Tom Hope would like to contact Bob Bartels. Address 53, Lloyd Road.

THE SYONAN TIMES

No. 2   FEBRUARY 21, 2602, SYOWA 17   5 cents

LARGE-SCALE ATTACK ON PORT DARWIN

Australia's Northern De...

Fate Of Java Foredoomed

Lisbon, Feb. 20.

At Allied concern over the Nipponese ... McEvoy, N.B.C. commentator and ...spondent in Tokyo, says in a broad-...scale reinforcements can arrive and ...ate of Java is foredoomed. ...reports from London indicate that ...over the question of where Allied re-...sent.

...rd summing up general opinion, ...disputable reasons why Burma should ...ava: firstly, the battle for Burma is ...einforcing Java; secondly, Malaya ...f using troops without aircraft pro-...insportation difficulties are less in ...in the case o Java. Dutch ...eeling of defea... m in Java. ...nothing short of a miracle can save ...utch East Indies is similar to that ...al collapse.

Thirt... 4...

THIRTEE... aircraft ... in Thursd... ponese nav... ters in To... 4.30 o'cloc... Nipponese ... large-scale bo... and naval base ... crippling dama... military establish...

The Meaning Of Syonan

IN naming Singapore Island Syonan, the Nipponese Government hopes to bring prosperity to all civilians in Syonan.

We think it appropriate to explain the meaning of Syonan. Some of you already know that this era in Nippon history is called Syowa. The meaning of Syo is "bright" or "brilliant" or "brilliance," and Nan means "south." Therefore, Syonan means "Brilliant South," commemorating the Nippon people or the Yamato race.

In this era of Syowa, Nippon troops have captured this strong fortress of Singapore and have attained their great southward expansion. The Nipponese Government wishes to give all coloured or Asiatic peoples peace and glory with the capture of Singapore, and hopes that all the coloured races will begin the construction of the New Order of East Asia.

TRAIN FROM INDO-CHINA TO SYONAN

(Special News Release by Press Agency)

ACCORDING to an announcement by a reliable source it was stated that an express train ran between Pnom-Penh (Indo-China) and Syonan that night.

This train is only for Army ...se, but it will be made avail...ble to all travellers in the ...ear future.

Gen. Isogai New Governor Of H.K.

Hong Kong Feb. 20.

...a ceremony held at the ...Peninsula Hotel in Hong ...General Isogai was ap-...ed the new Governor of ...Kong.

...neral Isogai was on the sta... ...e headquarters of the Nip-...e Army at the beginning of ...hinese incident. He has been ...e for several years and is ...ert in Chinese culture.

...ish Cabinet ...onstruction

Lisbon, Feb. 20.

...i. CHURCHILL, Br...i Prime Minister, has...

71

The Japanese renamed Singapore *Syonan* (Light of the South) and declared that the Japanese Government would give all "coloured or Asiatic peoples peace and glory". Lt Gen Yamashita also issued a declaration hoping to "promote social development by establishing the East Asia Co-prosperity Sphere".

72

A Japanese propaganda cartoon.

The British were often portrayed as intimidating masters who had exploited Asian labour and confiscated and looted Asian treasures. The Japanese projected themselves as the saviours (note the tight fist with the Japanese flag on the cuff at the top right corner) who had come to save the people from the "foxy, deceit (sic), cunning" British.

72

73

73

Looters were executed and their heads displayed on spikes in public places as a warning and deterrent to others.

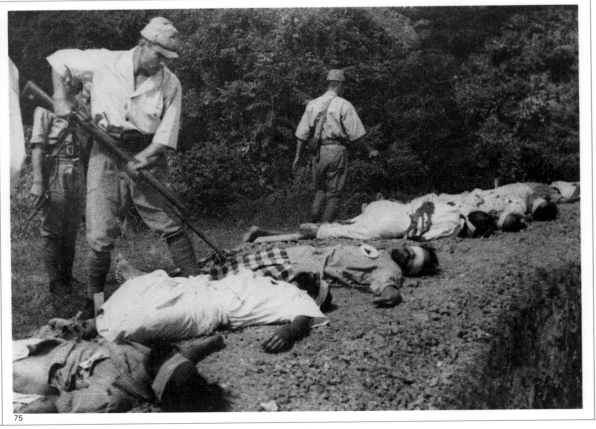

74/75
(Top) Sikh prisoners of war sit blindfolded with target marks hanging over their hearts as the Japanese take aim with their rifles.

When bullets failed, bayonets (right) came in handy.

75

76
Dr Lim Boon Keng, founder and chairman of the Overseas Chinese Association formed under Japanese directive to serve as a vehicle for conveying Japanese orders to the Singapore Chinese.

Born in Singapore in 1869 and educated at Raffles Institution, he was the first Chinese Queen's Scholar, and a founder member of the Straits Chinese British Association. Active in public life, his various involvements included membership of the Singapore branch of the Kuomintang and the Chinese Company of the Singapore Volunteer Corp. He was a Legislative Councillor from 1895 to 1902.

76

78

78
S C Goho, a lawyer and a prominent Indian leader in the 1940s.

As president of the Indian Youth League, he organised several hundred volunteers during the intense Japanese air raids before the Occupation to feed and shelter refugees streaming into Singapore from Malaya. Goho became a member of the Legislative Council in 1948.

77

77
The $50-million cheque given as "donation" to the Japanese military government in Singapore by the Overseas Chinese Association on behalf of the Chinese in Malaya and Singapore.

The Japanese had compelled the Chinese in both territories to donate this amount as a token of atonement for their past hostility to Japan. Singapore succeeded in raising its share of $10 million, but the Malayan Chinese managed to raise only $18 million. The balance was made up through loans repayable within a year from the Yokohama Specie Bank, which was operating from the Chartered Bank premises in Singapore. Yamashita received the "gift" in June 1942 at a ceremony held in the Chinese Chamber of Commerce.

Fighters for "Freedom"

79
Members of the Malayan People's Anti-Japanese Army (MPAJA) at a camp in Skudai, Johor.
 The British assisted the MPAJA during the Occupation years through air drops of arms, supplies and the provision of advisers.

79

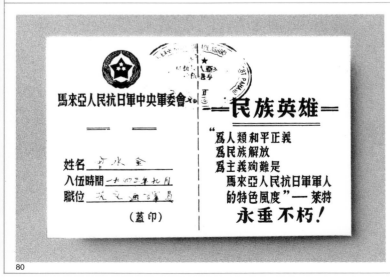

馬來亞人民抗日軍中央軍委會

民族英雄

姓名 黃水金
入伍時間 一九四三年九月
職位 英文通譯員

（蓋印）

"為人類和平正義
為民族解放
為主義殉難是
馬來亞人民抗日軍人
的特色風度"—萊特

永垂不朽！

80

80
A card of a member of the MPAJA.
 The card, issued in September 1943, bears a quotation from Lai Teck, secretary-general of the Malayan Communist Party: "To die for peace and justice of mankind, for national liberation and for a cause, is the distinguishing character of the servicemen of the Malayan People's Anti-Japanese Army."
 The MPAJA had its origins in the agreement reached between the British and the Malayan Communist Party in December 1941. Under the agreement, the British released communists from jail and provided communist-selected cadres with a few weeks of guerilla warfare training to enable them to fight a guerilla campaign in Japanese-occupied territory. The MPAJA remained under the control of the Malayan Communist Party.

81

81
The mammoth crowd that turned up at the Padang on 24 October 1943 to hear Subash Chandra Bose "declare war" against Britain and the United States.

Bose was the president of the Indian Independence League, an East Asia-wide organisation created to mobilise the support of overseas Indians for the freedom of India. Bose was also the head of the Indian National Army, which was formed to fight alongside the Japanese to win freedom for India from the British.

On 21 October 1943 Bose declared himself the head of the Provisional Government of India, which was promptly recognised by the Japanese Government.

82
Subash Chandra Bose inspects the Ranee of Jhansi Regiment, the women's regiment of the Indian National Army. He is accompanied by Captain Dr S Lakshmi, commander of the regiment.

82

Allied Prisoners of War

83

83
Australian and British prisoners at Selarang Barracks, Changi, where all European prisoners, including Lt Gen Arthur Percival and Governor Shenton Thomas were interned. In the foreground are makeshift shelters.

In August 1942, Percival and Shenton Thomas, together with 400 military and civilian prisoners (from Changi Prison) were removed to Taiwan.

This photograph (above), secretly taken by an Australian POW and concealed in the false bottom of a water bottle, was later presented to the Australian War Memorial.

84

85

84
(Left) POWs cooking their meal after a hard day's labour. Nearly all prisoners were forced to work at construction sites. Later, thousands of prisoners and civilians were sent to work on the Burma-Siam Railway, from where few returned alive.

FATHER FORGIVE THEM
THEY KNOW NOT WHAT THEY DO

86

85
Australians in a hospital ward at Changi POW camp at the time of the surrender of the Japanese.

86
Stanley Warren, a British prisoner, found solace from the torture and privations at Selarang Barracks by painting Biblical murals in St Luke's Chapel within the prison camp. Now known as the Changi Murals, the paintings (five in all) represent the triumph of the human spirit over trying conditions.

Life in Syonan

87

87
Food shortage was a serious problem during the Occupation. To encourage the people to grow their own food, the Japanese launched a "Grow More Food Campaign", and made vegetable gardening part of the school curriculum.

88
Students of St Joseph's Institution tend the vegetable plots in their school grounds under the guidance of teachers

88

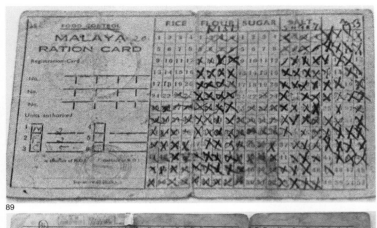

89

90

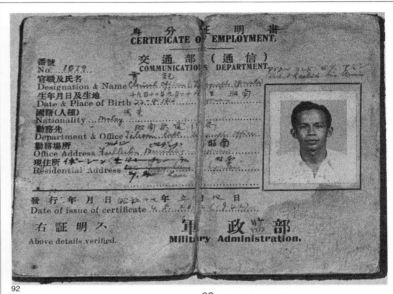

92

92
The Japanese issued all workers with certificates of employment detailing the nature of their work and personal particulars. This card, issued on 4 May 1942, was for a telegraph operator working in Fullerton Building.

89/90
Ration cards issued by the Japanese to control the supply of rice and other essential items to the residents.

Without these cards one could not get any provisions from shops. Each adult was authorised a ration of eight katis (4.8 kg) of rice per month and each child four katis (2.4 kg). In early 1944 the rice ration was reduced to six katis (3.6 kg) per month for adults.

91
The scarcity of most goods sent prices sky-rocketing and soon a thriving black-market was in operation. This table shows the prices of some commodities before the outbreak of the war and just before the war ended.

A SAMPLE OF PRICES IN PRE-WAR AND JAPANESE-OCCUPIED SINGAPORE	1941 $	1945 $
RICE 1 picul	5.00	5,000.00
EGG 1 dozen	0.24	120.00
PARKER PEN 1	15.00	5,000.00
QUININE POWDER 1 lb	1.50	15.00
BERIN VITAMIN B1 500 pills	26.00	45,000.00
SHOPHOUSE 1	5,000–6,000	160,000–250,000

Sources: Low and Cheng, *This Singapore* and M Turnbull, *A History of Singapore 1819–1975*

91

93

93
The Japanese issued these currency notes, featuring coconut palms and banana plants, to replace the Malayan currency. As the currency's value rapidly declined, "banana money", as it came to be known, was worth little more than scraps of paper.

94
New Japanese stamps depicted various Malayan scenes and activities. This card was postmarked at Orchard Road Post Office on 29 April 2603. (The year 2603 was based on the Japanese system then in use. It corresponded to 1943.)

94

95

95
Japanese (*Nippon-go*) was
made the official language and
people were ordered to learn it.
The first *Nippon-go* classes
were held to teach Japanese
songs to music teachers (above)
when schools reopened in April
1942. The teachers were to
teach their students to sing
them at the Japanese

Emperor's birthday
celebrations on 29 April 1942.
Thousands of students
participated in a parade at the
Padang waving Japanese flags
and singing the patriotic song,
Aikoku Koshin Kyoku, as Lt
Gen Yamashita reviewed the
parade from the balcony of the
Municipal Building (now City
Hall).

96/97
To make the learning of
Japanese easier, simple
Japanese books like these
(below) were issued.
   The *Syonan Shimbun* also
ran daily Japanese lessons.

96

97

98
The Japanese stage a masquerade, one of the many activities held in Syonan in celebration of the Japanese Emperor's birthday.

99
In less than a year, Singapore streets had taken on a Japanese look, as shown in these pictures taken on 8 February 1943. A Japanese-made bus cruises down North Bridge Road/ Coleman Street junction past Adelphi Hotel. Japanese billboards adorn the hotel's shops.

100

101

100
An electric tram car, the most common mode of public transport during the Occupation period, travels down Bras Basah Road. The Cathay Building is in the background.

101
With kimono-clad women, street signs in *Nippon-go* and Japanese soldiers, this street could pass for a street in Japan. But it is High Street during the Occupation.

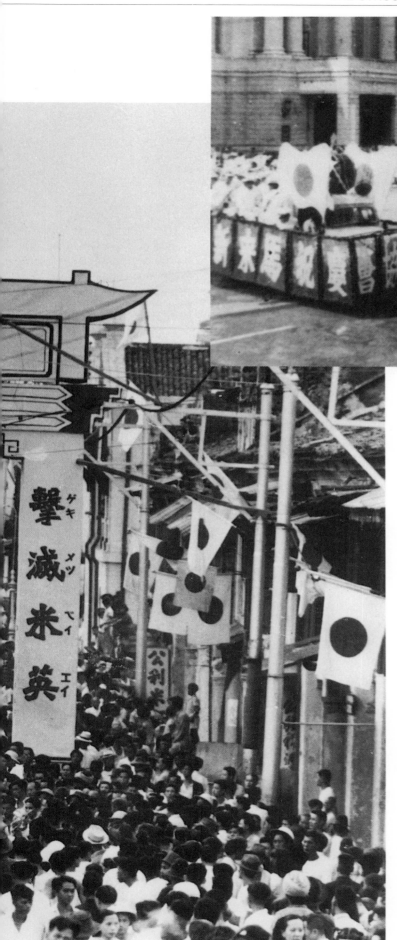

103

102/103
Celebrations marking the first anniversary of the fall of Singapore were staged on 15 February 1943. There was a procession of floats and the city was decorated with flags and arches.

The words on the centre of the arch say, "Celebration of Malaya's new birth". The other banners proclaim: "To accomplish and complete the holy war", "Long live Japan", and "Annihilate the United States and Britain".

The Return of the British

104

104/105
By the beginning of 1945, it was evident to the people of Singapore that the Japanese were losing the war and liberation was only a question of time. The war came to a sudden end on 15 August following the dropping of atomic bombs on Hiroshima and Nagasaki on 6 and 9 August respectively.

(Below) British troops arrive in assault craft on 5 September to repossess Singapore.

105

106/107
Overjoyed that the hardships of war are over, the people of Singapore welcome the British back with enthusiasm …

108

108
… lining the streets and waving British, American, Russian and Kuomintang flags …

109/110
… and holding street parades.

109

110

111
Japanese officers, in the process of handing over control of Singapore to the British, point out their troop dispositions to some British officers.

112
Two members of the much feared *Kempeitai*, the Japanese Military Police force.
Once the British returned, the *Kempeitai* were rounded up and placed in Pearl's Hill Jail to await trial for war crimes.

113
Some of the Japanese soldiers after being rounded up.

114

114/115
The formal surrender ceremony takes place in the Council Chamber of the Municipal Building (City Hall) on 12 September 1945. Admiral Lord Louis Mountbatten, Supreme Allied Commander, Southeast Asia Command, accepts the surrender of the Japanese forces in the area, whilst Lt Gen S Itagaki signs the Instrument of Surrender on behalf of the Japanese Commander-in-Chief of the Southern Army, Field Marshal Count Terauchi, who lay seriously ill in Saigon.

115

INSTRUMENT OF SURRENDER OF JAPANESE FORCES UNDER THE COMMAND OR CONTROL OF THE SUPREME COMMANDER, JAPANESE EXPEDITIONARY FORCES, SOUTHERN REGIONS, WITHIN THE OPERATIONAL THEATRE OF THE SUPREME ALLIED COMMANDER, SOUTH EAST ASIA.

1. In pursuance of and in compliance with :

    (a) the Instrument of Surrender signed by the Japanese plenipotentiaries by command and on behalf of the Emperor of Japan, the Japanese Government, and the Japanese Imperial General Headquarters at Tokyo on 2 September, 1945 ;

    (b) General Order No. 1, promulgated at the same place and on the same date ;

    (c) the Local Agreement made by the Supreme Commander, Japanese Expeditionary Forces, Southern Regions, with the Supreme Allied Commander, South East Asia at Rangoon on 27 August, 1945 ;

to all of which Instrument of Surrender, General Order and Local Agreement this present Instrument is complementary and which it in no way supersedes, the Supreme Commander, Japanese Expeditionary Forces, Southern Regions (Field Marshal Count Terauchi) does hereby surrender unconditionally to the Supreme Allied Commander, South East Asia (Admiral The Lord Louis Mountbatten) himself and all Japanese sea, ground, air and auxiliary forces under his command or control and within the operational theatre of the Supreme Allied Commander, South East Asia.

2. The Supreme Commander, Japanese Expeditionary Forces, Southern Regions, undertakes to ensure that all orders and instructions that may be issued from time to time by the Supreme Allied Commander, South East Asia, or by any of his subordinate Naval, Military or Air Force Commanders of whatever rank acting in his name, are scrupulously and promptly obeyed by all Japanese sea, ground, air and auxiliary forces under the command or control of the Supreme Commander, Japanese Expeditionary Forces, Southern Regions, and within the operational theatre of the Supreme Allied Commander, South East Asia.

3. Any disobedience of, or delay or failure to comply with, orders or instructions issued by the Supreme Allied Commander, South East Asia, or issued on his behalf by any of his subordinate Naval, Military or Air Force Commanders of whatever rank, and any action which the Supreme Allied Commander, South East Asia, or his subordinate Commanders, acting on his behalf, may determine to be detrimental to the Allied Powers, will be dealt with as the Supreme Allied Commander, South East Asia may decide.

4. This Instrument takes effect from the time and date of signing.

5. This Instrument is drawn up in the English language, which is the only authentic version. In any case of doubt as to intention or meaning, the decision of the Supreme Allied Commander, South East Asia is final. It is the responsibility of the Supreme Commander, Japanese Expeditionary Forces, Southern Regions, to make such translation into Japanese as he may require.

Signed at Singapore at O341 hours (G.M.T.) on 12 September, 1945.

    SUPREME COMMANDER   **SUPREME ALLIED COMMANDER,**
JAPANESE EXPEDITIONARY FORCES,   **SOUTH EAST ASIA.**
    SOUTHERN REGIONS.

116

116

The Instrument of Surrender of the Japanese Forces.

117
The sufferings of war are temporarily forgotten as the people scramble for vantage points atop the Supreme Court to witness the pomp and splendour of the victory parade at the Padang.

117

118
Lord Mountbatten leads the cheers for His Majesty the King at the parade of Allied service personnel on the Padang after the surrender ceremony.

118

119

119
The Cathay Building as it was on 27 November 1945, after the flags of the five Allies – Britain, the United States, China, France and the Netherlands – were hoisted.

The Cathay, then Singapore's only "skyscraper", was the centre of activity during and after the war. Just before Singapore fell to the Japanese, it was crowded with army deserters and war refugees from Malaya and Singapore; during the Japanese Occupation, Yamashita made it one of the many Japanese headquarters; and when the British returned in victory, the Cathay became the headquarters of Lord Mountbatten. The Broadcasting Station also operated from this building before it moved to Caldecott Hill.

120
The Cathay Building in 1983.

120

Memorials to the Dead

121

122

123

121/122
Mourners observe a minute's silence at Lim Bo Seng's memorial service held on the steps of the Municipal Building (City Hall) on 13 January 1946.

Lim died in Batu Gajah Jail on 29 June 1944 after suffering several months of torture at Japanese hands. He was then 34 years old.

After the war, the British brought Lim's remains to Singapore and reburied him with full military honours at MacRitchie Reservoir. He was also posthumously awarded the rank of Major-General by the Chinese Nationalist Government.

123
Lim Bo Seng's memorial at the Esplanade. It was unveiled in June 1954, the 10th anniversary of his death.

124

125

126

124/125/126

War's poignant legacies: the War Memorial across the Padang in Elizabeth Walk (left) which commemorates those who died in the two world wars; the Japanese Cemetery at Chuan Hoe Avenue (bottom left); and the Kranji War Memorial (centre).

The Kranji War Memorial contains the remains of all Allied soldiers killed in Singapore and the remains of Allied soldiers transferred to Kranji from the Saigon Military Cemetery during the late 1950s. The oval-shaped memorial with the towering obelisk in the background honours the unknown Allied soldiers killed in Southeast Asia and the Pacific.

The Japanese Cemetery is the resting place for Japanese servicemen and civilians who either committed suicide at the end of the war or died of natural causes. The ashes of Japanese officially executed in Changi Jail for war crimes in Malaya and Singapore are also buried at the cemetery under a single marker.

MEMORIAL TO THE CIVILIAN VICTIMS OF THE JAPANESE OCCUPATION
1942 – 1945

127

This Civilian Memorial in Beach Road is dedicated to the civilians of all races who were victims of the Japanese Occupation.

The memorial was partly financed with money paid by the Japanese Government to the Singapore Government as atonement for the atrocities committed during Japan's occupation of Singapore. The payment was in the form of a $25-million grant and a $25-million loan on liberal terms.

The civilian memorial was unveiled on 15 February 1967. The monument is a reminder to Singaporeans of what can happen to a conquered people.

3

EARLY POLITICAL STIRRINGS

128
The end of war brings no relief from misery. To this girl, and many others of her age, childhood does not mean carefree days of schooling and playing.

1945~1948

The defeat of the British in 1942 and the Japanese Occupation which followed had brought about a change in the attitudes of the people of Singapore towards their colonial rulers. The nationalist and anti-colonial feelings which would soon sweep through Asia were to change them further. On the international scene, the United States and the Soviet Union replaced the old European colonial powers as the most powerful and influential nations. Soon the Soviet Union would make aggressive moves to expand world communism by exploiting both the weakness of the European powers and the surge of the anti-colonial movements.

When the British returned to Singapore and resumed control in September 1945, they set up a military administration. A seventeen-member Advisory Council was formed in November to assist the British Military Administration. Members of the Council included prominent members of the Chinese Chamber of Commerce such as Lee Kong Chian, a businessman, Tan Chin Tuan, a banker, and Wu Tien Wang, a communist and former guerilla leader.

The first thing the British did was to free the British and European nationals from prison. They also started to repair the war damage, remove the wreck of ships from the harbour, and restore electricity, gas, and other essential services. Japanese prisoners were put to work to repair docks and airfields.

However, contrary to the expectations of the public, the return of the British did not result in a quick and significant improvement in living conditions. Crime reappeared on the streets and secret societies were active once again. Thousands of people remained unemployed. There was widespread hunger and malnutrition. Wages were low, inflation was high and the shortages of food, clothing and other commodities continued. All regulations to control prices of essential goods failed. The severe disruptions caused by the war to the world economy and to the production and supply of goods in many countries made it impossible to return to normal conditions immediately.

Unable to control prices, the British Military Administration distributed relief supplies. People's Restaurants, where food was sold at controlled prices, were opened. Such measures helped, but did not solve the basic problem of shortages. The population was now double the pre-war figure, and

the health services were in poor shape. Tuberculosis was widespread. Housing conditions were appalling, and thousands of people had no homes. The squatter population grew rapidly until about one-third of the population was living in squatter shacks.

Nevertheless, education made a quick recovery. In October 1945, the British started reopening schools, where, in addition to the normal intake, places had to be found for the over-aged children who had received no schooling during the Occupation years. Six months after the British returned, 62,000 children had gone back to school. The Medical College and Raffles College also admitted their first new intakes of students in October 1946.

The war crimes trials of the Japanese *Kempeitai* and their collaborators began in January 1946. In the trial of the 21 *Kempeitai* members who were accused of torturing and murdering European internees and civilians in Changi Prison on 10 October 1943, all the accused were convicted. The convictions were made possible by the testimony of the many who witnessed the gruesome events.

The outcome of the *Sook Ching* trials and the trials of the Japanese collaborators was, however, very different. There was a dearth of evidence which made it difficult to apportion individual guilt. Many accused collaborators escaped punishment, while of the seven accused in the *Sook Ching* trials, only two received the death sentence. The rest were given life sentences. This aroused the wrath of many who felt that the verdict did not do justice to the thousands killed by the Japanese.

The communists were ready to exploit the post-war

discontent. After the surrender of the Japanese they were the only organised local force, having both a guerilla army and a party network. They made political capital out of the fact that their Malayan People's Anti-Japanese Army had fought the Japanese during the war. Though their actual role in winning the war was negligible, and they had killed more local people than Japanese during the war years, they presented themselves as victors and as the people's heroes.

The Malayan Communist Party, a banned organisation operating clandestinely before the war, was now allowed to operate openly by the British authorities. Since the war was now won, the British asked the Malayan Communist Party to disband its army and to surrender its arms. However, the communists surrendered only some of their arms and secretly stored others for later use. They formally disbanded their guerilla army, but at the same time formed an ex-servicemen's association through which members of the army could be kept together. The communists were obviously not prepared to give up all the "assets" they had built up over the war years. Their goal was to bring Malaya and Singapore under communist rule, and nothing would deflect them from this ultimate objective.

During the war years, the communists had used "armed struggle" to fight the Japanese. Now circumstances dictated a change of tactics. Hence the Malayan Communist Party instructed its members to pursue "peaceful struggle" which would have the dual approach of cooperating with the British Military Administration at the official level while mounting agitation on the ground through trade unions and Chinese school students. They were to exploit public grievances and present the Malayan Communist Party as an anti-colonial movement, a champion of the masses. A new political party was also to be launched as a "front" behind which the communists could pursue their objectives.

The political party conceived by the Malayan Communist Party as its front organisation – ostensibly non-communist but covertly controlled by it – was the Malayan Democratic Union. It was formed in December 1945. Its leaders were the communist Wu Tien Wang and four others with strong communist or left-wing connections: Lim Kean Chye, Lim Hong Bee, John Eber and Gerald de Cruz. A British-educated Singapore lawyer, Philip Hoalim Sr, a non-communist with good reputation and social standing, was made chairman. The constitution of the Malayan Democratic Union, moderate in its objectives, called for self-government for a united Malaya, including Singapore, within the Commonwealth.

The Malayan Communist Party swiftly organised labour unions to spread its influence among the workers. In September 1945, within a month of the return of the British, the General Labour Union, a pre-war vehicle of the communists, had been revived. The Malayan Communist Party dominated the General Labour Union and controlled several other mass organisations. Small numbers of communist cadres who held key positions on the committees of labour unions were able to manipulate large masses of people, most of them non-communist. In October 1945 the General Labour Union staged a successful strike by port workers to obtain higher wages. This was soon followed by strikes by other groups of workers.

In January 1946, the Selangor High Court jailed Soon Kwong, a leader of the Selangor Malayan People's Anti-Japanese Army, on charges of intimidation and extortion. This brought matters to a head, with the General Labour Union staging a two-day general strike. It was meant to be a show of strength against the British Military Administration. Over 170,000 people stopped work, bringing business and transportation to a virtual halt.

On 15 February 1946 the communists inaugurated a Pan-Malayan Federation of Trade Unions (PMFTU) incorporating all the unions of the General Labour Union of Malaya and of Singapore. The Singapore unit was later registered as the Singapore Federation of Trade Unions with a membership of around 51,000. The communists tried to organise a procession for 15 February 1946, the anniversary of the fall of Singapore to the Japanese, with the intention of embarrassing the British. The British did not allow this, and on the eve of the planned procession the

authorities arrested 27 leading communists, later deporting 10 of them. Despite this setback, PMFTU-inspired strikes were a common occurrence in 1946.

The British, meanwhile, had been preparing constitutional changes for Malaya and Singapore. In October 1945, they revealed proposals to create a Malayan Union. The Union was to consist of the states of Malaya as well as the Straits Settlement territories of Penang and Malacca. Singapore was to be a separate Crown Colony.

The Malayan Union proposal was opposed for different reasons by different groups of people in Singapore and Malaya. In Malaya, the opposition came mainly from the Malays who felt that the setting up of a single state, the Malayan Union, would take away the distinct identity of the individual Malayan states and curtail the powers of the Sultans. Above all, the Malays protested that the citizenship laws proposed for the Malayan Union would endanger the political position of their community. Led by Dato Onn bin Jaafar, Malay leaders formed the United Malays National Organisation (UMNO) in March 1946 to resist the Malayan Union proposal. In Singapore, most of the politically conscious people were unhappy because the Malayan Union would separate Singapore from Malaya.

On 1 April 1946, Singapore returned to civilian rule as a Crown Colony under a British Governor and separate from the Peninsula. In Malaya, however, the Malayan Union plan was not implemented. The British had been receptive to UMNO protests against the scheme and, after secret negotiations with the Malays, had drawn up alternative proposals for a federation of Malayan states, stricter citizenship requirements, and more safeguards for the Malays

and the Sultans. The Malays in the Peninsula were happy to see Singapore excluded from the federation because they did not want the delicate racial balance in the proposed federation to be upset.

The Malayan Communist Party and the Malayan Democratic Union were initially in a dilemma over the Malayan Union scheme and the federation proposals. The Malayan Communist Party saw its struggle as pan-Malayan and did not want to see Singapore separated from the Peninsula. Also, ideologically, it should have been opposed to arrangements for the Peninsula which discriminated against the non-Malays. However, political expediency dictated that it should not alienate the Malays. The initial reaction of the Malayan Communist Party and the Malayan Democratic Union was, therefore, muted.

It was officially announced in October 1946 that the new constitutional proposals would be decided between the British and the Malays, and that the other ethnic communities would merely be asked to comment upon them. This aroused the apprehension of the Chinese. The Malayan Communist Party now had to take a clear-cut stand to retain the confidence of its mainly Chinese base. On 14 December 1946, it covertly sponsored the creation of a "Council of Joint Action" through the Malayan Democratic Union to agitate against the proposed federation scheme. The Council secured the support of Tan Cheng Lock, a prominent Chinese from Malacca who subsequently became president of the Malayan Chinese Association. He took on the chairmanship of the Council, with John Eber of the Malayan Democratic Union as secretary-general.

The Council was later renamed the "All-Malaya Council of Joint Action" (AMCJA). The Malayan Communist Party mobilised mass organisations, especially the Pan-Malayan Federation of Trade Unions, in support of it. AMCJA also had the support of Pusat Tenaga Rakyat (Centre of People's Power or PUTERA), formed by the left-wing Malay Nationalist Party which opposed the Malayan Federation plans.

At a protest mass rally in Farrer Park on 21 September 1947, AMCJA-PUTERA presented a "People's Constitution" as an alternative to the draft Federation Agreement. The Agreement already had the approval of UMNO and the Malay Sultans and had been made public by the British in May. The "People's Constitution" provided for a fully self-governing united Malaya (including Singapore) with a federal legislature, common citizenship, and equal rights for all. AMCJA-PUTERA agitation against the federation scheme culminated in a *hartal* (a stoppage of business activities) on 20 October 1947, with the full backing of the Chinese chambers of commerce in Malaya and Singapore. However, the British authorities rejected the proposals embodied in the "People's Constitution" and the Federation of Malaya became a reality in February 1948. The AMCJA-PUTERA movement started disintegrating from January 1948 when the Chinese chambers of commerce withdrew their support. The disintegration was complete in June 1948 when the communists decided to embark on a course of armed insurgency in Malaya. The Malayan Democratic Union, plagued by a pro-communist image and dwindling support, became irrelevant with the change in communist strategy.

The decision by the Malayan Communist Party to abandon "peaceful struggle" and opt for "armed struggle" was probably brought about by both international and local factors. In 1947 the tensions between the West and the Soviet Union had worsened, and the Cold War was on. In 1948 a new and harder Soviet line against the capitalist world emerged and communist parties worldwide took the cue. It is probable that directions given at an international meeting of communists in Calcutta in February 1948, at which the Malayan Communist Party was represented, signalled the move to violence in Southeast Asia. Communist insurgencies broke out in a number of Southeast Asian countries in 1948.

From 1947 circumstances in Singapore and Malaya had also become less favourable to the communists. As the worst of the shortages and hardships caused by the war were resolved, the grievances which the communists could exploit were reduced. Further, the British had begun to adopt a firmer stand against communist subversion of trade unions. In March 1947 the government began registering trade unions under the 1940 Trade Union Ordinance which gave the authorities a greater control over unions and made it

illegal to use union funds for political purposes. The unions were further weakened as workers became disillusioned with strikes which were often staged for political ends rather than for their betterment. The Malayan Communist Party, which had regarded control of major trade unions as crucial for "peaceful struggle", was now forced to consider other methods.

The majority of leading communists in Singapore left for the Federation of Malaya in May 1948. Armed insurgency began on 16 June 1948 when three British rubber planters were murdered by bands of communists near Sungei Siput in Perak. The British declared a State of Emergency in the Federation and outlawed the Malayan Communist Party. The murders were followed by a long series of killings by the communists of innocent people, mostly rubber tappers, miners and villagers, as well as attacks on security forces, and the destruction of public and private property.

A week later, a State of Emergency was also declared in Singapore, giving the authorities sweeping powers to deal with the communist rebellion.

Earlier, on 20 March 1948, the first election to the Singapore Legislative Council was held. The British were trying to educate the people of Singapore in democratic politics. Though they had no intention of relinquishing control of Singapore, the mood of the times dictated some movement, however gradual and limited, towards the election of Singapore representatives.

In anticipation of the elections, three London University educated lawyers – C C Tan, John Laycock and N A Mallal – had formed the Singapore Progressive Party on 25 August 1947. The party was dominated by English-educated pro-British professionals who shared the British belief that progress towards self-government should be gradual.

The 1948 election was for only six of the 22 seats of the Legislative Council. Although it was a milestone in the sense that it was the first election held in Singapore, it attracted little public interest. Only British subjects were qualified to vote. Yet out of 200,000 qualified to be voters, only about 23,000 bothered to register and of these about 14,000 finally cast their votes. The Malayan Democratic Union boycotted the election, leaving the field open to the Progressive Party and the independents. The Progressive Party secured three seats, and the remaining three went to independent candidates.

The Malayan Democratic Union, fearing government action under the Emergency Regulations, voluntarily dissolved itself in June 1948. In September 1948, the Singapore Labour Party was formed. The Labour Party called for full self-government by 1954, to be followed by merger with Malaya. Among the party's founder members were M A Majid, president of the Singapore Seamen's Union, and M P D Nair and Peter Williams, both from the Army Civil Service Union. A school teacher, Francis Thomas, was elected president of the Labour Party in 1949. The following year, Lim Yew Hock, a trade unionist and a nominee of the Governor in the 1948 Legislative Council, became its president. The party, however, disintegrated within a few years, leaving the field to the Progressives who were to dominate the legislative and municipal elections until 1955.

During the period 1945 to 1948 the main political forces on the Singapore scene were the colonial regime and the communists. Most of the people of Singapore were not yet interested in politics. Nevertheless the response to some of the activities of the Malayan Democratic Union, the elections of 1948, and the formation of the Singapore Progressive Party and the Singapore Labour Party reflected early political stirrings among the people.

Post-War Singapore

129

130

129
A panoramic view of Singapore in September 1945, soon after the British regained control. On the extreme right are the spires of the Chapel of the Holy Infant Jesus and the Cathedral of the Good Shepherd. In the foreground are Dhoby Ghaut and Prinsep Street with Bras Basah Road on the right.

130
A view of the harbour from Clifford Pier.

131

Two *Samsui* women on their
way to work pass a shop
bedecked with traditional
Chinese lanterns used in
funerals.

  Samsui women, known for
their ruggedness and
indomitable spirit, were a
common sight at construction
sites in Singapore till the 1970s.
Their characteristic attire was
black cotton *samfoo* (pantsuit),
a stiff red cloth head-dress, and
"sandals" made from old worn-
out car tyres cut to the shape of
their soles and held together
with strings.

132

133

134

132/133/134
Popular modes of transport in the post-war years. (Top left) Jinrickshaws and (above) trishaws, a few of which still ply Singapore roads. With cars within the reach of only a few, bicycles (top right) were prized possessions.

Shortages and Hardship

135/136

Within two days of their return, the British declared the Japanese currency worthless. However, as they did not circulate the new Malayan currency until a few days later, the people were left without money.

On the first day of the official announcement, some stall-holders generously gave away free food on production of food control cards.

As a relief measure, the British Military Administration distributed free rice, sugar and salt, but as *The Straits Times* said, "people cannot live entirely on these; nor can they live entirely without money".

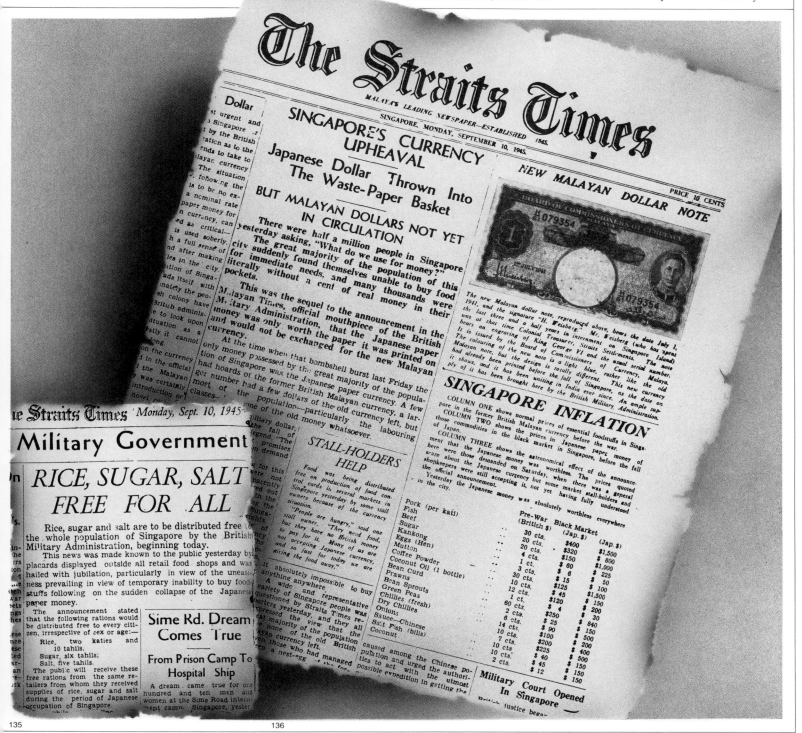

137

137/138
Japanese POWs and local women helping out in the Food Supply Depot which stored and issued food supplies in early post-war Singapore.

Food shortage was a major problem in the immediate post-war years. Rationing was enforced and People's Restaurants were set up to provide meals at controlled prices.

138

139

139
Having a square meal for 35 cents at a People's Restaurant.
The colonial government opened the first of such restaurants on 29 June 1946 to give lunch to workers at subsidised rates. The People's Restaurants functioned until August 1948. Besides the People's Restaurants there were Sponsored Restaurants, People's Kitchens and Family Restaurants. The Family Restaurants offered a meal to very poor families for as little as eight cents.

140

140
Prices of the limited fresh produce sold at roadside markets were beyond the means of many.

141

141

Children being fed at the Prinsep Street Clinic. Free food was served daily at this clinic from 9.30 am to 11.30 am.

SINGAPORE, SATURDAY, AUGUST 31, 1946.

Rice Eaters' Bread Queue

People of Singapore queueing up for their bread ration from the Lung Sing Bakery in Cross Street. A daily scene —Straits Times picture.

142

142

People queuing for their bread ration from Che Lung Sing Bakery in Cross Street.

Bread and rice queues like this became familiar scenes from April 1946 when rice rations were reduced from four pounds (1.8 kg) a week (for an adult male) to three pounds (1.4 kg) and to 1⅔ pounds (0.75 kg) per week in mid-August. In pre-war days, the normal consumption was 8¾-10½ pounds (3.99 kg – 4.76 kg) per person per week.

MAN IN THE STREET

Rice: Reports From The Public

FOLLOWING the announcement of a drastic cut in the rice ration, there was a general panic in the market. Prices of food have soared sky-high, and the poor man-in-the-street is in a dilemma.

Does Lord Killearn know that the public as a whole are losing confidence, due to the inconsistencies of official utterances made from time to time?

Has the "People's Restaurant" served its purpose? For the last two days, hundreds of city workers, if not thousands, have been turned away without a meal because they arrived too late.

The period of catering, as we understand it, is between 11.30 in the morning and 2 o'clock in the afternoon, but lately the meals have been sold out before 1 p.m., the time when most office workers begin to leave for their tiffin recess.

Many of us are also missing our morning bread, which is now not easily obtainable owing to the rice crisis. It appears that a good part of the flour is being turned into noodles, for which a higher price is demanded, and thus a loophole provided for unscrupulous bakeries.

The widely advertised "Rycena," a substitute for rice, is just as difficult to obtain in the market, although it is said to be plentiful in Australia. It is just

A Singaporean Sends This-

ODATE: Hello! Is that you, Killearn?
VOICE: No.
ODATE: Has he been recalled?
VOICE: Eh? Well ... er .... Who are you?
ODATE: Insignificant self is Odate... Sigeo Odate.
VOICE: What do you want?
ODATE: I wish to congratulate Killearn. You see, when I was Mayor of Syonan, I could never reduce the rice ration to under six katies for men. I was warned against trouble and black-market.
VOICE: Oh...er.. We're not interested in your regime. Besides, we've got good old Hamer. He's got the black-market well in hand. Hasn't he?
ODATE: Ahem! It's remarkable how you put over that Coconut Lunch stunt. I should have thought of it myself.
VOICE: Blast you, Jap.
ODATE: Thank you. We have been blasted. But it's never too late to learn. Well, I just wanted to congratulate you...... Goodbye!

This picture has been prompted by the letter from "A Chinese Citizen of Malaya" published in this page the other day. In submitting it, the artist, Mr. Goh Seng Lim, of Singapore, expresses the hope that it will help the movement to stage a buyers' strike and make the black-market kings take that grin off their faces!

144

143/144/145
With no end to corruption and food shortages, the people became more unhappy. Some vented their anger through cynical cartoons and bitter letters in the press.

146

147

146
A familiar post-war scene: people rummaging through discards in the hope of salvaging something usable.
   In this instance, the discarded planks served as fuel for cooking fires.

147
A mother carrying her son haggles over the price of eggs.

148

149

148/149/150
Three scenes of pavement
markets of the immediate
post-war years.

150

151

153

152

151
Several families lived in each of these dilapidated buildings, overflowing with garbage and festooned with the day's washing. Next to food, housing was the most acute problem faced by the people.

When the war ended, overcrowding worsened in the city area where the population density in low-rise shophouses could be more than 2,400 persons per hectare.

152
A cubicle in Queen Street with no water or sanitation. Cubicles like this housed families with eight to 10 members each. Overcrowding and malnutrition resulted in the spread of tuberculosis, which became the scourge of the population.

These overcrowded tenements also proved ideal spawning grounds for secret societies. Secret society violence was a common occurrence.

153/154
Public housing built by the Singapore Improvement Trust (SIT) in the mid-1940s: single-storey units at Balestier Road (far right) and five-storey blocks of flats at Tiong Bahru Road (above). The number of public houses built by SIT was totally inadequate.

155
Students at King Edward VII College of Medicine working in the biology laboratory, soon after the College was reopened in June 1946. The slides the students are using were recovered from outbuildings of the College.

154

155

Japanese Prisoners of War

156

157

158

156/157/158

History has come a full circle – it is now the Japanese, as prisoners of war (POWs), who dig trenches and do other forms of manual labour.

They fill in trenches at the Padang (top); pull a heavily-loaded cart to a worksite (above); and (left) shovel soil to fill in trenches along roads.

War Crimes Trials

159

160

159/160
During the Japanese Occupation, thousands lost their lives at the hands of the occupying forces. The British Military Administration found many unmarked graves.

In the foreground (above) are the remains of a victim unearthed from one such grave. (Left) A British soldier is examining a piece of cloth believed to have been used to blindfold the victim.

161
The British Military Administration set up a war crimes commission to investigate atrocities committed by the Japanese forces during their occupation of Singapore. Soon after, a special court was set up to try these cases.

The first trial opened on 21 January 1946 (above) and dealt with the treatment of Indian POWs. This was followed by the "Double Tenth Trial" in which 21 members of the *Syonan Kempeitai* were convicted of atrocities they committed in Changi Prison on 10 October 1943.

162
The accused at the January trial.

The Straits Times

MALAYA'S LEADING NEWSPAPER: ESTABLISHED 1845.

SINGAPORE, WEDNESDAY, MARCH 19, 1947.

PRICE TEN CENTS

Accused Japs face Court. From left: Capt. Hisamatsu Haruji (7), Maj. Onishi Satoru (6), Maj. Jyo Tomatatsu (5), Lt. Col. Yokota Yoshitaka (4), Lt. Col. Oishi Massayuki (3), Lt. Gen. Kawamura Saburo (2), Lt. Gen. Nishimura Takuma (1).

SINGAPORE JAPS KEPT 'REGISTER'

IT was revealed at the "Chinese Massacre" trial yesterday that, in rounding up Singapore Chinese, the Japanese used a "Register of anti-Japanese Chinese"—a "thick book" containing information compiled by resident Japanese in Singapore before the war.

This book contained personal histories and photographs of "wanted Chinese."

The case for the prosecution closed yesterday—the seventh day of the hearing—with the submission of affidavits by Japanese and sworn statements by the seven accused. The Court then adjourned until tomorrow, when the case for the defence will open.

Another finding of the Committee was:—

"On questioning Major General Kawamura (one of the seven accused), it was ascertained that during a tour of inspection General Yamashita (the "Tiger of Malaya," who was executed in Manila last year) impressed upon Kawamura the urgency of the question of dealing with anti-Japanese Chinese. General Yamashita was reported to have said to Kawamura 'This is not a private instruction: make a thorough job of it.'"

Tokio Inquiry

Reference to the "Register" was made in an affidavit by Japanese Major Hashizume Isamu, who stated that he was a member of the Prisoner of War Investigation Committee in Tokio (in September 1945) which investigated the mass round-up of Chinese in Singapore.

Hashizume stated that one of the findings of the Committee was: "Colonel Oishi (one of the accused) said that suspicion on the Chinese was based on the 'Register of Anti-Japanese Chin-

'Massacre Order'

One of the accused, Major Onishi Satoru, in a sworn statement said that the order he received from General Headquarters read: "Due to the fact that the army is advancing fast and in order to preserve peace behind us, it is essential to massacre as many Chinese as possible who appear in any way to have anti-Japanese feelings."

Full report of yesterday's hearing, Page 5

163

163
The *Sook Ching* trial opens at the Victoria Memorial Hall in March 1947.

Among the seven accused were General Saburo Kawamura, commander of the Syonan garrison, and Colonel Masyuki Oishi, head of the *Syonan Kempeitai*. Many prominent local Chinese, like Tay Koh Yat whose eldest son had been killed, came forward to give evidence. But the court was hampered by the dearth of conclusive proof of individual responsibility.

Among the chief persons responsible, Lt Gen Tomoyuki Yamashita had been executed in Manila by the Americans; Colonel Masanobu Tsuji, head of operations staff, had disappeared; and others had been killed in the war. Kawamura and Oishi were sentenced to death and five others to life imprisonment.

Communists Make Their Bid

164

Lord Mountbatten shaking hands with Chin Peng, the communist guerilla commander of the Malayan People's Anti-Japanese Army (MPAJA), after decorating him for resistance activities during the war.

He was awarded the Burma Star and the 1939/45 War Star. The ceremony took place at a parade held at the Padang on 6 January 1946. Some of the 16 leaders decorated with the Burma Star, dressed in the uniform of the MPAJA, saluted the Supremo with clenched fists, communist style.

The MPAJA, which was controlled by the Malayan Communist Party, had grown to about 10,000-strong by the time the war ended in 1945. Directed by the British, it disbanded itself in December 1945 and surrendered some of its arms and ammunition. The rest were secretly stored for future use against the British.

164

165

Port workers, demanding higher wages, stopped work in October 1945. This was the first major strike after the war. It was a prelude to the wave of strikes and work stoppages in 1946 and 1947, many of them communist-inspired.

The Malayan Communist Party was the only organised local political force in the immediate post-war years. The party was now allowed to operate openly. It went all out to exploit the difficult post-war conditions to expand its influence. Trade unions were a prime vehicle which the communists used for their political ends.

THE STRAITS TIMES

Monday, Oct. 22, 1945

WHARVES IDLE AS DOCKERS QUIT WORK

7,000 Men Involved: No Demands

The normal draft of about 7,000 Chinese and Indian dockside labourers stayed away from work at the wharves in the Tanjong Pagar dock area yesterday and the entire harbour area was idle so far as unloading of ships was concerned.

While no official demands have been made by the labourers, the Straits Times was informed by Mr. Loo Cheng, president of the Singapore Labour Union, that as far as he knew the labourers were staying away from work in protest against insufficient wages and against the loading of ammunition which, they allege, is destined for Java for use against the Indonesians.

He emphasised that the Labour Union had nothing to do with the labourers' action.

The Straits Times understands that yesterday morning about 2,000 labourers were on their way to work at the wharves but were stopped by a small party of agitators and warned to stay away.

Ten members of the Propaganda Corps of the Labour Union, eight men and two girls, were detained yesterday when they attempted to enter the wharf area in a truck.

The President of the Union who was yesterday trying to get the eight men and two girls released by the authorities claimed that his Propaganda Corps was on its way to inform dockside workers that the Union had food supplies available to assist them in the over their difficulties resulting from insufficient wages and the high cost of living.

Outside the Harbour Board police headquarters where the eight men and two girls were detained, a crowd of 500 gathered.

Crowd Dispersed

A platoon of paratroops arrived on the scene, followed by Military Police officers in

165

166

The communist-controlled General Labour Union organised a massive general strike on 29 January 1946 to protest the arrest of its secretary-general, Soon Kwong, a leader of the Selangor Malayan People's Anti-Japanese Army. The two-day strike involved over 170,000 workers.

In 1947, which has come to be known as the "Year of Strikes", around 700,000 man-days were lost in Singapore and Malaya in strikes and work disputes.

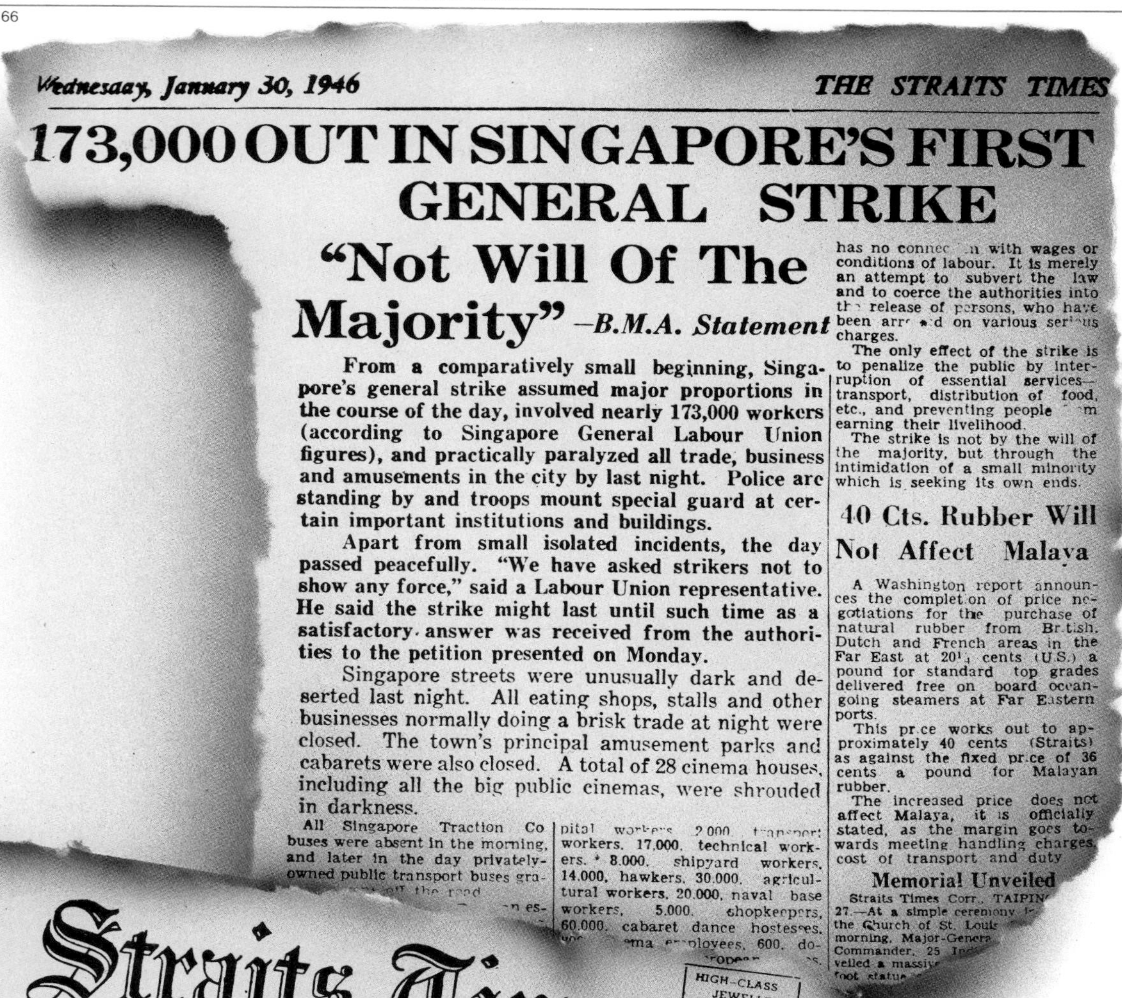

Wednesday, January 30, 1946 — **THE STRAITS TIMES**

173,000 OUT IN SINGAPORE'S FIRST GENERAL STRIKE

"Not Will Of The Majority" —B.M.A. Statement

From a comparatively small beginning, Singapore's general strike assumed major proportions in the course of the day, involved nearly 173,000 workers (according to Singapore General Labour Union figures), and practically paralyzed all trade, business and amusements in the city by last night. Police are standing by and troops mount special guard at certain important institutions and buildings.

Apart from small isolated incidents, the day passed peacefully. "We have asked strikers not to show any force," said a Labour Union representative. He said the strike might last until such time as a satisfactory answer was received from the authorities to the petition presented on Monday.

Singapore streets were unusually dark and deserted last night. All eating shops, stalls and other businesses normally doing a brisk trade at night were closed. The town's principal amusement parks and cabarets were also closed. A total of 28 cinema houses, including all the big public cinemas, were shrouded in darkness.

All Singapore Traction Co buses were absent in the morning, and later in the day privately-owned public transport buses gra... ... the road ... es-

... pital workers, 2,000 transport workers, 17,000 technical workers, 8,000 shipyard workers, 14,000 hawkers, 30,000 agricultural workers, 20,000 naval base workers, 5,000 shopkeepers, 60,000 cabaret dance hostesses, ...ma employees, 600, do-...

has no connec.. n with wages or conditions of labour. It is merely an attempt to subvert the law and to coerce the authorities into the release of persons, who have been arr...ed on various serious charges.

The only effect of the strike is to penalize the public by interruption of essential services—transport, distribution of food, etc., and preventing people ..m earning their livelihood.

The strike is not by the will of the majority, but through the intimidation of a small minority which is seeking its own ends.

40 Cts. Rubber Will Not Affect Malaya

A Washington report announces the complet on of price negotiations for the purchase of natural rubber from Br.tish, Dutch and French areas in the Far East at 20¼ cents (U.S.) a pound for standard top grades delivered free on board ocean-going steamers at Far Eastern ports.

This pr.ce works out to approximately 40 cents (Straits) as against the fixed pr.ce of 36 cents a pound for Malayan rubber.

The increased price does not affect Malaya, it is officially stated, as the margin goes towards meeting handling charges, cost of transport and duty.

Memorial Unveiled

Straits Times Corr., TAIPIN, 27.—At a simple ceremony t. the Church of St. Louis... morning, Major-Gener... Commander, 25 Ind...veiled a massive... foot statue...

The Straits Times

MALAYA'S LEADING NEWSPAPER ESTABLISHED OVER A CENTURY

SINGAPORE, WEDNESDAY, JANUARY 22, 1947.

PRICE TEN CENTS

SCIENTIFIC EYE EXAMINATION — QUALIFIED OPTICIAN — EVERBRIGHT OPTICAL CO.

HIGH-CLASS JEWELLERY — PLATINUM & DIAMONDS — P. H. HENDRY

MUNICIPALITY CALLS ON TROOPS

4,000 Singapore Workers Strike

JAPANESE surrendered personnel and Army specialists helped out Singapore Municipality yesterday on the first day of the strike called by seven municipal labour unions.

Both Japanese and Army men were devoted to the maintenance of essential services.

Although the precise number of men involved in the strike could not be given by the Municipal authorities, it is understood by the Straits Times that about 4,000 out of the municipal labour force of 6,400 have struck work.

The Town Cleansing Department had 1,300 men on strike.

The strike yesterday affected particularly the Water, Town Cleansing and Anti-Malarial Departments. Men from all seven striker unions, however, were on strike.

Men of the Gas Department and St. James's Power Station carried on their duties as usual.

The Straits Times was informed by a Government spokesman that the Japanese surrendered personnel...

Settlement Move At ...ng

...dent ...ay. ...vern- ...on in ...strike ...e In...

Committee Meeting

The Central Executive Committee of the Singapore Municipal Labour Unions are to hold a meeting today at 4.30 p.m. to discuss steps to be taken "in view of the fact that the auth... have been employing Japa...

At a conference with the S...pore press last night the C...mittee's secretary, Mr. Sur...raju, said:

"Until our living condition... ...mproved we are determin... stay out. We are even willi... work elsewhere, and if ne... return to our homelands."

Questioned about the d... replies given to a union... m.nth, Mr. Sundararaju sa... Town Cleansing Superinten... replied that it was impos...increase the workers' pay...they would be given a dai...crement of one cent after... years' satisfactory service...two cents after ten years' se... After 20 years' service they w... be paid a gratuity of one mon... pay for each year worked if... were medically unfit and... under 45 years of age.

TIN PRICES

LONDON. Tues.—The Mi... of Supply has ar...d...

In the middle of ... are several hundred ... ...namese who have sv ... rather than surrende ... ger may force thr ... to break out.

Vietnam irregular ... British and Chin ... c.rrying their ...

167

Through their unrealistic and insensitive response to workers' demands, the British authorities sometimes aggravated the situation.

The use of Japanese prisoners of war to break the Municipal strike, and the offer of a two-cent pay rise after 10 years' service, insulted and angered the workers. The press was unanimous in expressing sympathy with the strikers.

168

169

170

168/169/170/171
Philip Hoalim Sr, John Eber and Gerald de Cruz, three of the leaders of the Malayan Democratic Union. (Below) Leaders of the Malayan Democratic Union addressing a rally in Farrer Park.

The Malayan Democratic Union, formed in December 1945, was conceived by the Malayan Communist Party as its front organisation. Several of its leaders were either communists or had communist connections.

Though the Malayan Democratic Union was able, with the support of the communists, to organise agitation over a few specific issues, it never had any real mass support. When the Malayan Communist Party embarked on armed insurgency in 1948, the Malayan Democratic Union dissolved itself.

171

Communist Insurgency

172

173

172/173
Chin Peng (left), the man who became secretary-general of the Malayan Communist Party in 1947, and launched it on the path of armed insurgency.

The party's previous secretary-general, Lai Teck (right), had absconded with party funds when the party discovered his treachery: he had been an agent of the French, the British and the Japanese in turn.

174
The Malayan Communist Party signalled its launching of armed insurgency on 16 June 1948 by killing four people in Perak (three were British planters) and another, a Chinese, in Johor, Malaya. Other acts of violence followed in quick succession. The British banned the MCP and declared a State of Emergency in Malaya. The communist insurgency was to continue for 12 years, claiming the lives of thousands of civilians and security forces. It had a profound effect on the daily lives of many people and on the political evolution of Malaya.

174

175

175
Most of the communist terrorist activities were confined to Malaya, but a State of Emergency was also declared in Singapore.

Here security forces prepare for a night patrol.

176
Identity cards were introduced soon after the declaration of Emergency, and it became an offence for anybody to be found without one.

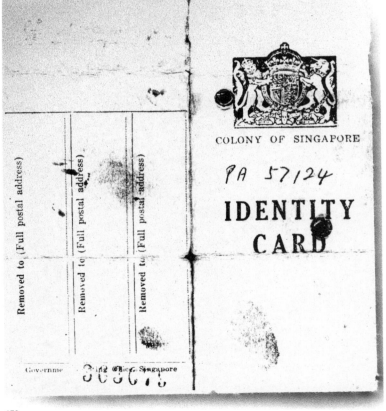

176

178

177

177
Police road blocks were a familiar sight in Malaya and Singapore during the Emergency period. Passing vehicles were stopped and the identity cards of occupants checked to prevent the movement of communist terrorists and to stop supplies from reaching them.

178
The Jungle Squad of the Singapore Police Force escorting suspected communists from a village in Johor.

Members of the Singapore Police Force often assisted their Malayan colleagues in the operations against communist terrorists.

Constitutional Development

The Straits Times

B. P. de SILVA Ltd.
(Incorporated in Ceylon)
Singapore & Penang.

OPTICAL COMPANY
19, Chulia St., Tel. 4421
QUALIFIED OPTICIANS

* Scientific Eye Examination
* Modern Eyewear

MALAYA'S LEADING NEWSPAPER ESTABLISHED OVER A CENTURY
SINGAPORE, TUESDAY, APRIL 2, 1946.

PRICE 10 CENTS.

ELECTORAL REPRESENTATION FOR NEW SINGAPORE COUNCIL

No Official Majority, But Governor Has Casting Vote

MALAY RULERS

Yesterday's Ceremony

Mr. P. A. B. McKerron appending his signature to document at the completion of the installation ceremony in the cipal Council Chamber yesterday when he

RADIOS
KEE HUAT RADIO Co.
122-124 ORCHARD RD.
TELEPHONE 6566
— SINGAPORE —

Times

NEWSPAPER ESTABLISHED OVER A CENTURY

SINGAPORE, THURSDAY, MAY 30, 1946.

PRICE 10 CENTS.

"NOBODY IN MALAYA IN FAVOUR OF UNION" SAYS M.P.

Gammans On How Treaties Were Forced On Rulers

From Our Special Correspondent
KUALA LUMPUR, Wednesday.

Floods In New York State

NEW YORK, Wed.—Eleven persons were known dead and 13 others were missing today as rivers in southern Pennsylvania and central

The Conference of Malay Rulers in Session with the British Parliamentary Delegation at the Astana Iskandriah, Kuala Kangsar. The Sultan of Perak, presiding, is seen with Lt.-Col. D. R. Rees-Williams, M.P., on his right and Capt. L. D. Gammans, M.P., on his left.

SIAM SENDS
TEST

Cable Rates Halved

LONDON, Wed.—From June 1 cable rates between Malaya and the United States are halved, the new rates being £5 cents (Straits) for one word, deferred 35 cents, night letter rate 20 cents. Reuter.

SENATORS OPPOSE
TRUMAN'S ANTI
STRIKE BILL

WASHINGTON

179

With the end of British Military Administration on 31 March 1946, Singapore becomes a Crown Colony under a British Governor.

Thus for the first time Singapore was separated from the Peninsula. Before the war it had formed part of the Straits Settlements comprising Malacca, Penang and Singapore. The new Constitution, implemented in 1948, provided for a partly elected Legislative Council.

Under the constitutional proposals announced by the British in October 1945, Peninsular Malaya would have become a Malayan Union and Singapore a Crown Colony. However, the Malayan Union scheme was not implemented because of opposition from the Malays on the grounds that the proposed citizenship laws would give non-Malays a political status equal to that of the Malays. Instead, in 1948, the Federation of Malaya scheme was implemented.

180

180
The Municipal Commission, forerunner to the Municipal Council, in session in 1946.

The Commission's 24 members were nominated by the Governor. In 1947 the Commission was changed into a Council providing for the election of 18 out of a total of 27 members. The Progressive Party won 13 of the seats in the first Municipal Council election held in 1949.

When Singapore was granted city status in 1951, the Municipal Council became the City Council. What is now City Hall was then the Municipal Building and housed the Municipal offices.

181

181
As in other parts of the British Empire, the opening of the Assizes in Singapore is accompanied by traditional pomp and ceremony. The building in the background, the headquarters of the Social Welfare Department, formerly housed the Supreme Court. Since renovated, it is now Parliament House.

182
Singapore's Advisory Council headed by the Governor, Sir Franklin Gimson, at a regular session at the Municipal Building on 16 June 1947. Seated left to right (straight table): J D M Smith (Financial Secretary); E J Davies (Attorney-General); Sir Franklin Gimson (Governor); P A B McKerron (Colonial Secretary); L Rayman (President, Municipal Commission) and Sir Han Hoe Lim.

The Advisory Council was set up in November 1945 under the presidency of Maj Gen H R Hone, Chief Civil Affairs Officer, British Military Administration. Among the members of the first Council were: Major H R S Zehnder, Wee Swee Teow, P Samy, G A Potts, R Jumabhoy, Tan Chin Tuan, Ng Seng Choy, Syed Ibrahim Omar Alsagoff, Lien Ying Chow, Tsai Hui Sheng, Wu Tien Wang, Lee Kong Chian, Tan Chor Lam, Miss Lee Kiu, Dr Abdul Samat and Dr Chen Su Lan. When the British Military Administration ended, the Council continued to function but was headed by the Governor.

In April 1948, the Legislative Council replaced the Advisory Council.

182

183

184

185

183/184/185
C C Tan, John Laycock and N A Mallal, the three founder members of the Singapore Progressive Party formed in August 1947.

Laycock and Mallal had served as municipal commissioners in the 1930s. C C Tan, who became the party's first chairman, appeared in public life only in 1946 when he became a non-official member of the Advisory Council.

186

186
The first post-war Legislative Council.

Six of the 22 members were elected under Singapore's first-ever polls held on 20 March 1948. Only British subjects, numbering 200,000, were qualified to vote. However, only 23,000 of them bothered to register themselves as voters and less than 14,000 actually cast their votes.

The Progressive Party, the only party to contest the election, won three of the six seats while the remaining three went to independent candidates. All six seats were held by lawyers; three were Indians, one Chinese, one European and one Malay. Front row (left to right): Maj-Gen L H Cox (General-Officer-Commanding);

R Jumabhoy; J Laycock; E M F Fergusson; P A B McKerron (Colonial Secretary); Sir Franklin Gimson (Governor); E J Davies (Attorney-General); Tan Chin Tuan; L Rayman (President, Municipal Commission); M J Namazie; A Gilmour (Secretary for Economic Affairs).

Back row (left to right): P F de Souza; Thio Chan Bee; S C Goho; N A Mallal; Dr W J Vickers (Director of Medical Services); L W Donough (Clerk of Council); C C Tan; W A Sennett (Commissioner of Lands); J B Neilson (Director of Education); Sardon bin Haji Zubir; E R Koek; and Lim Yew Hock. J D M Smith (Financial Secretary) is not in the picture.

4

COMMUNISTS LAY THE GROUNDWORK

187
Chinese middle school students
in a clash with the riot police
during an anti-national service
demonstration in 1954.

1949~1955

The 1950s saw profound changes in the expectations and political attitudes of the people of Singapore. These changes were the result of the interaction of a number of factors, which included the socio-economic conditions, the policies and actions of the Malayan Communist Party, moves by the British to allow greater local participation in political affairs, and the influence of external events.

It was during this period that the anti-colonial movement gathered momentum among the subject peoples of Asia and Africa. Colonialism was coming to an end, and several countries formerly under colonial rule had been given their independence. These newly independent countries were acquiring a voice of their own in world affairs under charismatic leaders like Pandit Nehru, President Sukarno and President Nasser, and through forums like the first Afro-Asian Conference, which was held in Bandung in 1955. Such developments had an influence on the intelligentsia in Singapore.

In 1949, Mao Zedong had defeated the Kuomintang

and unified China under communist rule. This, coupled with the ability of the Chinese army to fight the Americans to a stalemate in Korea in 1951 to 1953, enormously enhanced the prestige of China among Chinese everywhere, including those in Singapore.

The social and economic conditions prevailing in Singapore at this time were difficult. Singapore's population grew from 961,856 in 1948 to 1,167,682 in 1954. There was serious unemployment and an acute housing shortage. Accommodation in the city area often consisted of one cubicle for an entire family, and many lived in squatter colonies and in rural areas where they had no electricity, modern sanitation, or piped water.

In the early 1950s, the people of Singapore thought of themselves essentially as Chinese, Malays or Indians. Colonial rule and colonial policies on education, language and citizenship had stifled the emergence of any feeling of sharing a common destiny and identity. Racial and religious sensitivities lay close to the surface and, if mishandled, could give rise to trouble, as happened in the Maria Hertogh riots.

The riots from 11 to 13 December 1950 were the result of a lawsuit over the custody of a 13-year-old girl, Maria Bertha Hertogh. She had been brought up as a Muslim by a Malay couple after her Dutch parents were interned in Indonesia during the Japanese Occupation. Now the courts in Singapore ruled that she be returned to her natural parents. The colonial government's

failure to appreciate the religious and racial sensitivities in this case, and the arousal of emotions by press photographs and articles, contributed to the outbreak of the riots which left 18 dead and 173 injured.

Chinese education was a major problem area. English was the only official language, yet nearly half the school population was enrolled in Chinese-stream schools where the curriculum was primarily China-oriented and which, unlike English-stream schools, did not enjoy adequate government support or full recognition. Their teachers were poorly paid. Chinese school graduates could not secure jobs in the civil service. They could not gain entry to the English-medium University of Malaya or the Teachers' Training College. All this caused much resentment among Chinese school students, teachers and the Chinese population in general. Chinese schools were therefore fertile ground for exploitation by the communists.

The communist takeover of China in 1949 closed most avenues for tertiary education in the Chinese-medium. This was because the British barred those who had gone to communist China for higher studies from returning to Singapore for fear that they would spread communist influence. The local Chinese community therefore wished to have a Chinese university in Singapore. In January 1953, Tan Lark Sye, a wealthy rubber merchant and industrialist who had started off as a penniless immigrant from China, proposed the establishment of such a university at a meeting of the Hokkien Huay Kuan (a dialect group association). The proposed university would cater to the needs of Chinese-educated students in Singapore, Malaya and the rest of Southeast Asia.

Tan Lark Sye's proposal met with criticism and suspicion from the colonial government and from the other communities in Singapore and Malaya. It was felt that such a university, by reinforcing Chinese distinctness, would make the nation-building process more difficult. However, the Chinese community responded enthusiastically, and Chinese from all walks of life, including taxi drivers and trishaw riders, contributed to the building fund. The British, though suspicious of the project, did not stop it. However, they refused to grant tax-exemption for donations to the university which was eventually built entirely by the efforts of the Chinese community. Three years later, on 15 March 1956, the Nanyang University was formally declared open by Tan Lark Sye.

The declaration of Emergency in Malaya and Singapore in 1948 had driven the Malayan Communist Party underground. Though the communist insurgency was concentrated more in the Peninsula, from the beginning of 1950 there was a spate of violent acts in Singapore. In April 1950 an attempt was made to assassinate Governor Gimson. In July 1950 the Aik Ho Rubber Factory was burnt down. In the month of September alone one major godown, 16 buses and 18 taxis were destroyed.

In addition to violence, there was quiet but active subversion of Chinese middle school students. The communists had left behind secret cells in these schools when they went underground in 1948. In May 1950 the government brought into force the School Registration Ordinance which empowered it to search or close any school used "as a meeting place by an unlawful society" or for spreading "political propaganda". In June 1950,

two leading Chinese schools – Chinese High School and Nanyang Girls' High School – were closed for two months after the police discovered subversive material in them. Sixty-seven students and seven teachers were expelled.

The government began a campaign to track down and arrest communists and pro-communists. In May 1950 the entire

120

Singapore Town Committee of the Malayan Communist Party was arrested. This was followed by the arrest in January 1951 of 34 members of the Anti-British League, the main satellite of the Malayan Communist Party. Among the 34 arrested were John Eber, a lawyer, C V Devan Nair of the Singapore Teachers' Union, and James Puthucheary of the University of Malaya. In all, more than 1,200 people were detained between 1948 and 1953 under the Emergency Regulations.

In 1951, after three years of insurgency, the Malayan Communist Party realised that armed rebellion was not likely to have an easy or early success. This prompted a change in strategy. A directive went out to cadres to complement armed struggle with greater emphasis on united front work which the party had neglected since 1948. This meant a revival of efforts to make use of legally established and non-communist mass organisations as fronts to further the communist cause. In line with this directive, the communists in Singapore stepped up infiltration, propaganda and organisational work among trade unions, Chinese schools and other organisations. They exploited any issue that was available or could be created: for example, among students, the issue of safeguarding Chinese education and culture; among workers, better wages and working conditions; among women, equal treatment and pay; and above all, across all sectors, the anti-colonial issue.

In the early 1950s, the British decided to ease restrictions on the organisation of trade unions and political parties so as to prepare Malaya for independence and Singapore for self-government. These moves coincided with and facilitated the increase in communist united front activity, especially as some prominent pro-communist detainees were released. While the relaxation of rules helped to encourage people to come forward to participate in political and trade union activities, it also provided the communists with new opportunities to extend their influence in trade unions, Chinese schools and political parties. The majority of those who participated in communist-manipulated demonstrations, strikes or riots in subsequent years were not communists. Many were not even aware that they were being made use of by the communists; they participated because of anti-colonial sentiments and genuine grievances of one kind or another.

The two most prominent communist united front activists were Lim Chin Siong and Fong Swee Suan, both born in Malaya in 1933 and 1931 respectively.

As cell leaders of the student branch of the Anti-British League, both had organised the class boycotts which led to the police raid on Chinese High School in 1950. Now they took low-paid jobs with bus companies and devoted their energies to building up communist influence among workers and students.

In 1954 the communists began to use their front organisations to challenge the colonial government. The first opportunity was provided by the national service issue.

The National Service Ordinance, passed by the Legislative Council in December 1953, came into force on 1 March 1954. It required all males between the ages of 18 and 20, who were British or Federation of Malaya subjects, to register for part-time national service. The Malayan Communist Party incited Chinese middle school students to oppose national service registration, by presenting it as a plot by the colonial authorities to use the local people to fight for the preservation of colonial rule.

On 13 May 1954 clashes erupted between students and the police when lorry loads of students congregated to go to the Governor's residence to present a petition against national service registration. The police broke up the demonstrations and arrested 48 students. This triggered off further student protests in six schools, together with demands for the release of those arrested. This was the first time in the post-

war period that students were used in public demonstrations and confrontations against the authorities.

In May 1954, the Singapore Factory and Shop Workers' Union (SFSWU) was registered, with Lim Chin Siong as its secretary-general. Within 10 months its membership increased from 375 to nearly 30,000. Through a succession of small, well-organised strikes, the union gained better conditions for its workers – the first improvements in many years. From then on, workers needed little persuasion to join this union, and it soon had 30 industrial unions under its wing.

The majority of members of the SFSWU were ethnic Chinese, while the union's executive committee consisted of both English- and Chinese-educated militants. Among these militants were Fong Swee Suan, general secretary of the Singapore Bus Workers' Union, and C V Devan Nair, adviser to the Singapore Traction Company Employees' Union. During this period three others who came to prominence in the labour movement were James Puthucheary, assistant secretary of the SFSWU; Jamit Singh, secretary of the Harbour Board Staff Association; and S Woodhull, secretary of the Naval Base Labour Union.

Another development in 1954 was the demand made by Chinese middle school students to have their union registered. Since the colonial government did not immediately permit this registration, it remained a simmering issue between the authorities and the students during 1954 and 1955. The problems of Chinese education in general had also become more acute. From 1954 more and more Chinese school students were going to China for further education, either because they could not gain entry into the University of Malaya or because they wanted to avoid national service. The colonial authorities barred almost all who went to China from returning to Singapore.

However, the British soon decided that the best political weapon against the communist insurgency in Malaya would be to grant national independence to a moderate and broadly based local leadership. This would deprive the communists of their justification for insurrection: that they were anti-colonial freedom fighters. The UMNO-MCA-MIC Alliance under the leadership of Tunku Abdul Rahman, the president of UMNO, was a moderate, broadly based political organisation which represented the interests of the main races in Malaya. The British therefore felt they could hand over power to an Alliance government after some years of preparation. Political activity increased in Malaya and the cry of *Merdeka* or "Freedom", echoed throughout the Peninsula.

In step with their policy towards Malaya, the British decided to give some measure of internal self-government to Singapore. In October 1953 the Colonial Office appointed a Constitutional Commission, headed by Sir George Rendel. This Commission included the Attorney-General, the President of the City Council, and Chinese, Malay and Indian representatives nominated by the non-official members of the Legislative Council.

In its report released in February 1954, the Commission recommended a Legislative Assembly of 32 members, of whom 25 would be elected for a four-year term. The other seven would be made up of three British officials and four non-officials, nominated by the Governor. There was to be a council of nine ministers to advise the Governor, six of whom would be from the political party which had the largest representation in the Assembly as a result of the election. The other three ministers would be British officials and they would take charge of finance, the judiciary and the information services. The Governor would have absolute control of external relations, public service, defence and internal security. The Commission also recommended a fully elected city council. To ensure wider participation in the electoral process, registration of qualified voters was to be made automatic.

Though the recommendations of the Commission were a significant advancement from the past, they meant only a limited step towards self-government, as the control of not only external affairs and defence but internal security, the civil service, finance and law were to remain in British hands. The Governor was to retain his power to veto legislation.

The British Government accepted the Commission's recommendations, and the first election for the Legislative Assembly was scheduled for April 1955.

The prospect of elections under the new Constitution stimulated political activity in Singapore. Existing political parties prepared for the coming election and new parties were formed. The most prominent political party at that time was the Progressive Party, which had won six of the nine elected seats in the 1951 Legislative Council election. However the 1951 election was no different from the 1948 election: it was meant to give only a token representation in the Council to local people without affecting British power in any way. Though in 1951 there were more registered voters than in the 1948 election, they still numbered only 48,155, a tiny segment of the population; and of these only 51 percent voted on election day, many of them middle-class, English-educated people.

Under the Rendel Constitution, the Progressive Party leaders faced an entirely new situation. They were out of touch with the problems and aspirations of the ordinary masses. The automatic registration of voters would greatly increase the size of the electorate, and many more people were expected to vote than in previous Legislative Council elections because of a heightening of political interest and consciousness. Furthermore, the majority of the new voters would be working-class Chinese.

New political parties were also formed. In late 1954, two former Labour Party leaders, Lim Yew Hock and Francis Thomas, and a prominent lawyer, David Marshall, formed the Labour Front. Lim Yew Hock was a trade unionist who had once been in the Progressive Party and who had been a nominated member of the Legislative Council representing the interests of labour. He was an anti-communist who believed in removing communist influence from trade unions. The leader of the Labour Front, however, was David Marshall, who was known to be strongly anti-colonial. This did not endear him to the British. Under David Marshall, the Labour Front stood for immediate independence and merger with Malaya. It also promised to Malayanise the civil service within four years, abolish the Emergency Regulations and introduce multi-lingualism.

In February 1955, some members of the Singapore Chinese Chamber of Commerce founded the Democratic Party. This party of rich Chinese merchants made an attempt to appeal to the Chinese population by championing the cause of Chinese education, language and culture.

The People's Action Party (PAP) was formed in November 1954. Its origins could be traced to a group of young men who had returned to Singapore in the early 1950s after studying in British universities, and who were committed to the removal of British colonialism and the establishment of an independent non-communist Malaya, including Singapore. Foremost among them were Lee Kuan Yew, Goh Keng Swee, Toh Chin Chye, and S Rajaratnam. English-educated, of middle-class origins and with little or no

political experience, their problem initially was to win a mass following for their ideas from people who were mostly poor and non-English speaking and among whom the Malayan Communist Party, with its long experience and organisational and propaganda skills, was increasingly active.

Lee Kuan Yew became legal adviser to a number of trade unions and in this capacity he acquired a reputation, beginning with the strike of postal workers in 1952, as a lawyer who successfully defended the interests of the workers. His work as legal counsel brought him into contact with many anti-colonialists, and with communists and pro-communists in the trade unions and among Chinese middle school students and university students – including members of the Anti-British League.

Goh Keng Swee was a civil servant, and together with a colleague named Kenneth Byrne, he united the civil service unions and associations behind a Council of Joint Action, created to fight for improved conditions and terms of service for local officers. The Council, formed in 1952, helped to turn the question of Malayanisation of the civil service into a major anti-colonial issue.

Putting an end to colonialism was the first priority of Lee Kuan Yew and his colleagues. They calculated that this could be achieved only with the support of the Chinese-educated public and the communist-controlled trade unions. They therefore decided that they could not afford to adopt an anti-communist stand. Instead they declared themselves to be non-communist – neither for the communists nor against them. They were aware that ultimately the communists would want to set up a communist Malaya, and that after independence from the British had been won, there would have to be a showdown with them. However, until then, the realities of politics in Singapore made an anti-colonial united front with the communists necessary.

The inauguration of the PAP on 21 November 1954 was attended by 1,500 people, among whom were Tunku Abdul Rahman, president of UMNO, and Tan Cheng Lock, president of the MCA in Malaya. Others present included communists and pro-communists like Samad Ismail, Devan Nair, Fong Swee Suan, and Chan Chiaw Thor who were now members of the new party.

The PAP declared that it wanted immediate independence for Singapore through union with Malaya. It called for the abolition of Emergency Regulations, a common Malayan citizenship, complete Malayanisation of the civil service, equal pay for women, and free primary education.

The communists thought they could use the PAP for their own political objectives, just as they had earlier used the Malayan Democratic Union as a front organisation, and it was for this purpose that they and their supporters joined the PAP.

The moderate leaders tried to ensure their control of the central executive committee of the party. The first Committee had three communist united front leaders in it out of a total of 12 members, but Lee Kuan Yew and his colleagues sought to make a distinction between themselves and the communists by constantly stressing, in public, the party's objective to establish a non-communist, independent state.

The elections for the 25 seats in the Legislative Assembly under the Rendel Constitution were held on 2 April 1955. For the first time, Singapore was gripped by election fever and candidates were locked in spirited contest. Surprisingly the Labour Front, which had hoped only to be a strong opposition in the Assembly,

won 10 of the 17 seats it contested. The Progressive Party, which was the major party in the colonial Legislative Council and which the British had hoped would dominate the new Assembly, secured only four of the 22 seats it contested, while the Democratic Party secured two out of 20. The People's Action Party, which fielded only four candidates, won three seats. The Alliance (United Malays National Organisation, Malayan Chinese Association and Singapore Malay Union) contested five seats and won three.

The election results showed that politics in Singapore had undergone a major change. The people had rejected the pro-British and conservative parties and voted for parties which favoured drastic changes, including the removal of colonial rule and rapid improvement in social and economic conditions. With automatic registration, the number of eligible voters, all British subjects, had increased to more than 300,000 and the majority of these were working-class Chinese. About 53 percent of the electorate turned out to vote, more than six times the number that had voted in the 1951 election for the Legislative Council.

Influence of External Events

188

External events had an important bearing on political developments in Malaya and Singapore in the 1950s. These included the surge of the anti-colonial movement in Asia and Africa, the attainment of independence by countries like India and Indonesia, and the capture of China by the communists.

188
Indonesia, under the leadership of Sukarno and Hatta, proclaimed itself independent on 17 August 1945, two days after the surrender of Japan in World War II. Dutch attempts to regain their former colonial territory by military force resulted in a war with Indonesian nationalists. Finally the Dutch agreed to the transfer of sovereignty to Indonesia at the end of 1949.

(Above) Dutch troops man a position on the streets of Jogjakarta in December 1948.

189

189
Pandit Jawaharlal Nehru, Prime Minister of India, salutes the national flag during Independence Day ceremony at Red Fort, New Delhi on 15 August 1947.

190

Chairman Mao Zedong proclaiming the founding of the People's Republic of China on 1 October 1949.

191

The opening of the Afro-Asian Conference at Bandung, Indonesia on 18 April 1955.

The Conference, with delegates from 29 nations, saw Chou En Lai, Nehru, Nasser and Sukarno on the centre stage. The Conference brought together, for the first time, developing and newly independent countries to make an impact on world opinion.

Social and Economic Conditions

192/193

Two scenes typical of the housing conditions in the 1950s. Many shophouse owners in the city centre sub-divided rooms into tiny cubicles and rented them out to families of eight or more.

Unemployment and the housing shortage were serious problems during the 1950s.

192

193

194

An official of the Government Employment Exchange registers applicants for jobs. The Exchange, opened by the Department of Labour in 1946, found jobs for 8,100 applicants in 1950.

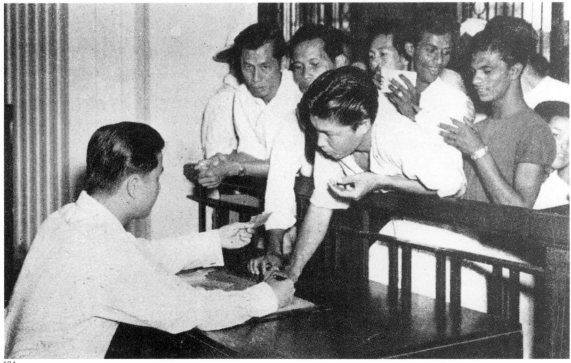

194

195

A satay seller. Itinerant hawkers like him were a common sight on Singapore streets. He would move from one area to another with his portable hawker-stand slung over his shoulder on a bamboo pole. In 1952, a satay stick cost 10 cents, a price that remained unchanged till the mid-1970s.

Owing to the lack of employment and educational opportunities many turned to hawking. The unhygienic handling of food by these hawkers was a health hazard.

196

196
Young and old gather round a Chinese pavement library, a common sight in many Chinatown streets. For a few cents, one could read for as long as one pleased.

197

197
There were also the story tellers to narrate fables and tales of ancient China to rapt street audiences.

English Education and Chinese Education

198

198
The Bukit Timah campus of the University of Malaya, as it was in 1949. Raffles College with its Arts and Science faculties and the King Edward VII College of Medicine with its departments of Medicine, Pharmacy and Dentistry, merged in 1949 to form the University of Malaya.

The university admitted only English-educated students, and served Singapore, the Federation of Malaya, British North Borneo, Sarawak and Brunei.

The English-educated formed a privileged group in society. Only they could aspire to join the civil service, the university and the Teachers' Training College.

199

200

199
A section of Raffles College.

200
A graduand receiving her degree from Malcolm MacDonald, the Chancellor of the University of Malaya and British Commissioner-General for Southeast Asia, at the university's first convocation in July 1950. Seventy-two degrees, including three postgraduate, were awarded at this convocation.

With Malaya becoming independent in 1957 and with the number of students seeking admission on the increase, the university split into two autonomous bodies in 1959, one operating in Kuala Lumpur and the other in Singapore.

Three years later, the two units became separate universities, the University of Singapore and the University of Malaya.

201

203
Sir Sydney Caine, first Vice-Chancellor of the University of Malaya.

204
Dr Lin Yu Tang, first Vice-Chancellor of Nanyang University.

201/202
Chinese High School (above) and Nanyang Girls' High School (right). These two leading Chinese schools were among the main centres for pro-communist student activities. In June 1950, both schools were closed for two months and 67 students and seven teachers expelled when communist propaganda material was discovered in the classrooms.

The Chinese-educated were an underprivileged group. Chinese-medium schools did not receive any government support and the teachers were poorly paid. The Chinese-educated had no avenues for tertiary education; nor could they aspire for jobs in the civil service.

202

206

203

204

205

205
Tan Lark Sye. Born in 1896, he came to Singapore from China as a youth and became a wealthy rubber merchant and industrialist as well as a leader of the Chinese community. In 1953 he proposed the establishment in Singapore of a Chinese-medium Nanyang University to serve the higher education needs of the Chinese-educated in the region.

206
Nanyang University. Tan Lark Sye's proposal, announced at a meeting of the *Hokkien Huay Kuan* was not welcomed by the colonial government. The Chinese community, however, showed tremendous enthusiasm donating generously towards the building fund. The *Hokkien Huay Kuan* donated 212 hectares of land at Jurong for the university and Tan Lark Sye pledged $5 million.

Construction began in late 1953 and the first batch of students started preparatory classes in June 1955 in borrowed premises.

Maria Hertogh Riots

207

The people of Singapore, living in different ethnic, religious and cultural groupings, lacked a sense of common identity. The colonial authorities were not always sensitive to the racial and religious feelings which lay beneath the surface of social relations. The lack of such sensitivity was a factor behind the mob fury and riots from 11 to 13 December 1950. Malay, English and Tamil newspapers also contributed to the outbreak of violence by playing up emotional and religious issues thoughtlessly.

The Maria Hertogh Riots, as they are called, arose out of a law suit over the custody of Maria Bertha Hertogh, a Dutch Catholic girl brought up by a Muslim family when her parents were interned by the Japanese. Maria's marriage to a Muslim was declared null and void, and the court ruled that she be returned to her natural parents. Till her return to Holland, she was placed in a Catholic convent.

208

207
Steel-helmeted troops with fixed bayonets prevent a crowd of spectators from entering the riot area near the Supreme Court.

208
Maria with her foster mother.

132

209

209
At the hearing of the appeal on the custody of Maria, the entrance to the Supreme Court is packed with observers.

210
The aftermath of the riots. In the riots, 18 people were killed, 173 injured, 72 vehicles burnt, and 119 others damaged.

210

Communist Insurgency Continues

211/212/213
The communist insurgency in Malaya continued during the 1950s. Three results of violent communist activities in Malaya: a passenger train derailed through sabotage; a burnt-out village and rubber plantation; and a mutilated rubber tree.

The communists tried to disrupt the economy through such acts but failed to achieve their goal of ousting the British and seizing power.

214

Though the focus of insurgency
was Malaya, Singapore was not
spared. In April 1950, the
communists unsuccessfully
attempted to assassinate
Governor Sir Franklin Gimson
as he was leaving a sports
stadium. The Governor was
injured by the grenade thrown
at him.

215

The communists often resorted
to arson. In 1950, in the worst
case of arson, the Aik Ho
Rubber Factory was completely
destroyed, with a loss of $12
million.

215

30 Held In S'pore Security Check-Up

ABOUT 30 men were arrested in the Sims Avenue-Al-Junied Road area last night during one of the biggest security check-ups Singapore has seen since the Emergency.

Screening of men, women and children and thorough searching of houses in the area were still going on in the early hours of today.

Over 400 uniformed police and officers, 100 plainclothesmen, and many policewomen took part in the operation.

The force was drawn from all the Divisions and also from the Training Depot.

At 6 p.m. armed police parties, equipped with walkie-talkies and portable searchlights, went through the houses from all sides of the area bounded by Sims Avenue, Al-Junied Road, MacPherson Road and Paya Lebar Road.

After 90 minutes the police went away, but they were back again at 10.30 p.m.

Superintendent C. J. A. Haines, in charge of the operation, set up headquarters at the telephone hut at the junction of Sims Avenue and Al-Junied Road—the one Communists twice have tried to burn down—and kept in touch with the men carrying on the screening by radio.

Last night's check was the second since Sunday when a Malay constable guarding a Rediffusion junction was shot by two Chinese and had his revolver stolen.

'SPY' SURRENDERS

SINGAPORE police screening passers-by at the junction of Sims Avenue and Al-Junied Road last night in one of the biggest security checks yet carried out in the Colony.—Straits Times picture.

INSPECTOR A. WILSON, of the Kandang Kerbau Station, examining the yellow top taxi which was fired by Communist terrorists in Dickson Road. The tin near the driver's seat held petrol used for starting the fire.—Straits Times picture.

Another 'Yellow Top' Destroyed

216/217
Aspects of the Emergency in Singapore: security checks and the burning of taxis.

217

136

218

219

218
The defence of Singapore was the responsibility of the British and there was little involvement on the part of the local population, except in the volunteer force and in civil defence.

Here personnel of the Singapore Volunteer Corps (SVC) practise gun drill in 1951.

The SVC was founded in 1854. During World War II, the volunteers fought alongside the regular British and Allied troops in the battle for Singapore. In 1963, when Singapore was part of Malaysia, the SVC was designated the 10th Battalion Territorial Army. In 1965 it was redesignated the 10th People's Defence Force (PDF), and in 1974 renamed the 101 PDF.

219
A Civil Defence Squad, forerunner to the present Civil Defence Force, at a training exercise. Its duties included fire-fighting, debris clearance, first aid, and evacuation. It was disbanded during the Japanese Occupation, but revived in 1951.

United Front Activity Revived

220

221

220/221
The Malayan Communist Party, which had embarked on a path of armed insurgency in 1948, changed its strategy three years later. According to the new strategy, while armed struggle was to continue, much more attention would also be given to united front work. The new strategy was especially important in Singapore's context.

The central politburo of the party, in a directive issued on 1 October 1951, told its members that their "first urgent mission" was to "expand and strengthen the mass organi-sations", "mobilise the masses to wage political struggles", and "make maximum use of different types of open, lawful or other forms of mass organisations to extensively unite the masses".

222

222
The conditions in Singapore favoured a united front strategy, especially since the British were soon to lift restrictions on the organisation of trade unions and political parties so as to prepare Singapore for self-government.

Two prominent communist united front cadres were Lim Chin Siong and Fong Swee Suan (left). They began their careers as Chinese middle school student leaders who organised the boycotts of classes and other militant pro-communist activities. During a police round-up, Fong gave the police the slip and left school while Lim was expelled in 1952. Working in bus companies, both strove diligently to build up communist influence among workers and students. In May 1954, Lim became the secretary-general of the newly formed Singapore Factory and Shop Workers' Union, which was to play a major role in the many industrial strikes of the 1950s.

Agitation Against National Service

223/224
In 1954, the British Government introduced part-time national service as part of the process of preparing Singapore for eventual self-government. Registration (left) began in early 1954 and the first batch of 400 national service recruits reported for training in July 1954 (below).

223

224

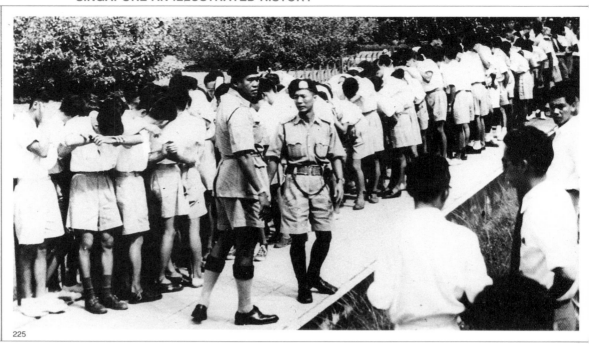

225

226

Estd. 1845

SINGAPORE, FRIDAY, MAY 14, 1954

15 CENTS.

CHOOLBOYS BATTLE POLIC
26 injured in street clashes

Girls join in protest on call-up

FIVE HUNDRED Chinese schoolboys and girls demonstrating against National Service clashed twice with the Singapore Police yesterday as they tried to march on Government House.

A police sergeant is in hospital with a suspected fracture of the skull received when he was hit by a flying stone. Six more policemen got slight stab wounds, but were not kept in hospital.

About 20 schoolchildren, some of them girls, were injured in struggles—first in Clemenceau Avenue and later in Penang Road.

Police arrested 14 boys and a girl. She was released on arrival at the Central Police Station. The boys, who are all over 16, are being detained.

Police watch while boys hold meeting

Later last night about 1,000 schoolboys locked themselves in the Chung Cheng High School in _____ Road to hold a meeting. Police stood by for any further trouble.

_____ boys posted sentries at all the entrances and _____ to allow anyone to enter.

_____ sentries _____ young girls in pig tails and boys in shorts _____ had orders to stop outsiders getting. Only certain pupils, those on errands _____ were allowed to leave _____ and relatives who had come for their _____ were allowed brief interviews through the _____ gates.

The sentries kept assuring worried mothers who _____ outside for hours not to worry.

"Go back and sleep," said one of the sentries, a bespectacled boy. "Your children are all right and they have enough to eat."

All troops in Singapore were recalled to their barracks last night by loudspeaker jeeps which toured the city and notices flashed on cinema screens. All local leave was cancelled.

Yesterday afternoon, the boys and girls, some of them as young as 12 years old, came mainly from the Chung Cheng High School. They were joined later by others from the Chinese High School in Bukit Timah Road.

Twenty lorries drive into town

Youths not wearing any school uniforms were also seen demonstrating with them.

Both schools recently sent petitions to the Government asking for exemption from National Service. On Wednesday the Officer Administering the Government, Mr. W. A. C. Goode, agreed to meet a delegation of eight.

At 2 p.m. yesterday 17 lorries loaded with boys and girls left the school in Goodman Road. They went through the town to Fort Canning Road, where they were diverted by police into Clemenceau Avenue.

By this time another three lorries from the Chinese High School had joined the procession.

In Clemenceau Avenue the schoolboys got out of their lorries and formed up in three and fours on the pavement alongside the King George V Park, making a column about 200 yards long.

WITH MUSCLES tense and determination on their faces, these boys hold fiercely to each other as the police try to separate them.

The struggle is over and these boys—among the 36 who were arrested in Clemenceau Avenue are escorted to a waiting police van.

225/226/227

National Service was not popular with many youths. The communists exploited this issue to mobilise Chinese school students against the government. They incited the students to boycott the registration teams visiting the schools.

On 13 May 1954, nearly 1,000 students congregated in front of Government House (the Istana) to lodge their protest against national service. When they failed to disperse, the Riot Squad was called in.

Soon after this picture (top left) of a "camera-shy" section of the crowd was taken, the demonstrators clashed with the police (left). Over 20 people were injured and 48 students arrested.

228

228
Subsequently, 10 middle
schools were closed by bringing
forward the mid-term holidays
by two weeks. On the day this
was announced, 2,500 students
locked themselves in for a few
days at Chung Cheng High
School, well-fortified with food
and supplies brought in by their
pro-communist supporters.

229
By 1954, hundreds of Chinese
students were leaving for
China, many for further
education, some to avoid
national service. Almost all
were barred from returning to
Singapore as the authorities felt
they would spread communism.

229

Political Evolution

230

230

In 1951 the number of elected seats in the Legislative Council was increased from six to nine. The Progressive Party, which held three of the elected seats in the 1948 Council, won six seats in the 1951 election.

Members of the 1953 Legislative Council: front row (left to right): Elizabeth Choy; T P F McNeice (President, City Council); John Laycock; E J Davies (Attorney-General); Tan Chin Tuan (Deputy President, Legislative Council); Sir John Nicoll (Governor/President, Legislative Council); W L Blythe (Colonial Secretary); C C Tan; W C Taylor (Financial Secretary); E M F Fergusson; Thio Chan Bee.

Back row (left to right): G W Davis; M P D Nair; H J C Kulasingha; Ahmad bin Mohamed Ibrahim; N A Mallal; Dr W J Vickers (Director of Medical Services); P F de Souza; L W Donough (Clerk of the Legislative Council); Lim Yew Hock; J A Harvey (Commissioner of Lands); A McLellan; C H Butterfield (Solicitor-General); C R Dasaratha Raj; Dr C J P Paglar; A Gilmour (Director of Commerce and Industry).

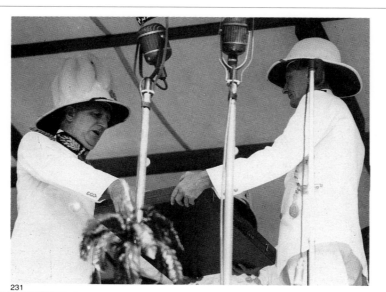

231

231

Singapore was proclaimed a city on 22 September 1951. The Governor, Sir Franklin Gimson (left), presents the Royal Charter conferring city status to Singapore to the President of the Municipal Council, T P F McNeice. Thenceforth, the Municipal Council became City Council.

232

232
An estimated 25,000 people thronged the Padang to see and participate in the City Day celebrations which included a procession of floats (above), a fireworks display and an illuminated dragon gliding across the sea front.

233

234

233
The Rendel Constitutional Commission. The Commission had nine members including its chairman, Sir George Rendel. Five of the members were nominated by the unofficial members of the Legislative Council. They were N A Mallal and Lim Yew Hock (first and second on the left), Tan Chin Tuan and C C Tan (second and third from the right), and Ahmad Ibrahim (sixth from the right).

The Commission recommended partial internal self-government for Singapore. There was to be a Legislative Assembly of 32 members of whom 25 were to be elected,

and a council of nine ministers. Singapore's elected representatives would be in charge of internal affairs, except for internal security, law and finance, which were to remain under British control. Britain would also be in charge of defence and external affairs.

234
In early 1952, the Postal and Telecommunications Uniformed Staff Union which had a pay dispute with the government, engaged a young lawyer, Lee Kuan Yew, as its legal adviser. His successful negotiations with the government on behalf of the postmen who were on a three-week strike, earned him the support and goodwill of workers. Soon he was to become legal adviser to several unions.

(Above) Lee Kuan Yew (third from the right) at the beginning of an arbitration in the dispute between postal clerks and the government, 9 April 1953.

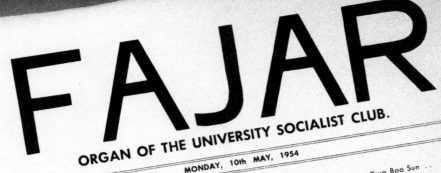

FAJAR

ORGAN OF THE UNIVERSITY SOCIALIST CLUB.

20 cents

MONDAY, 10th MAY, 1954

No. 7

CONTENTS

Comments .. .. .. Page 1
Singapore Socialist Party—Francis Thomas 3
Seamen's Strike—Lam Khuan Kit 3
Indo-China Story 4

Pan-Malayan Labour Party—Kwa Boo Sun .. Page 5
Book Review— 6
Indonesian Poetry and Nationalism—Ali Abdullah .. 7
International Socialism 8

AGGRESSION IN ASIA

Looming large in Asia once again is the threat of Western aggression. The West has been the aggressor in modern history and Asia has suffered bitterly from Western barbarity. The bitterness of these memories is not easily removed. They will greatly influence Asian thinking for a long time, until the West proves itself worthy of trust and friendship. This day is yet to come and vigilance is needed to prevent any form of Western imperialism getting a foothold in Asia again. Recent events in Asia give great cause for alarm.

We see signs all over Asia that the West is still a menace. In Indo-China the French, backed by American arms, are striving to suppress the Vietminh Nationalists in their struggle for freedom. Republican China is being denied her rightful place in the United Nations, whilst an **emigre** government is being maintained in Taiwan under the protection of the U.S. navy. Republican India is being dragged into the theatre of war by the purchase of American military bases in Pakistan. Now we are told that Asia is to be defended, whether she likes it or not. A military pact is being formed against Asian objections and without Asian participation. We view this as being, in Mr. A. Bevan's words, "for the purpose of imposing European colonial rule."

Little attempt is made to maintain more than a pretence of con-

sulting Asian opinion. The time is past, however, when European nations could make decisions binding on Asia. But this is still not recognised. The South East Asian "defence" pact is the latest example of Western interference. Its immediate object is to stamp out the freedom movement in Indo-China. Its long term object is to prevent the development of any movement in Asia that will stand up against the West. Asian nations must take a firm stand now before it is too late. We must warn the West to "Hands off Asia."

Clearly Asian friendship cannot be won under such hostile conditions. Asia needs Western technical knowledge and we welcome Western friendship. But there can be no compromise with colonialism in any form. "The dramatic change, the psychological revolution" that Jennie Lee speaks of is needed. Anti-communism is not a substitute for this. Yet apparently this negative philosophy is all that the West can offer.

The prospect of Asia "going communist" has been responsible in a large measure for every major Western concession ranging from Indian Independence to land for the Chinese squatter in Malaya. Is it therefore surprising that the spectre of Communism haunting the West should leave Asia unperturbed? Is it any wonder that Asia will have nothing to do with

anti-communist fronts? For that is not our problem. We need peace and freedom. The solidarity of Asia is the solidarity of the suppressed. This alone is our fight and we will be dragged into no other. Our sympathies are with all people like us who are thirsting for peace and freedom. We are therefore comrades, of the African struggling for the most elementary human rights, of the Indo-Chinese fighting for his freedom. Our enemies are those who would deny us these rights.

Malaya, however, cannot choose. It is one more pimple on the face of Asia where a Colonial Power rules with the help of quislings. As such our interests will always be sacrificed to imperial expediency. Thus we see our country being committed into a military alliance, the SEATO, without the sanction of its people. Our young men are being conscripted; our land is being turned into a military base. Our country is to fight in wars over whose making it will not have any say. We must collaborate in crushing the Indo-Chinese people. We are to be the allies of petite fascists like Syngman Rhee, Chiang Kai Shek and Phibun Songgram who stand for totalitarian tyranny. We would rather stand with Republican India, Republican China, Republican Burma and their allies in Asia and Africa. The people of this country do not identify themselves with the actions of the Colonial government.

235

235

One of the five articles in *Fajar*, the organ of the University of Malaya Socialist Club, which angered the colonial authorities. Eight undergraduates connected with the publication were brought to

court on charges of sedition. The trial, from 23 to 25 August 1954, put the colonial government in a poor light. The court ordered the discharge of the students.

However, the trial brought

into the limelight Lee Kuan Yew who was keen on working for Singapore's independence. He had acted as junior counsel to D N Pritt, QC, on behalf of the students.

236

237

238

239

236/237/238
The release of the Rendel Report in February 1954 aroused political interest and led to the formation of new political parties.

The People's Action Party (PAP) held its inaugural meeting at the Victoria Memorial Hall on 21 November 1954. The party's founder members included Lee Kuan Yew (lawyer), Dr Toh Chin Chye (university lecturer) and S Rajaratnam (journalist).

More than 1,500 people from all walks of life pack the Victoria Memorial Hall, many spilling into the foyer to witness the birth of the PAP.

239
Tunku Abdul Rahman, president of the United Malays National Organisation in Malaya, and Tan Cheng Lock, president of the Malayan Chinese Association are among the invited guests.

240
Election fever comes to Singapore, and for the first time election rallies are lively, boisterous affairs. The general election in April 1955 under the Rendel Constitution paved the way for Singapore's first government with elected ministers. Seventy-nine candidates, including two women, contested the 25 elected seats in the Legislative Assembly. Sixty-nine represented six political parties. while 10 were independents.

241/242
Labour Front leaders addressing a rally under the "Old Apple Tree" at Empress Place (below left·), and PAP supporters on the campaign trail (below). More than 40 rallies were held during the month-long campaign leading up to the polling on 2 April 1955.

243
Polling staff setting off to man their respective stations in the 25 electoral districts. Ample publicity on polling procedures and automatic registration of voters provided for by the Rendel Constitution, ensured a large turnout at the polls. A total of 160,395 voters, out of an electorate of 300,299 cast their votes – an almost seven-fold increase over the 24,580 votes cast in 1951.

243

244

244
The three PAP candidates who were elected. (From left): Goh Chew Chua, Lim Chin Siong and Lee Kuan Yew. On the right is Ahmad Ibrahim who won as an independent. The PAP's fourth candidate, Devan Nair, lost by a narrow margin.

245
Lee Kuan Yew, secretary-general of the People's Action Party, and David Marshall, leader of the Labour Front, after their victory at the polls. Marshall, whose party won 10 seats, became Chief Minister and formed a coalition government with the UMNO-MCA Alliance, which won three seats.

The election results amounted to a clear rejection by the people of the pro-British and conservative political parties. Instead, they voted for parties which stood for an early end to colonial rule and the rapid improvement of economic and social conditions.

The Progressive Party, which was the dominant party in the Legislative Council, won only four seats. The PAP won three seats. The Democratic Party won two seats, while the Singapore Labour Party failed to win any. Three independents were elected.

245

5

TURBULENT YEARS

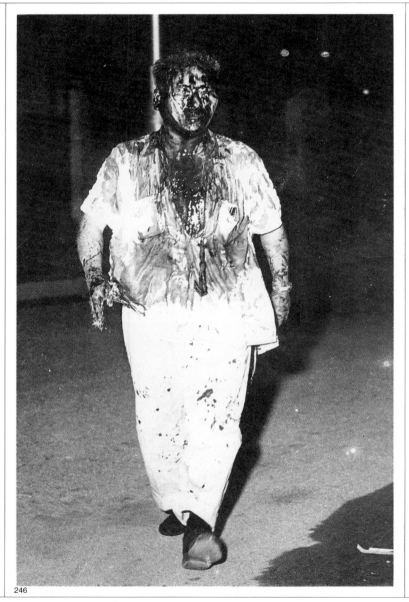

246
Violence, destruction and death marked the communist-inspired troubles of 1955 and 1956. Detective Corporal Yuen Yan Peng suffered severe burns when his car was set on fire by a mob during the Hock Lee riots in May 1955. He died a week later.

1955~1959

avid Marshall became Singapore's first Chief Minister at the head of a Labour Front Government. In addition to 10 Labour Front Assemblymen, the government had the support of two UMNO-MCA members, three ex-officio members, and two nominated members, forming a group of 17 in the 32-member Assembly.

From the start the Labour Front Government was beset by problems. The most serious challenge came from the communist united front. No sooner had the government assumed power than it was faced with communist-instigated strikes and student unrest. In fact, throughout the period of the Labour Front Government under Marshall, the communists used the Singapore Factory and Shop Workers' Union (SFSWU) and the Chinese middle school students to confront the government and to expand communist control and influence among workers and students.

The first clash came in April 1955, soon after the formation of the Marshall Government. The immediate cause was a strike by some Hock Lee Bus workers belonging to the Singapore Bus Workers' Union

whose general secretary was Fong Swee Suan. Although a settlement seemed likely at one stage, the pro-communists in the union were not interested in this. They were more interested in exploiting the dispute to whip up the emotions of the workers and to have a confrontation with the government. Large numbers of Chinese school students were brought in to encourage the striking bus workers. When police tried to break up the illegal picket line a major riot broke out on Thursday, 12 May, which has come to be known as "Black Thursday". Four people died and 31 were injured. The strike was seen as a victory for the workers because the strikers were reinstated with no loss of income. In the follow-up action, several students and workers involved in the riots were arrested.

fter this Singapore was beset by strike after strike. Altogether there were 275 strikes in 1955, with 946,354 man-days lost. Student agitation also continued. When the government threatened to close Chinese High School, Nanyang Girls' High

School and Chung Cheng High School if students involved in the Hock Lee riots were not expelled and discipline restored, 2,000 students barricaded themselves in Chung Cheng High School. They threatened

to camp there until the government released their arrested leaders, and repealed legislation which empowered the authorities to close schools if students indulged in subversive activities.

Marshall refused to take stern action, partly because he felt it would ultimately be politically damaging to his party, and partly because he believed that Chinese teachers and students had genuine grievances caused by the colonial education policy. Instead, he appointed an all-party committee to study the Chinese education problem. Marshall agreed to the committee's suggestion that the ultimatum to close the schools be set aside till the committee had looked into the education problem. In October 1955, he also agreed to register the Singapore Chinese Middle School Students' Union (SCMSSU), on condition that it kept out of politics. The students accepted the condition; but they had no intention of honouring it.

There was also constant conflict between Marshall and the colonial government over the respective powers of the Governor and the Chief Minister. Marshall did not want to be a mere figurehead while most of the power lay with the colonial government – the Chief Secretary, the Financial Secretary, the Attorney-General and the Commissioner of Police were all British, answerable only to British authority.

The Emergency Regulations which Marshall had pledged to repeal were one point of contention. The British wanted to retain these Regulations so as to contain the communist threat. Marshall's desire to repeal some of the regulations was strengthened by the fact that the PAP, which also strongly opposed them, would have made political capital out of any reluctance on his part to have them repealed. In the end, the Regulations were replaced in October 1955 by the Preservation of Public Security Ordinance, which retained detention without trial, but with a tribunal allowing for review and appeal.

When the new Governor, Sir Robert Black, refused to allow Marshall to appoint four new assistant ministers, he threatened to resign unless Singapore was given early internal self-government. The Colonial Office in London agreed to hold constitutional talks the following year and instructed that, in the meantime, the Governor act on the Chief Minister's advice.

The constitutional talks, popularly referred to as the Merdeka Talks, opened in London on 23 April 1956. Marshall led a 13-member all-party mission comprising six Assemblymen from his government and six Opposition members, including Lee Kuan Yew and Lim Chin Siong of the PAP. The 10-man British side was led by Alan Lennox-Boyd, Secretary of State for the Colonies.

At the talks, the British were prepared to grant full internal self-government to Singapore. There would be Singapore citizenship for those born in Singapore, or of long residence; a fully elected legislature and Cabinet; and Malayanisation of the civil service; but Britain would retain control of foreign affairs and defence. The talks, however, broke down over the issue of the control of internal security. The British insisted that they should have the decisive say in the proposed Defence and Internal Security Council. They wanted the three British and three Singapore representatives on the Council to be under the chairmanship of the British High Commissioner in Singapore, who would have the casting vote. They wanted the Commissioner of Police to have the right to report direct to the High Commissioner, bypassing the minister-in-charge.

The British were determined to control internal security. They regarded the Marshall Government's handling of the pro-communists as weak and the Chief Minister's general attitude to the communist threat as lacking in realism. Singapore was an important military base. The British were not prepared to take the risk of placing security in the hands of an elected government in a politically volatile situation.

Marshall was forced to resign as Chief Minister on 6 June as he had pledged that he would not stay in office if he failed in his bid for internal self-government. Lim Yew Hock succeeded him as Chief Minister on 8 June, retaining Marshall's entire Cabinet.

Lim Yew Hock was prepared to deal firmly with the communists. The first year of his government was therefore marked by a showdown with the communist united front. In June and July students of the SCMSSU held a number of sessions, which were also attended by trade union cadres, to prepare for a campaign of agitation against the government. Strong government action followed in September and October, starting on 19 September. Two communist united front organisations were deregistered; seven persons, including the president of the Singapore Factory and Shop Workers' Union (SFSWU), were banished; and the SCMSSU was dissolved. The students retaliated by holding an illegal celebration of China's National Day on 1 October. This resulted in the arrest of four of their leaders.

The students then camped at Chung Cheng High School and Chinese High School. They organised meetings and demonstrations, and food was brought in from outside by parents and left-wing elements. This went on for two weeks. Finally, on 24 October, the government issued an ultimatum that parents should remove their children from the schools by 8.00 pm the following day, or it would take strong action to remove them.

On 25 October, at about 5.00 pm, Lim Chin Siong and others made inflammatory speeches at a protest meeting in Bukit Timah village, and afterwards several hundreds of those who had attended this meeting joined the crowds assembled outside Chinese High School. The mob became rowdy, and began attacking the police and overturning their cars. The violence moved down Bukit Timah Road and into the town, and subsequent rioting lasted five days, from 25 to 29 October. A curfew was imposed on the island and troops were brought in from Johor to control the

situation. Thirteen people were killed, over a hundred were injured, more than a hundred vehicles were burnt or damaged, and over 900 people were arrested. This was one of the bloodiest riots Singapore had experienced up to that time.

The communist united front was crippled, at least for the time being, by the large number of arrests. Among those arrested were some of its more prominent leaders, including Lim Chin Siong, Fong Swee Suan, Devan Nair, James Puthucheary and S Woodhull. The two Chinese middle schools involved in the student camp-in were closed, and in February 1957 the SFSWU was dissolved. But the use of force against school children by British and British-controlled security forces enraged the Chinese public and the communist united front propaganda was able to depict the Lim Yew Hock Government as a tool of the British colonialists.

However, the tough line taken by Lim Yew Hock pleased the British. They now had more confidence in his willingness to use force to maintain internal security, and were therefore prepared to make concessions when he led a five-member all-party delegation to London in March 1957 for a second round of constitutional talks to discuss internal self-government.

During the month-long talks the controversial issue of the Internal Security Council was resolved by doing away with the British majority and giving the casting vote to a representative of the Federation of Malaya. Thus the seven-member council was to have three Britons, three Singaporeans and one Malayan. The Head of State would be a local Yang di-Pertuan Negara instead of a British Governor. Singapore would have its own citizenship laws. The Commissioner of Police would be responsible only to the elected

government. However, the British would have the right to suspend the Constitution.

The mission returned home to a hero's welcome, and the Legislative Assembly agreed to the constitutional proposals which were to be finalised by a third all-party mission to London in 1958.

Meanwhile, though there was relative quiet for the time being among the trade unions and Chinese school students, the communists were stepping up pressure within the PAP. By 1956, before the party was even two years old, the moderate leaders realised that they were virtual prisoners of the communists. Led by Lim Chin Siong, the pro-communists in the party controlled many of the mass organisations on the island and had strengthened their hold on the party branches. In the party's central executive committee, the moderate leaders were still in the majority and this gave them some room for manoeuvre, at least in public statements on the party's policy, goals and thinking on the issues of the day. The communists wanted to bring the party's policies and public pronouncements under their firmer control, while retaining the key moderate leaders as front men. They tried to do this by winning a pro-communist majority in the central executive committee.

At the 1956 annual general meeting of the party, the pro-communists had increased their representation in the central executive committee from nothing to four out of 12. (At the annual meeting of the party in 1955, the pro-communist faction had agreed to give up all representation in the committee.) They had also pressed unsuccessfully for changes in the party's constitution which would allow branch committees, in which they had strong influence, to nominate members to the central executive committee. Their next effort to control the central executive committee was made at the annual general meeting held on 4 August 1957. The pro-communists packed the meeting with their supporters. Membership admission cards, which had been posted to members who gave trade union premises as their addresses, were instead distributed to non-members who would vote for the pro-communists. The result was an increase in the representation of the pro-communists in the central executive committee from four to six out of 12.

The six moderate leaders (Toh Chin Chye, Lee Kuan Yew, Ahmad Ibrahim, Goh Chew Chua, Chan Choy Siong and Tann Wee Tiong) would not accept a situation where they would be a front for the leftists and nothing more. They refused to take office, thereby exposing the pro-communists (Tan Chong Kin, Tan Kong Guan, Chan Say Jame, Goh Boon Toh, Ong Chye Ann and T T Rajah) and leaving them with no choice but to assume the top posts of the party.

However, this change in the leadership of the PAP was short-lived. On 21 and 22 August 1957 the Lim Yew Hock Government arrested 35 pro-communists, including five of the six (the exception was T T Rajah) who had become members of the central executive committee of the party. On the following day the government issued a White Paper which revealed, among other things, how the communists had been reorganising since the security action taken against them in 1956, and how they had expanded their infiltration and control of various existing organisations, including trade unions and PAP branches.

The arrest of the pro-communists in August 1957 enabled Lee Kuan Yew and his moderate colleagues to regain control of the PAP. The moderate leaders were determined that they should never again lose control of the central executive committee to the pro-communists. For this reason, the party's constitution was amended in November 1958 to introduce cadre members, making it impossible for ordinary members to interfere in the elections to the central executive committee.

Elections for the first fully elected City Council, provided for under the Rendel Constitution, were held on 21 December 1957. For the first time any voter literate in one of the four main languages could stand for election as long as he was a British subject and lived within City Council electoral divisions. Eighty-one candidates contested the 32 seats.

The PAP, which campaigned vigorously on an anti-corruption platform, emerged as the leading party winning 13 of the 14 seats it contested. The Liberal Socialist Party contested all 32 seats but won only seven. The Labour Front won four out of 16, UMNO-MCA Alliance two out of three, and independents won two seats. The Workers' Party formed by David Marshall only two months before the elections won four out of the five seats it contested. This surprisingly good performance was achieved with the help of communist supporters, a fact which David Marshall seemed unaware of. While the PAP was their main vehicle, the communists viewed their backing of the Workers' Party as a useful threat which might enable them to keep the recalcitrant PAP moderates in line.

The Council elected Ong Eng Guan, a founder member and treasurer of the PAP, as Mayor on 24 December 1957. As events turned out, he was to be Singapore's first and last Mayor. Ong Eng Guan moved quickly to attack colonial symbols and colonial attitudes in the City Council. The public gallery was packed daily as labourers and hawkers flocked to hear the Mayor revile British colonialism and ridicule the English-educated civil servants.

Ong Eng Guan's style aroused the wrath of the Opposition Councillors, who lodged a complaint with the Lim Yew Hock Government. When the Council seemed headed for an open confrontation with the Mayor, the govern-ment took over some of its functions in March 1959. The following month, Ong Eng Guan and the other PAP Councillors resigned.

The Mayor's style was unconventional and populist. Though he did much to boost his own image, he also made political gains for the PAP. He made the people see the shortcomings and faults of the colonial government and the colonial psychology. Under the PAP, the City Council had proved itself effective in improving the water supply, markets, the condition of hawkers, and sewerage – areas which touched upon the day-to-day life of the people. Within weeks, numerous bus shelters and standpipes had been installed, and five public dispensaries were opened in crowded and generally neglected areas. The PAP's experience and achievements in the City Council from 1957 to 1959 benefited it in the 1959 general election, though some of the English-educated, especially the civil servants, were alienated by the Mayor.

After successive purges of their united front cadres, the communists had been planning their next move. Some weeks before Lim Yew Hock again led a mission to London to finalise details of the new Constitution, the Malayan Communist Party – alarmed by its estrangement from the PAP after it had supported David Marshall in the City Council elections – sent a high-level emissary to meet Lee Kuan Yew in order to come to some understanding before elections were held under the new Constitution. The emissary, Fong Chong Pik, who was subsequently referred to as "The Plen" (short for Plenipotentiary), met Lee Kuan Yew four times before the 1959 election. His main purpose was to find out if Lee Kuan Yew was prepared to let the communists work together with the PAP in a united anti-colonial front.

In April 1958, Lim Yew Hock led the third all-party mission to London. An agreement which provided for a constitution for a State of Singapore with full powers of internal self-government was signed on 28 May. In August 1958 the British Parliament changed the status of the island from a Colony to a State. Under the new

Constitution the British would retain control of foreign affairs and defence, while internal security would be in the hands of an Internal Security Council in which the Federation of Malaya representative would have the casting vote. The British also insisted that individuals with records of subversive activity would not be allowed to stand for election, and they retained the power to suspend the Constitution if necessary. Voting was made compulsory, and the first election to bring the new Constitution into effect was scheduled for May 1959.

From the outset, the PAP set the pace and direction of the election campaign. The Labour Front, already damaged politically by its strong action against pro-communist activities in trade unions and Chinese schools, was now hit by a major scandal. Campaigning on a platform of an efficient and incorruptible government, the PAP revealed in February 1959 that Chew Swee Kee, Minister of Education in the Labour Front Government, had been receiving funds from American sources. A Commission of Inquiry confirmed the charge. The findings of the Commission and the extended media publicity given to the case discredited the Lim Yew Hock Government.

It was a hard-hitting election campaign with daily rallies drawing mammoth crowds. People were interested not just in the promise of self-government. They were looking for jobs and freedom from poverty and squalor. The PAP leaders made clear in their speeches the distinction between themselves and the communists and stressed that they stood for a non-communist independent state. Lee Kuan Yew, in an election speech at Clifford Pier on 26 May 1959, said

that the real fight after the election would be between the PAP and the communists – "the PAP for a democratic, non-communist, socialist Malaya, and the Malayan Communist Party for a Soviet Republic of Malaya".

Candidates from 10 different parties, including David Marshall's Workers' Party, and 39 independents, contested the 51 seats. The PAP fielded candidates in all constituencies.

The electorate had nearly doubled to 587,797 because under the new citizenship laws more people, including many who were China-born, had become citizens and were therefore eligible to vote – and for the first time voting was compulsory. On polling day, 30 May 1959, around 90 percent (524,420) of the electorate turned out to vote. The PAP romped home to a spectacular victory winning 43 of the 51 seats. The

Singapore People's Alliance which was led by some of the former Labour Front leaders was routed, winning only four out of the 39 seats it contested. The Liberal Socialist Party, which fielded 32 candidates, failed to win any seat. Three were won by the UMNO-MCA Alliance and one by an independent candidate. Lim Yew Hock was returned but David Marshall was defeated, and the Workers' Party, which had won four out of the five seats in the City Council elections in December 1957, now did not win any of the three it contested. The reason was simple: the communists had abandoned the Workers' Party.

Initially the PAP's clear victory triggered off uneasiness among both the business community and the English-educated middle class. There was a flight of capital, and some foreign firms moved their headquarters to Kuala Lumpur.

During the election campaign Lee Kuan Yew had pledged that the PAP would assume office only if the eight pro-communist PAP detainees arrested in 1956 and 1957 were freed. When on 1 June he was invited by Governor Sir William Goode to form the government, he therefore insisted on and secured an agreement for their release. The new Constitution came into force on 3 June when Sir William took his oath of office as Singapore's first Yang di-Pertuan Negara. The eight detainees were released the following morning, but only after Lee Kuan Yew had obtained a pledge from six of them, in signed statements, that they would strive for a "united, independent, democratic, non-communist and socialist Malaya by peaceful means" and renounce revolutionary violence.

On 5 June Lee Kuan Yew and his eight-member Cabinet were sworn in. It was a young Cabinet with an average age of 37. The Prime Minister, Lee Kuan Yew, was only 36 years old. Five of the released detainees – Fong Swee Suan, Lim Chin Siong, Devan Nair, Chan Chiaw Thor and S Woodhull – were

appointed political secretaries to various ministries, while James Puthucheary was made manager of the Industrial Promotion Board.

The years 1955 to 1959 were transitional ones in Singapore politics. They were a period of intense political education and arousal of the masses for which the communists were not the only ones responsible. The two non-communist leaders with ability and popular appeal, David Marshall and Lee Kuan Yew, played important roles. Though Chief Minister for only about a year, David Marshall did much to awaken the people to the ills of colonial rule during the campaign for the 1955 election, in debates in the Legislative Assembly, and by drawing attention to his problems with the colonial authorities. But he underestimated the threat the communists posed and never fully appreciated their mode of operation.

Lim Yew Hock was Chief Minister for three years. He successfully completed the constitutional talks and achieved self-government for Singapore. He showed a willingness to take firm action against the communists, though he paid a political price for this. But by so acting he was able to win concessions from the British and keep the left-wing in check, which in turn helped the moderate PAP leadership to consolidate its position within the party. However, towards the end of his

tenure as Chief Minister increasing corruption undermined his government.

With essential powers in British hands and with frequent communist-inspired strikes and agitation, the Labour Front Government was unable to deal with the growing social and economic problems of Singapore, such as housing and unemployment. There was also a steady increase in secret society activity during this period. Many crimes were committed by gangs connected with secret societies, including kidnapping for ransom, extortion from hawkers, trishaw riders and others, as well as murder.

However, the Labour Front did identify certain important grievances and initiate action to resolve them. In August 1955 the Marshall Government appointed the Sreenivasan Commission on Malayanisation of the civil service. The Legislative Assembly accepted the Commission's report which advocated the complete localisation of administrative posts in two years, and of the rest of the service in four. Marshall also appointed an all-party committee on Chinese education. Its report, made public in 1956, recommended the introduction of a common bilingual primary education, parity for the four main language streams, equal pay for teachers, equal opportunities for entry into government service, and the banning of students from active politics. These recommendations were embodied in the Education Ordinance of December 1957 enacted by the Lim Yew Hock Government.

Legislation in October 1957 created Singapore citizenship, an essential qualification for electors under the Constitution which was to give full internal self-government to Singapore. All those born in the island automatically became Singapore citizens. Those born in the Federation of Malaya, and citizens of the United Kingdom and the Colonies as well as citizens of Commonwealth countries, could acquire Singapore citizenship by registration if they had resided in Singapore for two years. All others, including those born in China, qualified for citizenship provided they had resided in Singapore for eight years. In an initial registration drive which ended in December 1958, a total of 325,000 residents born outside Singapore acquired citizenship. Among them were the majority of 220,000 China-born residents who had until then been denied the right to vote.

Labour Front Forms Government

247
David Marshall, Singapore's first Chief Minister and a founder member of the Labour Front. A lawyer by profession, he fought with the Volunteers during the Japanese invasion, and as a prisoner of war, he worked in the coal mines of Hokkaido.

248
Governor Sir John Nicoll reviews a guard-of-honour before opening the Legislative Assembly on 22 April 1955.

249
The first Council of Ministers under the 1955 Rendel Constitution. Back row (left to right): Francis Thomas (Communications & Works); T M Hart (Financial Secretary); Lim Yew Hock (Labour & Welfare); Haji Abdul Hamid bin Haji Jumaat (Local Government, Lands & Housing); A J Braga (Health); J M Jumabhoy (Commerce & Industry). Front row (left to right): Chew Swee Kee (Education); David Marshall (Chief Minister); Sir John Nicoll (Governor); William Goode (Chief Secretary); E J Davies (Attorney-General).

252
Sir George Oehlers.

250/251
Marshall taking the oath as Member of the Legislative Assembly and (below) members preparing to leave at the end of the first session. The government bench is on the left and facing them are the opposition members. Singapore's first Speaker, Sir George Oehlers, is in a dark suit, full wig and robe. Oehlers, a lawyer, was not a member of the Assembly.

250

252

251

253

253
People waiting at the Assembly House for a "Meet-the-People" session. Marshall introduced this programme soon after he became Chief Minister to enable him to meet the people and listen to their problems. The programme, however, was short-lived.

Riots and Strikes

254

254
The Marshall Government's strength and resolve were soon to be tested by the communist united front of trade unions and Chinese middle school students.

On 23 April 1955 some workers of the Hock Lee Amalgamated Bus Co, who were members of the pro-communist Singapore Bus Workers' Union, went on strike (above) in protest against new work rosters and the formation of rival unions. The strikers attempted to stop the buses from leaving the depots. The dispute dragged on into the early weeks of May, with Chinese middle school students and other sympathisers joining the strikers in a show of support.

255

255
Chinese middle school students on one of their many donation drives in support of the strikers. Students not only brought food and money for the striking workers, but also entertained them with songs and dances.

256

257

258

256/257
Afternoon of 12 May: students of Chung Cheng High School and Chinese High School converging in a convoy of 20 lorries on Alexandra Road Circus, near the Alexandra Road Depot of the Hock Lee Bus Company, soon after a bus was attacked at 1.45 pm. By 3.00 pm all Hock Lee buses had stopped running, their crew intimidated by the strikers.

258/259/260
The police resort to water-cannon and tear gas to disperse the mob which (far right) retaliates by stoning the policemen and buses.

259

260

261

262

263

261
By nightfall, violence has spread to the adjoining areas and the police are attacked with sticks, stones, and *cangkuls*.

Among the policemen set upon by the rioting mobs were Volunteer Special Constable Andrew Teoh Bok Lan (seen seated in his car between two *cangkul*-wielding rioters) and Detective Corporal Yuen Yan Peng (who died after his car was set on fire).

262
Andrew Teoh Bok Lan lies critically injured on the road; he died in hospital soon after.

Others killed in the riot were Gene D Symonds, the Southeast Asia manager for United Press International, and a 16-year-old student, Chong Lon Chong.

263
A section of the crowd (below) that turned up at the General Hospital mortuary to accompany Chong Lon Chong's hearse.

Chong, who sustained a head injury during the rioting, was paraded around by the mob for more than three hours instead of being rushed to the nearby General Hospital for treatment. He died, and the communists used him as a martyr to whip up public emotions.

264/265
Students of Chung Cheng High School stage a sit-in on 17 May 1955 protesting against the government's demand that student leaders involved in the Hock Lee strikes and riots be expelled, while (above) other students protest over the same issue with banners and placards.

The government also threatened to close the three Chinese middle schools involved in the riots if discipline was not restored. However, the ultimatum was withdrawn on the recommendation of the all-party committee appointed to study the education problem. The students saw this as a victory and this spurred them on to further involvement in labour disputes and riots.

266

Throughout the period 1955 to 1959, the communist united front sought to discredit the Labour Front Government and to radicalise the population through a series of confrontations. Strikes and work stoppages were the common means used. During this four-year period, there were 393 strikes and lock-outs with over 1.6 million man-days lost. The worst year was 1955:

there were 275 strikes and lock-outs, the highest for the decade, with a loss of 946,354 man-days. Only a third of these were for better working conditions and wages; the others were either sympathy strikes or demands for the release of detained trade union leaders.

266
Striking Singapore Harbour Board (SHB) workers picketing

the entrance to Government House (the Istana) at Orchard Road Circus on 30 May 1955. The Governor and the Harbour Board negotiators were holding talks inside to end the two-month-old strike of 1,300 monthly paid employees of the SHB. The Chief Minister (with finger raised) is arguing with the pickets.

267

267
Workers at a mass rally organised by the Singapore Trade Union Working Committee on 7 October 1955 to protest against the Emergency Regulations. The banner reads: "Those who are enslaved, arise".

268

268
Motorists, turned away from petrol stations where attendants had gone on strike, created major traffic jams in May 1955. This scene was repeated at all the stations which opened for business. The strike brought public transport to a halt.

269

269
City Council workers went on strike on 20 August 1955, disrupting the cleansing and public utilities services of the city.

270

270
Workers of Diamond Restaurant and Wing Choon Yuen Restaurant in Great World register their protests during their strike on 4 November 1955.

Baling Talks

271

271/272
On 28 and 29 December 1955 a meeting was held in Baling, Kedah, between Tunku Abdul Rahman, Chief Minister of the Federation of Malaya, and Chin Peng, secretary-general of the Malayan Communist Party (MCP), to discuss an end to the communist insurgency. The Tunku was accompanied by David Marshall and Tan Cheng Lock, president of the Malayan Chinese Association (MCA).

The talks failed. The MCP demanded that party members and insurgents who gave themselves up should not be subjected to any security action or investigation. The party should be accorded recognition as a legal and legitimate political party with the right to take part in constitutional politics.

Tunku Abdul Rahman could not accept these demands because they would have

272

amounted to giving the MCP all the opportunities to expand its strength and influence through legal means. The Emergency was to continue until 1960 when the remnants of the MCP insurgent force withdrew to southern Thailand. Top picture

(right to left): Tan Cheng Lock, (president, MCA); Tunku Abdul Rahman (Chief Minister of the Federation of Malaya); and David Marshall (Chief Minister of Singapore). (Above) Chin Peng (centre) flanked by two MCP central

committee members, Rashid Mydin (left) and Chen Tien.

Showdown with Communist United Front

273
Lim Yew Hock, Singapore's second and last Chief Minister. A former clerk and trade unionist, he was a Legislative Councillor from 1948 to 1955. He was also a founder member of the Labour Party, the Labour Front, Singapore People's Alliance and the Trade Union Congress.

273

274
The first year of the Lim Yew Hock Government saw a showdown with the communist united front which had been flexing its muscles ever since the Labour Front Government took office. Lim Yew Hock was not prepared to tolerate communist-inspired agitation. In September 1956, he de-registered two pro-communist organisations, and the Singapore Chinese Middle School Students' Union (SCMSSU) was dissolved.

The students retaliated by camping at Chung Cheng High School and Chinese High School. They organised meetings and demonstrations (below) and were supported by pro-communist trade unions.

This went on for two weeks. On 24 October, the government issued an ultimatum that the schools be vacated. On 25 October, as the deadline approached, rioting started in front of the Chinese High School, where several hundred supporters of Lim Chin Siong had gathered.

The riots soon spread to other parts of the island. They lasted five days, leaving 13 people dead and more than 100 injured.

Hundreds of people, including prominent communist united front leaders were arrested. The pro-communist Singapore Factory and Shop Workers' Union was dissolved.

274

275

275
The arm of the law holds back a suspect.

276/277/278
British and Gurkha troops were brought in from Johor to help put down the riots which exacted a heavy toll in lives and property.

276

277

278

THE CRISIS OVER, NEW SECRETARY SAYS: 'WE ARE ALL UNITED'

'We will do our best to promote party's aims and implement non-Communist resolution'

PAP: LEFTISTS TAKE OVER

THE NEW BIG THREE

Tan Chong Kin
—CHAIRMAN

T. T. Rajah
—SECRETARY

Ong Chye Aun
—TREASURER

By LEE KHOON CHOY

THE LEFTWING GROUP of the People's Action Party last night took over the key posts of the central executive committee.

This ended the week-old crisis in the party following the refusal by the "moderates," led by Mr. Lee Kuan Yew, to take office.

After a three-and-a-half-hour meeting behind closed doors in the party's Neil Road headquarters last night the new general-secretary, Mr. T. T. Rajah, told the Press:

"The crisis is now over. We will do our best to implement the resolution passed at the fourth annual conference."

THE NEW OFFICIALS

(He was referring to the resolution moved by Mr. Lee two Sundays ago "to strive for an independent, non-Communist socialist Malaya, to re-organise the party and amend its constitution.")

Mr. Rajah then announced the names of the new officials:

MR. TAN CHONG KIN, chairman;
MR. TAN KONG YUAN, vice-chairman;
MR. T. T. RAJAH, general secretary;
MR. TAN SAY JAN, assistant secretary;
MR. ONG CHYE AUN, treasurer;
MR. GOH BOON TOH, assistant treasurer.

He said the new officials would strive and do their best "to promote the aims and objects of the party."

When the meeting ended last night, Mr. Lee Kuan Yew told reporters on leaving the conference room:

"I am no more the general-secretary. You must see the new general-secretary for a statement."

Mr. Lee, Inche Ahmad Ibrahim, Mr. Goh Chew Chua, Dr. Toh Chin Chye, Mr. Tann Wee Tiong and Miss Chan Choy Siong will remain as committee members of the central executive.

HE STEPS INTO LEE'S SHOES

..he takes over from Mr. Lee Kuan Yew.

BOOK-KEEPER

The chairman, Mr. Tan Chong Kin, and Mr. Rajah are the only English-educated members of the Leftwing camp.

Mr. Tan is a Chinese book-keeper.

The vice-chairman, Mr. Tan Kong Yuan, is also vice-chairman of the party's Bukit Timah branch.

Mr. Tan Say Jan, the assistant general-secretary, was once a paid secretary of the Singapore Bus Workers' Union in the days when Mr. Fong Swee Suan was honorary secretary.

A CLERK

The new treasurer, Mr Ong Chye Aun, is a clerk in a Chinese firm. He is vice-chairman of the party's Farrer Park branch.

Mr. Goh Boon Toh, who was regarded as an important leader of the Leftwing faction accepted a minor position as assistant-treasurer.

Mr. Goh is the secretary of the Singapore Cycle and Motor Workers' Union.

Before leaving for his home, Mr Rajah claimed that all the 12 members of the committee agreed that there was only one group in the party. "We are all united," he said.

279

Estd. 1845. SINGAPORE, SATURDAY, AUGUST 24, 1957 ★ 15 CENTS

QUOTE ❝It is evident that once again a serious threat is developing. Communists and their agents are back in key positions...If the situation is allowed to deteriorate, it will become increasingly difficult to check the threat, and decisive action will be resisted with consequent rioting and blood-shed. ❞ — FROM THE WHITE PAPER

ARRESTS: MORE TODAY

AND ThE TENGKU SAYS: 'WELL DONE!'

THE Federation Chief Minister, Tengku Abdul Rahman, who was in Singapore yesterday, praised the Labour Front Coalition Government's firm action against subversive elements. Mr. Lim and others concerned in this action to promote peace and happiness, he said at Singapore Airport.

"This sort of security measure will benefit both territories and this is a courageous and good government."

But he added smiling, "I do not know whether this will lead to a merger of our territories."

'A coincidence'

It was a coincidence that the 'mass arrests' took place on the eve of the arrival of the Tengku in Singapore. Approached for a statement, Mr. Lim Yew Hock said: "Ask me tomorrow."

Mr. F. K. Tan, secretary-general of the Liberal Socialist Party said.

White Paper on Red plot

MORE arrests are expected today following the detention of 35 people, including five leading members of the People's Action Party, by the Singapore police.

In a White Paper issued yesterday explaining its action, the Government charged that in recent months the Communists had been successful in gaining control of the PAP and were posing a threat to public security.

EMPHATIC

He said: "The long-term objects of the party re-affirmed at the party conference is to establish an independent, democratic, non-Communist Socialist Malaya.

"The activities of any member which are in pursuance of the above aims cannot possibly be subversive."

The former chairman and secretary-general, Dr. Toh Chin Chye and Mr. Lee Kuan Yew said they had not decided whether

RAJAH ALONE

THESE ARE THE PAP 'BIG FIVE' DETAINED BY THE POLICE

TAN CHONG KIM Chairman / TAN KONG GUAN Vice-Chairman / ONG CHYE AUN Treasurer / GOH BOON TOH Assistant Treasurer / TAN SAY KUM Assistant Secretary

Red hold on PAP— here's proof

Mr. Rajah issued a statement last night after a meeting with the six other remaining members of the PAP central executive, in which he expressed concern over the arrests of party members.

branch, in charge of education and culture.

Yeo Chye Hi—committee member, central education.

Ang Cheng Han—secretary, Paya Lebar branch.

Heng Hock Guan—president Queenstown branch and secretary education and culture education

Lam Ping — secretary of education and culture committee. Farrer Park branch.

Tai Chew Seng—secretary, Farrer Park branch.

The unionists were:

Chua Wee Kiat—treasurer Singapore General Employees' Union.

Chye Hai—executive committee member, Singapore General Employees' Union. Supervisor of propaganda and education sections. Taxi Drivers Union. National Union of Building and Construction Workers and S.G.E.U.

Lim Say Tah—executive committee member, Singapore General Employees' Union: Lee Cheng Wah secretary National Union of Building and Construction Workers; Yang Kr-Choo—assistant secretary, National Union of Building and Construction Workers; Ling Inn Peng—president, Singapore Taxi Drivers' Union.

HERE IS THE LIST OF NAMES OF PEOPLE NOW IN CUSTODY

Tan Bok Teng — Paya Lebar branch.

ployees' Union and Amalgamated Malayan Pineapple Workers' Union.

STC MAN

Lou Juan—former executive vice-president, Singapore Traction Company Employees' Union; Tong Chi—

Sin Pao office deserted

ALTHOUGH no Government action has been taken against the Singapore Chinese newspaper, Sin Pao, its office in Cecil Street was deserted yesterday except for a watchman. Four people including an aging director Mr. Fu Wu, have been detained under the Preservation of Public Security Ordinance.

Late yesterday one of the newspaper's two reporters told the Straits Times that the management had not given him any instructions.

The paper comes out every Tuesday, Thursday and Saturday. There is also a Sunday edition. A reporter said that there might not be publication today.

STOP PRESS

GIRL DIES AFTER ACCIDENT

Schoolgirl Tan Guan Sim, nine knocked down by taxi in Serangoon Road, died in General Hospital early today.

Five people injured at 1 a.m. when car crashed into post near garage. Seriously injured: Siah

280

279

In a bid to control the PAP, the pro-communists within the PAP got themselves elected to six seats in the 12-member central executive committee at the party's fourth annual general meeting on 4 August 1957. But the moderates led by Lee Kuan Yew refused to hold office in the party because, with the new composition of the committee, they would be little more than front men for the pro-communists. This precipitated a major crisis in the party. After a week of wrangling, the leftists were forced to come to the forefront and assume the top posts in the party.

280

The leftists' control of the party was, however, short-lived. Within two weeks, the Lim Yew Hock Government, in a major sweep of pro-communists, arrested 35 people including five members of the PAP's central executive committee. The moderates regained control of the party. Subsequently they amended the party's constitution to prevent a recurrence of such a takeover attempt.

City Council Elections

281
Elections for the first fully elected City Council, held on 21 December 1957, arouse public interest and thousands flock to the rallies. Intense electioneering preceded the polls which saw 81 candidates contesting the 32 constituencies. The PAP, one of the five contesting parties, won 13 of the 14 seats it contested. Three women, Chan Choy Siong and Hoe Puay Choo of the PAP, and Mrs F Leon-Soh of the Liberal Socialists, were among those elected.

281

282

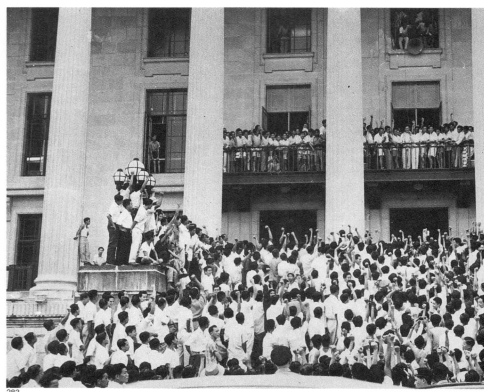

283

282/283/284

Ong Eng Guan, treasurer of the PAP, was elected Mayor at the City Council's first meeting on 24 December 1957. An Australian-trained accountant, his emotional, anti-colonial speeches at Council meetings attracted large crowds.

284

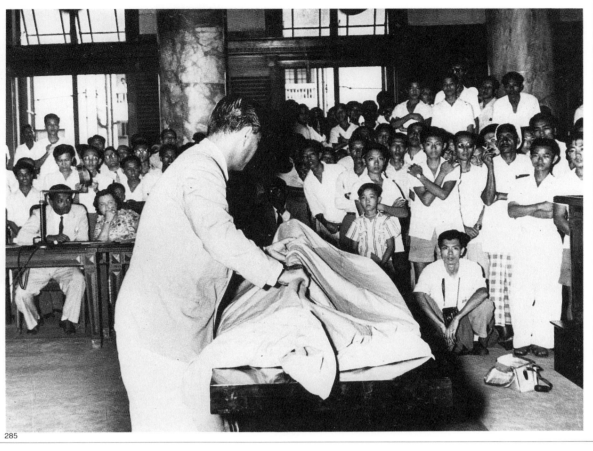

285

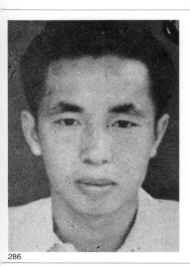

286

285

The Mayor's first act was to remove all "symbols of colonialism". At the Council's first sitting, the Mace, which the Mayor considered a relic of colonialism, was removed from the Council Chambers. The Mayor also discarded the official wig and wore white trousers and an open-necked white shirt.

For the first time, the City Council meetings were conducted in four languages, according to the policy laid down by the Legislative Assembly during David Marshall's government.

286

In 1956 and 1957 the PAP was a virtual prisoner of the communists who had strong influence in trade unions, Chinese schools and PAP branches. Relations between the moderates and the pro-communists in the party became more difficult when the communists tried to capture the PAP's central executive committee at the 1957 annual general meeting and then supported David Marshall's Workers' Party in the City Council elections of December 1957.

In March 1958 the communists sent a high-level emissary to meet Lee Kuan Yew to mend relations and establish cooperation. The timing of the move was significant because the third round of talks with the British to wrap up constitutional arrangements for full internal self-government were to take place soon. Further, the City Council elections had shown that there was a good chance of the PAP winning the general election and forming the government under the new constitution.

The Malayan Communist Party representative who met Lee Kuan Yew in March 1958 was Fong Chong Pik (left). He also pressed Lee Kuan Yew to work for the abolition of the Internal Security Council. Lee Kuan Yew later referred to him as "The Plen", short for plenipotentiary, and met him at least five times, the last on 11 May 1961.

Education Aviation Citizenship

287

288

290

289

287
Paya Lebar Airport was opened by the Secretary of State for the Colonies, Alan Lennox-Boyd, on 20 August 1955.

288
The civil airport at Kallang (above) was closed to traffic the next day. Aircraft movements during 1955 were 11,473; and 159,948 passengers arrived and departed through the airport.

289
Engineering students at the Singapore Polytechnic. The polytechnic started functioning in 1957 on borrowed premises while its four-hectare campus was being built. By 1959, the polytechnic was offering courses in electrical and mechanical engineering, architecture, commercial studies and nautical studies. In that year it had 1,240 full-time students, and 2,306 part-time students.

290

A section of the 30,000-strong crowd that came to witness the official opening of Nanyang University by Governor Sir William Goode on 30 March 1958. Taxi drivers and trishaw riders had donated a day's earnings towards the university's building fund.

291

M P D Nair, Assistant Minister to the Chief Secretary, registers as a Singapore citizen after the Singapore Citizenship Bill was passed on 16 October 1957. Under the new legislation all those born in Singapore became citizens automatically. Citizens of the United Kingdom and the Colonies were eligible to apply for citizenship after two years of residence, while others were eligible after eight years of residence.

At the end of an initial three-month registration period, 325,000 people were registered as Singapore citizens. The new citizenship laws allowed a large number of "alien" Chinese who were born in China to become citizens. The Chinese-educated now became a significant factor in determining the outcome of the general election in 1959.

291

Road to Full Self-government

292

293

294

292
A section of the crowd of 25,000 at the All-Party Merdeka Rally held at the old Kallang Airport grounds (at present the People's Association headquarters) on 18 March 1956. The rally, organised to demonstrate the people's desire for independence to a visiting six-member British Parliamentary delegation, was preceded by a campaign which collected over 160,000 signatures in favour of *Merdeka* (independence).

295

293
The Chief Minister, David
Marshall, being whisked away
by security men following the
collapse of the makeshift stage
on which he stood only minutes
after the start of the rally.

294
Lee Kuan Yew appeals for calm
as pandemonium breaks out. In
the melee, 50 people, including
20 policemen, were injured.

The disorder must have made
a poor impression on the
visiting British MPs and
aroused further doubts in
London about the ability of the
Marshall Government to
control internal security.

295
The first Constitutional Talks
(Merdeka Talks) open at
Lancaster House, London, on
23 April 1956.

Singapore's 13-member all-
party delegation was led by
Chief Minister David Marshall.
(Left to right): Lim Cher
Kheng; Lim Koon Teck;
William Tan; Lim Choon
Mong; A J Braga; Lim Yew
Hock; David Marshall; Haji
Abdul Hamid bin Haji Jumaat;
J M Jumabhoy; Seah Peng
Chuan; Wong Foo Nam; Lee
Kuan Yew; and Lim Chin
Siong.

The talks lasted till 15 May

but ended in failure over who
should control internal security.
The British wanted to have the
decisive say in the proposed
Defence and Internal Security
Council. On his return,
Marshall resigned as Chief
Minister. Lim Yew Hock
became Chief Minister on
8 June, retaining all the
ministers of Marshall's Cabinet.

296

297

298

299

296/297
Having demonstrated his willingness to deal firmly with communist subversion, Lim Yew Hock, who had succeeded David Marshall as Chief Minister, led an all-party delegation for the second Merdeka Talks in London from 11 March to 11 April 1957. (Top left) Lim Yew Hock and the all-party delegation at the talks and (far left) the Singapore and British delegations during an informal break.

This time the talks were successful. The contentious issue of the control of internal security was resolved by allowing a Federation of Malaya representative to sit on the Internal Security Council and to have the casting vote. The final agreement, which paved the way for Singapore's internal self-government, was signed on 28 May 1958, at the third round of constitutional talks.

298
The second Merdeka delegation to London, led by the Chief Minister, Lim Yew Hock (in the front car), returns home to an enthusiastic welcome.

299
While Singapore was moving towards full internal self-government the Federation of Malaya became independent on 31 August 1957.

303
People wait patiently in queues to cast their votes on polling day, 30 May 1959. Of the 587,797 electors, 55 percent were new citizens voting for the first time.

300
Over a million leaflets and more than 150,000 posters in Malay, English, Chinese and Tamil urged voters to exercise their voting rights in the 1959 general election. Voting was now compulsory.

301
Canvassing for votes.

302
The political apathy of the 1940s is a thing of the past as people flock to election rallies held before the 1959 general election. This PAP lunchtime

rally at Fullerton Square draws an attentive crowd.

Candidates from 10 parties and 39 independents contested the 51 seats in the Legislative Assembly.

302

303

304

305

304/305

(Above) The Liberal Socialist Party contested 32 constituencies, winning none, while (right) the Singapore People's Alliance won only four out of the 39 seats it contested.

The PAP was elected to form the government, winning 43 of the 51 seats in the Legislative Assembly. It polled 53.4 percent of the total votes.

306
Thousands of people attend the rally the PAP held at the Padang on 3 June 1959 to meet the people. Of the 16 elected members of the previous Assembly who contested the election, only the three members of the PAP and two of the former ministers were re-elected.

307
The prime minister-designate, Lee Kuan Yew, addresses an enthusiastic audience in Malay, Chinese and English.

306

307

308

309

308
At the mass rally, all 51 PAP candidates who contested the election are present on the City Hall steps to meet the people.

309
The PAP had said during the election campaign that it would assume office only if the eight pro-communist PAP detainees were freed. Lee Kuan Yew kept this pledge. In return, he asked the detainees to give a written pledge that they would work for a non-communist Malaya.

The detainees were released on 4 June 1959, five days after the PAP's election victory. Six of the eight detainees (with garlands) free caged pigeons to symbolise their release from prison. (Left to right): Fong Swee Suan, S Woodhull, Chan Chiaw Thor, Lim Chin Siong, Tan Chong Kin and Devan Nair. On their release, the detainees affirmed their loyalty to the PAP and to the PAP's objective of achieving " … a united, independent, democratic, non-communist and socialist Malaya … by peaceful, democratic and constitutional means".

6

TOWARDS NATIONHOOD

310
The mass rally of 25,000 people at the Padang to celebrate the launching of Loyalty Week in December 1959.

With self-government, it was necessary to develop a sense of belonging to Singapore among a people of diverse races and cultures.

1959~1961

The new PAP Government faced formidable problems. Singapore's long history of colonial rule had developed in many people a subservience to – and dependence on – the colonial rulers. Managing their own affairs was a new experience for which they were psychologically unprepared. The sense of belonging to Singapore was still weak among many who lived on the island. The people were also cocooned in their different ethnic, linguistic and cultural groupings, and viewed each other with uneasiness and suspicion.

To be able to govern themselves the people needed to have a sense of unity, of belonging to Singapore irrespective of their ethnic origins. The English-educated, who had fared better than the others under colonial rule, had to be persuaded to share their rights and privileges with the others. The Chinese-educated needed to be persuaded to be loyal to Singapore.

On the economic and social fronts, the serious unemployment and acute housing shortage continued. After many years of work stoppages, strikes and demonstrations, most of which had been communist-instigated, discipline, hard work, and law and order were urgently needed. Moreover, the communists were still determined to exploit any economic, social or communal grievance to further their cause. And they were in the PAP, in an uneasy alliance with the moderate leaders.

Confronted with so many problems, the new government had to act quickly on many fronts. It moved to instil a sense of unity, common identity and belonging to Singapore. A Ministry of Culture was set up and entrusted with the task of creating new opportunities for the three main ethnic groups to intermingle and to develop an appreciation for each other's cultures. The open air cultural concerts known as *Aneka Ragam Ra'ayat* which the ministry organised had this objective. The government, recognising that communalism was a real danger to a multi-racial and multi-religious society, adopted a policy of equal treatment for all the races.

Singapore's own flag, anthem and crest were introduced soon after the installation of Yusof bin Ishak as Singapore's first local Yang di-Pertuan Negara on 3 December 1959. Born in Perak in 1910, Yusof had been editor-in-chief and managing director of *Utusan Melayu* for many years. The installation of the Head of State was followed by a National Loyalty Week.

Malay, Chinese, Tamil and English were made the official languages of Singapore and all four languages were used in the Legislative Assembly for simultaneous interpretation. Changes were made in the education system to ensure that students developed a common sense of belonging to Singapore irrespective of the language stream in which they studied.

Soon after coming to power, the new government reduced the salaries of ministers and parliamentary secretaries and cut the cost of living allowances of civil servants in the middle and upper salary brackets as part of a general paring of public services expenditure. These moves were intended to symbolise the need for austerity. The civil service "pay cut" was also intended to jolt the service into a quick understanding that times had changed and that it now had to be responsive to an elected government which was in a hurry to get things done. The "pay cut" was unpopular and affected civil service morale adversely. The government later realised that it must have the confidence of the service if its programmes were to be implemented, and the allowances were restored in 1961.

In August 1959 a Political Study Centre was set up to educate senior civil servants in the needs of a self-governing nation. In lectures given by ministers and others they were told of Singapore's economic and social problems and provided with an insight into the politics of the island-state from the perspective of an elected government. The sessions also enabled them to get to know the ministers and their thinking.

The new government meanwhile eliminated the advantage enjoyed by citizens of the United Kingdom and British Colonies in their eligibility for Singapore citizenship. An amended Citizenship Bill passed in May 1960 disallowed dual nationality, and made the period of residence to qualify for Singapore citizenship eight years for all applicants, including British subjects.

In an attempt to improve the lot of the Malays, the largest and poorest of the minority races, the government set up a Malay Education Advisory Committee in 1959, opened the first Malay secondary school in 1960, and provided free education up to tertiary level for all Singapore Malays. Malay was also made the national language, in line with the PAP Government's belief that Singapore could achieve independence only through unification with Malaya. Malaya had already attained full independence in 1957.

A new education policy which drew upon recommendations embodied in the Education Ordinance of December 1957 (enacted but not fully carried out by the Lim Yew Hock administration) was now implemented. Education was to be made available to all children in Singapore. A crash programme was therefore launched to build new schools and to train hundreds of new teachers. Education in all four language streams was given equal treatment, and a unified education service with a common syllabus and a common Primary School Leaving Examination for all language streams was introduced. Facilities were provided for the study of local languages with the aim of making pupils bilingual and if possible trilingual.

From 1960 the government also created integrated schools, enabling students of different language streams to intermingle by studying under the same roof and sharing the same playground.

An area calling for urgent attention was housing. During its 32 years of existence the Singapore Improvement Trust had constructed only 23,300 housing units. This fell far short of meeting the housing demands of a rapidly increasing population, which by 1960 had passed 1.6 million. The new government had thus inherited a tremendous housing problem. A crash building programme was the only way to solve it. The Housing and Development Board was set up on 1 February 1960 with Lim Kim San, a successful banker and industrialist, as its chairman, and provided with adequate resources to undertake large-scale construction. The Board's first Five-Year Building Programme had a target of over 51,000 housing units.

The other major problem was the high rate of unemployment. Trade and commerce could not provide the jobs needed in sufficient numbers to mop up unemployment as well as raise individual incomes and revenue for the government to finance development and social services; only large-scale industrialisation could do so. However, there was no tradition of manufacturing in Singapore. From the earliest times, Singapore's main economic activity had been trading — buying and selling goods and acting as the middleman. There was a dearth of technical skills and the people had a strong prejudice against blue-collar factory jobs.

The local market was also too small to sustain large industries and the markets of neighbouring countries were not readily accessible. Indonesia and Malaya, now both independent countries, wanted to set up their own industries and protect their domestic markets. One solution for Singapore was to attract foreign multi-national corporations, which had their own worldwide markets, to invest in the island. The government also hoped that unification with Malaya would provide a wider common market for Singapore's industries; but at this stage Malaya was not interested in merger.

Undaunted by these obstacles, plans for industrialisation were prepared under the supervision of the Finance Minister, Dr Goh Keng Swee. At the invitation of the government, a UN Industrial Survey Mission visited Singapore in late 1960 and again in March 1961. It was led by a Dutch economist, Dr Albert Winsemius. The Commission reported that Singapore had the basic requirements for industrialisation, including a resourceful people and that with suitable

promotion by the government and close cooperation between employers and labour, it could successfully carry out an industrial expansion programme. An Economic Development Board with Hon Sui Sen, a senior civil servant, as its chairman, was set up in August 1961 to act for the government in a programme which would include promoting Singapore as a manufacturing base for the advanced countries of the West.

Dr Goh Keng Swee had earmarked Jurong as the main industrial estate. Initially, 1,600 hectares of wild swampy land were to be cleared. Incentives in the form of tax holidays for pioneer industries, low rates of taxation for export-oriented manufactures, and temporary protective tariffs were offered to attract local and foreign investors.

Recognising how important good industrial relations were to winning investors' confidence, the government had already enacted an Industrial Relations Ordinance under which an Industrial Arbitration Court had been set up in October 1960. Decisions of the court were to be binding on employers and employees. The government also began to reorganise the labour movement with a view to preventing agitators from calling strikes for political purposes. However, the left-wing within the PAP and in the unions obstructed these moves and Singapore's industrialisation programme could make little headway during the first term of the PAP Government, owing to persistent political turmoil and industrial strife.

The new government had an external orientation from the outset, a concern with foreign contacts and an interest in being able to put across its views to others, especially the non-aligned countries. Special attention was paid to fostering friendly ties  with Malaya and Indonesia. The Prime Minister, Lee Kuan Yew, visited Kuala Lumpur on 13 June 1959 to hold talks with the Malayan Prime Minister, Tunku Abdul Rahman. In October, Dr Subandrio, the Indonesian Foreign Minister, visited Singapore, and on 19 January 1960 Lee Kuan Yew went to Jakarta, where he had discussions with President Sukarno.

The People's Action Party had assumed power in 1959 despite serious ideological differences between the moderates and the pro-communists within the party, which were bound to result in open conflict sooner or later. These differences had to be resolved before undivided attention could be given to social and economic development.

Initially the pro-communist leaders in the PAP kept a low profile, though they continued to be active in the trade union field. A public appearance of solidarity with the moderates was maintained. However, by March 1960 tension between the two groups had markedly increased. This led to an inevitable open conflict and parting of ways, following a series of developments which started with a by-election in Hong Lim necessitated by the expulsion of Ong Eng Guan from the party.

Ong Eng Guan, the former mayor and now the Minister for National Development, ran his ministry with the same disruptive and authoritarian style that had marked his administration in the City Council. To prevent further damage to the party and the government and to get the housing programme moving, the Prime Minister took responsibility for the Harbour Board and local government, including the HDB, out of Ong's portfolio. In retaliation Ong tabled 16 resolutions at a PAP conference in June 1960, in which he criticised the government and its policies and challenged the party leadership. He evidently believed that the pro-communists in the PAP, who were already exhibiting signs of impatience with many of the government's policies, would back him. This was a misjudgement. Ong was dismissed from the Cabinet and expelled from the party. He resigned from his Hong Lim seat in December.

In the Hong Lim by-election on 29 April 1961, Ong defeated the PAP candidate, Jek Yeun Thong, in a straight fight, even though the PAP had many more campaign workers and organisers. Ong was popular with his constituents and support for him was strengthened by the feeling that he was an underdog whom the PAP had victimised. Ong's electoral success was a blow to the PAP. Flushed by his victory, Ong formed the United People's Party.

The PAP's Hong Lim defeat triggered developments which were to force an open breach between the moderates and the pro-communists in the party. The by-election result had been noted with concern by the Malayan Government in Kuala Lumpur. It was read to mean that the PAP might lose control and could be defeated by parties with a Chinese chauvinist and pro-communist appeal. This raised the spectre of a Cuba on Malaya's doorstep. Merger with Singapore, hitherto deemed undesirable by the Kuala Lumpur

authorities, now appeared to be the only way to contain the threat of a communist or pro-communist Singapore. In a speech which he made to the Foreign Correspondents' Association of Southeast Asia in Singapore on 27 May 1961, Tunku Abdul Rahman, the Prime Minister of the Federation of Malaya, floated the idea of an association of states that would incorporate not only the Federation of Malaya and Singapore, but also Sarawak, British North Borneo (Sabah) and Brunei.

Tunku Abdul Rahman's surprise suggestion was welcomed by the PAP moderates who had all along sought merger with Malaya, but it caused great consternation among the pro-communists in the party. They feared merger because control of security would pass into the hands of the anti-communist government in Kuala Lumpur which would not hesitate to take firm action to prevent them from establishing a pro-communist regime in Singapore.

Events moved rapidly after this. On 2 June, six pro-communist leaders, the "Big Six" of the trade union movement – Lim Chin Siong, Fong Swee Suan, S Woodhull, S T Bani, Dominic Puthucheary and Jamit Singh – publicly demanded the release of all political detainees; the scrapping of the Internal Security Council; and freedom of press, speech, assembly and organisation. On 3 June, Lee Kuan Yew accepted the Malayan Prime Minister's proposal in principle. On 9 July PAP chairman Dr Toh Chin Chye attacked the "Big Six" for opposing merger and preferring the continuation of colonial rule. Suspicion spread among the communists and pro-communists that union with Malaya had already been agreed upon by the Kuala Lumpur government, the British, and the PAP leaders. They mounted an all-out effort to get trade unions, PAP branches, PAP Assemblymen, the People's Association and the Work Brigade on their side. The Work Brigade, set up with the assistance of the People's Association and under the control of the Minister for Labour, was a uniformed organisation to absorb and discipline unemployed youth.

The sudden death of the PAP Assemblyman for Anson, Baharuddin bin Mohamed Ariff, led to another by-election. The pro-communists in the party chose the Anson contest, scheduled for 15 July 1961, to demonstrate their strength to the moderates and to make them more amenable to their stand on merger and on security and political issues. Accordingly, they withdrew their support from the PAP candidate, Mahmud bin Awang, president of the Trade Union Congress (TUC). Six days before the election, six left-wing members of the 10-man secretariat of the TUC, led by Lim Chin Siong, S Woodhull and Fong Swee Suan, published a statement demanding the release of all political detainees and declaring that the abolition of the Internal Security Council was more important than merger. The pro-communists then threw their support behind David Marshall of the Workers' Party, one of the five contestants.

Two days before the by-election, eight PAP Assemblymen led by Dr Lee Siew Choh, Parliamentary Secretary to the Ministry of Home Affairs, issued a statement alleging a lack of democracy within the PAP and supporting Lim Chin Siong's stand. Forty-three trade unions immediately endorsed the statement.

David Marshall won the by-election with a majority of 546 votes, and the final showdown followed, first in the trade union movement, then in the PAP itself. On 19 July the moderate leaders of the TUC accused Lim Chin Siong and the pro-communist unionists of treachery. This led to a split in the TUC and its eventual dissolvement. Lim Chin Siong and his group then applied for registration of a new Singapore Association of Trade Unions (SATU) on 13 August 1961, and the moderate union leaders, Mahmud bin Awang and Devan Nair, formed the National Trades Union Congress.

At the same time Lee Kuan Yew decided to force the issue in the Legislative Assembly by calling for a vote of confidence on 20 July. The pro-communists were not happy with this. Since they dominated the PAP branches they preferred to achieve their objectives within the PAP framework by pressurising and intimidating the moderates, or, if that failed, by taking over the government, even forming a new party. Apart from working on PAP Assemblymen and PAP officials to join their ranks, they had been sounding out the British to discover what the colonial power would do if they (the pro-communists) acquired power. S Woodhull, James Puthucheary, Lim Chin

Siong and Fong Swee Suan met Lord Selkirk, the British Commissioner-General for Southeast Asia, to seek an assurance that the Constitution would not be suspended should Lee Kuan Yew resign and they themselves take office. The British apparently led them to believe that they would be free to govern, provided they remained within the law.

When the Assembly met at 2.30 pm on 20 July to debate the vote of confidence motion, the pro-communists in the PAP denounced the proposed merger with Malaya as an imperialist plot, and a heated debate raged all through the night. When the division came at 4.00 am on 21 July, 13 of the PAP Assemblymen (some of whom were political or parliamentary secretaries) and three others abstained. Lee's Government won the motion by 27 votes to eight, but was left with a majority of only one in the Assembly.

There was no longer any question of the moderates and pro-communists working together in the party. On 21 July, three dissident political secretaries, five parliamentary secretaries, and eight other Assemblymen were expelled from the party and 14 PAP branch officials were suspended.

The split cost the PAP organisation dearly. Thirty-five out of 51 PAP branch committees defected to the pro-communists, as did 19 of the 23 paid branch organising secretaries. Large numbers of the cadres defected, and many PAP branches were vandalised.

The People's Association, which had been established in 1960 as a second line of defence against the communists as well as to provide recreational outlets for the public, had been infiltrated and could no longer be relied upon. The Work Brigade had also been infiltrated by the communists, and mutinied against the government.

On 13 August 1961 the PAP dissidents registered a new political party, the Barisan Sosialis (Socialist Front), with Dr Lee Siew Choh as chairman and Lim Chin Siong as secretary-general.

New Government Takes Charge

311

312

314

311
Lee Kuan Yew, Singapore's first Prime Minister and founder member of the PAP. He was a student at Raffles College at the time of the Japanese invasion. When the war ended, he went to Cambridge University and took a double first in law. During his student days in England he became keenly interested in issues of colonialism and freedom and acquired the determination to play a part in freeing Singapore from colonial rule.

He returned to Singapore in August 1950 as barrister-at-law (Middle Temple). After a year in chambers, he practised as an advocate and solicitor and became legal adviser to several trade unions.

In 1954, he became the secretary-general of the PAP and was elected to the Legislative Assembly in 1955. He was 36 years old when he became Prime Minister.

312
On the afternoon of 5 June 1959, members of the elected party and their supporters gathered at City Hall to witness the taking of the Oaths of Allegiance and of Office by Cabinet members before the Yang di-Pertuan Negara, Sir William Goode.

Arriving at the City Hall, back row (left to right): Low Por Tuck; Chan Sun Wing; and Wong Soon Fong. Front row (left to right): Oh Shu Chen; Fung Yin Ching (partly hidden); Chan Choy Siong; Sahorah bte Ahmat; and Hoe Puay Choo. (Low, Chan Sun Wing, Wong, Fung and Hoe were to defect to the Barisan Sosialis when the PAP broke with the communists in 1961.)

313

313
Members of the first Cabinet of the PAP Government in front of City Hall after being sworn in by the Yang di-Pertuan Negara, Sir William Goode. (Left to right): Yong Nyuk Lin, Minister for Education; Ong Eng Guan, Minister for National Development; S Rajaratnam, Minister for Culture; Ahmad Ibrahim, Minister for Health; Ong Pang Boon, Minister for Home Affairs; Goh Keng Swee, Minister for Finance; Toh Chin Chye, Deputy Prime Minister; K M Byrne, Minister for Labour and Law; and Lee Kuan Yew, Prime Minister.

314
The PAP Assemblymen, led by Prime Minister Lee Kuan Yew and the Deputy Prime Minister, Dr Toh Chin Chye, march from City Hall to the Assembly House for the first sitting of the Legislative Assembly on 1 July 1959.

315

315
The Speaker, Sir George Oehlers, in ceremonial wig and robe, receives Sir William Goode, Singapore's first Yang di-Pertuan Negara, at the Assembly House entrance.

Sir William read the policy statement of the government in Malay. For the first time, simultaneous interpretations into Malay, English, Chinese and Tamil were available in the Assembly.

316

318

316
Prime Minister Lee Kuan Yew, moments after taking the Oath at the first meeting of the Legislative Assembly. Lim Yew Hock, the former Chief Minister, became leader of the Opposition which had eight members. The Assembly passed 26 Bills by the end of the year.

317
Sir William Goode, the last British Governor and the first Yang di-Pertuan Negara, bids Dr Toh Chin Chye, Deputy Prime Minister, farewell. Sir William served as Singapore's titular Head of State for six months.

317

318
Yusof bin Ishak takes the oath of office on 3 December 1959 as Singapore's first Malayan-born Yang di-Pertuan Negara. Son of a civil servant, Yusof bin Ishak was a prominent journalist and nationalist and a founder and managing director of *Utusan Melayu*, a Malay language newspaper.

Looking on are (left to right): Sir George Oehlers, the Speaker; Lee Kuan Yew, Prime Minister; Sir Alan Rose, the Chief Justice; and Ahmad Ibrahim, the Attorney-General.

Nation Building

319

320

322

319/320
People flock to the first *Aneka Ragam Ra'ayat* (People's Cultural Concert) held at the Botanic Gardens on 2 August 1959 (top); and (above) a section of the 50,000 people who turned up at the Padang on 16 August 1959 to watch a similar concert. Culture Minister Rajaratnam (fourth from right) and Prime Minister Lee Kuan Yew (in white) are seated in the front row.

For the first time Malay, Chinese and Indian songs and dances were featured in the same concert. This was one of the means used by the government to promote better understanding among the main races and cultures in Singapore. The programmes of Radio Singapore (which had become a separate entity from Radio Malaya on 4 January 1959) were also reoriented to help achieve this objective. *Aneka Budaya Tunggal Suara* ("From Many Cultures – One Voice") became the motto of Radio Singapore.

321
Operation *Pantai Chantek*, the campaign to beautify the state and instil in the people a pride in their environment, was launched soon after the government took office. Culture Minister Rajaratnam joins thousands of volunteer workers in sprucing up the Nicoll Highway promenade. Other ministers and government officials also participated.

322
More volunteer workers sacrifice their weekends to clean the sea front along Beach Road.

323

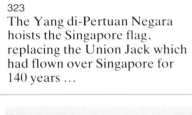

323
The Yang di-Pertuan Negara hoists the Singapore flag, replacing the Union Jack which had flown over Singapore for 140 years …

324/325
… and (below) addresses the crowd which turned up at the Padang to witness this historic occasion.

324

325

326
The Yang di-Pertuan Negara inspects a guard-of-honour formed by the First Battalion of the Singapore Infantry Regiment outside City Hall. The Head of State's installation marked the opening of Loyalty Week during which Singapore's flag, crest and anthem were introduced.

327

327
The Singapore flag. The red symbolises universal brotherhood and the equality of man; the white stands for purity and virtue; the crescent moon represents a young growing nation; and the five stars symbolise democracy, peace, progress, justice and equality.

328
The state crest. The animal supporters of the armorial crest are the Singapore lion and the Malayan tiger, the latter signifying Singapore's close links with Malaya.

MAJULAH SINGAPURA

328

329
The National Anthem, *Majulah Singapura* (May Singapore Progress), which replaced the colonial anthem "God Save the Queen".

Introduced during Loyalty Week, the anthem calls upon Singaporeans to move in unison towards happiness and success.

330
Zubir Said, the composer of the National Anthem.

331

332

331
Prime Minister Lee Kuan Yew inaugurates the Political Study Centre which was set up to give senior civil servants a better understanding of the needs of a self-governing nation. There were 19 senior government officers at the first course which was held on 17 August 1959, two days after the inauguration of the Centre.

332
The People's Association (PA) is officially inaugurated by Prime Minister Lee Kuan Yew on 20 August 1960.

The PA, which started functioning on 1 July 1960, was formed to bring cultural, recreational and sporting activities to the people; to help break down racial and cultural barriers; and to provide opportunities for young people to develop leadership talents through involvement in various activities. It was also meant to be the second line of defence against the communists whose supporters had a strong influence in PAP branches.

Within the first six months of its existence, the PA, under the Prime Minister's chairmanship, had set up 18 community centres and two holiday camps.

333

334

333/334
The Registry of Singapore Citizenship on 28 October 1959. Large numbers of people had been turning up at the registry to apply for citizenship since the Citizenship Bill had been passed in 1957. In May 1960, the residential requirement for citizenship for those not born in Singapore was standardised at a minimum of eight years. This did away with the privileged position of citizens of the United Kingdom and the Colonies, who, under the 1957 legislation, needed only two years of residence in Singapore to be eligible for citizenship.

335
Silat Primary School, one of the first integrated schools established to break down the barriers between pupils of different language streams.

In 1959 there was an acute shortage of schools. There were places for only 85 percent of children needing primary education and for only 23 percent of those in need of secondary education.

335

Acute Problems: Housing and Jobs

336

338

336/337
Conditions in 1959 hardly held promise for the better life the people were expecting: many lived in appalling, congested conditions, without piped water, proper sanitation or electricity.

341

337

338/339/340
The existing manufacturing industries were mainly small establishments involved in pineapple canning (left), rubber grading (right), and producing things like soap (below), biscuits, cooking oil, sauce, and aerated water. These establishments each employed only a few workers. The British military bases were Singapore's largest employer.

340

339

342

341
Unemployment was high and increasing, and 20,000 new job-seekers were entering the labour market yearly. Trade, Singapore's main economic activity, could hardly absorb all the unemployed.

342
Blocks of flats at Upper Pickering Street, built by the Singapore Improvement Trust (SIT), which was replaced by the Housing and Development Board (HDB) in 1960.

In its 32-year existence, the SIT had constructed some 23,000 housing units. In addition, there were another 20,129 units of public housing managed by bodies like the Public Works Department, the City Council and the Singapore Harbour Board. This fell far short of the housing needs of the population.

343

347

On the afternoon of 25 May 1961, a Hari Raya Haji public holiday, fire swept across Bukit Ho Swee, turning the attap huts of the squatter colony into a raging inferno. Prompt government help and public support brought speedy relief to the victims. By February 1962 all families affected by the fire had been rehoused in government-built low-cost flats. The fire left four people dead and 16,000 homeless.

343
Residents watch helplessly as the fire rages.

344/345
All that is left of Bukit Ho Swee. An area of about 25 hectares was devastated.

346
The Bukit Ho Swee name plate remains unsinged. Bukit Ho Swee has the tragic record of having been razed to the ground three times by major fires: in 1934, in 1961, and in 1968.

347
The Bukit Ho Swee Housing Estate in 1983.

344

345

346

Towards Industrialisation

348

348
Large-scale industrialisation was the solution to the unemployment problem. In 1960, Jurong – a wide expanse of swamp land – was chosen to be the industrial heart of Singapore. A UN mission surveyed the area and made recommendations on the types of industries to establish in Jurong.

Here, Dr Goh Keng Swee (third from left), Minister for Finance and the mastermind behind Jurong's development, inspects the site with some members of the government.

349

350

349
Dr Goh Keng Swee with government officials on one of his many site visits to Jurong.

Earth-moving operations in Jurong began in September 1961 and by the end of 1963, 728.4 hectares of land had been prepared by cutting down hills and filling in swamps. 18.4 million cubic metres of earth had been moved in the process. Yet Jurong, as of December 1963, had only two factories in production – the National Iron and Steel Mills and Pelican Textiles, between them employing 90 workers.

350
The 20-ton furnace at the National Iron and Steel Mills, the only one of its kind in Southeast Asia at the time. The company was a joint venture between local entrepreneurs and the Singapore Government, which held 29.9 percent of the equity. Built on what was formerly a 24.4-metre hill, the mill began production on 3 August 1963.

351

351
Dr Albert Winsemius, an industrial economist from Holland. He first came to Singapore with the UN team and later became an adviser on economic development to the government. In 1967, he was awarded the Distinguished Service Medal for his contributions to the nation. He relinquished his position as adviser at the end of 1983.

352

352
Local and foreign investors were wooed to invest in Singapore with incentives such as tax exemptions. By 1961, 18 industries and 62 products had been given "pioneer" status.

One of the industries to receive the pioneer status was Magnolia Dairies Ltd, whose representative is receiving the pioneer certificate from Dr Goh Keng Swee.

353
The $30-million Shell Refinery, opened in July 1961, was one of the major foreign investments of the time. It was the first oil refinery in Singapore.

353

For Better Industrial Relations

354

354
Workers throng the Jalan Besar Stadium for the May Day Rally organised by the Trade Union Congress (TUC) on 1 May 1960. At the rally, the TUC leaders pledged to support the new policy of achieving and maintaining industrial peace. However, the pro-communist leaders were soon to renege on their pledge.

356

355

357

355
Prime Minister Lee Kuan Yew reiterated at the rally that his government would not allow itself to be exploited, either by the British or by the communists for their own selfish ends. Seated (from right to left): Fong Swee Suan; Lim Chin Siong; S T Bani; Chan Sun Wing; G Kandasamy; Jamit Singh; Prime Minister Lee Kuan Yew; and K M Byrne (Minister for Labour and Law).

356
In June 1960 the TUC was revamped in an effort to unify the labour movement. Members of the new 10-man TUC secretariat posing for the camera are (from left to right): Buang Omar Junid; Dominic Puthucheary; Fong Swee Suan; Lim Chin Siong; G Kandasamy; S Woodhull; Jamit Singh; S T Bani; and Ow Kheng Tor. Devan Nair is not in the photograph.

357
The Industrial Arbitration Court in session. The Court was set up in October 1960, a month after the introduction of the Industrial Relations Ordinance 1960. The object was to abolish labour exploitation through freely negotiated collective agreements and to establish conditions conducive to industrial peace.

Where negotiations fail, labour disputes are settled by the Arbitration Court. The president of the Court, who has the powers and immunities of a High Court judge, is assisted by panels of employers' and employees' representatives.

Ties with Neighbours

Estd. 1845 — SATURDAY, JUNE 13, 1959

IT'S A GOVT.-TO-GOVT. MEETING NOW

Lee to bring two more Ministers to capital

TALKS: SURPRISE MOVE

Razak team is also built up

KUALA LUMPUR, Fri.— Tomorrow's meeting between the Prime Ministers of Singapore and the Federation has developed unexpectedly into what is to be a conference between the two Governments.

Originally, the Singapore Prime Minister, Mr. Lee Kuan Yew, was to have been accompanied by two of his Cabinet colleagues — Mr. Ong Eng Guan (National Development) and Mr. Ong Pang Boon (Home Affairs).

Two names

Today, the names of two more Cabinet Ministers, Dr. Goh Keng Swee (Finance) and Inche Ahmad bin Ibrahim (Health) were announced.

In addition, Mr. Lee's private secretary, Mr. Henry Armstrong, will also come.

358

358
Soon after assuming power, the PAP Government took steps to strengthen Singapore's relations with its immediate neighbours, the Federation of Malaya and the Republic of Indonesia. On 13 June 1959 Lee Kuan Yew and four of his ministers went on a goodwill visit to Kuala Lumpur.

359
The Indonesian Foreign Minister, Dr Subandrio visited Singapore in October 1959.

359

360

361

360
On 19 January 1960, Prime Minister Lee Kuan Yew, accompanied by two Parliamentary Secretaries and four Assemblymen, began a week's official visit to Indonesia. He is seen here with President Sukarno (sixth from right) of Indonesia.

The Prime Minister spoke of his visit as a Southeast Asian "bridge builder" and the official statement promised closer economic and cultural ties.

361
The Yang di-Pertuan Negara, Yusof bin Ishak, and Prime Minister Lee Kuan Yew are greeted by the Sultan of Brunei at Brunei Airport in September 1960. Both had been invited by the Sultan, Sir Muda Omar Ali Saifuddin, for his 44th birthday celebrations. From Brunei, Lee Kuan Yew went on to visit North Borneo and Sarawak to establish closer ties with the two British territories.

Split in the PAP

362
One of the many rallies of the People's Action Party (PAP) for the Hong Lim by-election on 29 April 1961. The by-election was brought about by the resignation from the Assembly on 29 December 1960 of Ong Eng Guan, who had also been Minister for National Development. He had earlier been dismissed from the Cabinet and expelled from the party. The by-election had been delayed till 29 April 1961 to allow a Commission of Inquiry to investigate Ong's allegations of nepotism against the Prime Minister and the Minister for Labour and Law. The Commission found the allegations totally unfounded.

By the time of the Hong Lim by-election, tensions between non-communist and pro-communist leaders in the PAP had worsened. The pro-communists had been expanding their influence in PAP branches, in trade unions and in the People's Association. Although a public appearance of solidarity with non-communist leaders was maintained, the policies of the PAP were being quietly undermined.

362

363
The by-election campaign lasted 49 days and almost every voter was visited several times by both the PAP candidate Jek Yeun Thong, Political Secretary to the Prime Minister, and Ong Eng Guan, who stood as an independent.

Dr Lee Siew Choh, a Parliamentary Secretary, is seen here at one of the by-election rallies urging the people to vote for Jek Yeun Thong.

Despite the PAP's superiority in organisation and in numbers of campaign workers, Ong won a landslide victory because of his personal popularity and the feeling among people that he had been victimised by the PAP. In June 1961 he formed the United People's Party.

The communists now stepped up efforts to bend the PAP's policies towards their goals. On 11 May, "The Plen" met Lee Kuan Yew and urged him to work for the abolition of the Internal Security Council.

The result of the Hong Lim by-election and the chauvinist issues raised during the campaign caused uneasiness in Malaya. The fear that the PAP could lose control and be succeeded by a pro-communist government in Singapore led the Malayan leaders to reconsider their earlier opposition to the inclusion of Singapore in the Federation.

363

364
The Prime Minister of Malaya,
Tunku Abdul Rahman,
delivering the historic speech at
the Foreign Correspondents'
Association of Southeast Asia,
Singapore, on 27 May 1961,
that set in motion plans for the
formation of Malaysia.

Tunku Abdul Rahman
envisaged a federation
incorporating Malaya,
Singapore, British North
Borneo (Sabah), Sarawak and
Brunei.

365
David Marshall of the Workers'
Party campaigning during the
Anson by-election. The seat fell
vacant following the sudden
death of PAP Assemblyman
Baharuddin Mohd Ariff, on
20 April 1961, nine days before
the Hong Lim by-election. The
three main contenders were
Mahmud Awang (PAP), David
Marshall (Workers' Party) and
Dr Chee Phui Hung (UMNO-
MCA Alliance and SPA).

ANSON BY-ELECTION TEST FOR PAP—See page 9

Call for conference of party executives

8 BACK UNION-SIX

TUC 3 'sack us' challenge to Lee

Open challenge to PAP leadership

SINGAPORE, Thurs.— Three political secretaries all former detainees tonight challenged the Prime Minister, Mr. Lee Kuan Yew, to require their resignations from their posts.

At the moment to state whether he did or did not give an assurance that all political detainees would be released within three to six months of the P.A.P. coming into office.

The dare was contained in a statement signed by Mr S Woodhull, one of the political secretaries.

It was a direct reply to last night's speech by Mr Devan Nair, a leading trade unionist who was freed together with Messrs. Woodhull Lim Chin Siong and Fong Swee Suan.

Four points

After attacking their present tactics on the detainee issue, Mr. Nair tonight asked "Why is it that they have continued their association with the PAP Government as political secretaries all this time, and

EIGHT P.A.P. members of the Singapore Legislative Assembly today declared their support for the six Trades Union Congress leaders who have been criticising the party's policies.

They back the six unionists' demands for immediate anti-colonial measures and for full internal self-government by 1963.

They have also called for a conference of the executives of the 51 branches of the Peoples' Action Party to discuss and examine the current role of the PAP and the present political situation.

This conference, the eight Assembly members said, should particularly discuss:

● THE QUESTION of merger or super-merger.
● THE SITUATION arising

The signatories

out of the Press statements of the six TUC leaders.

● INTERNAL democracy in the PAP.

The support of the eight Assembly members for the "union six" and their call for a conference of party executives is contained in a letter to the party chairman, Dr. Toh Chin Chye, which they released tonight.

The signatories are Dr. Lee Siew Choh (Queenstown), Mr. Wong Soon Fong (Toa Payoh), Mr. Fee Kim Leng (Pasir Panjang), Mr. Tan Cheng Tong (Jalan Kayu), Mr. Teo Hock Guan (Changi), Mr. S.T. Bani (Thomson), Mr. Lin You Eng (Moulmein) and Miss Fung Ying Ching (Stamford).

Mr. Bani is one of the "union six," along with Messrs. Lim Chin Siong, Fong Swee Suan, S. Woodhull, Dominic Puthucheary and Jamit Singh.

Dr. Lee Siew Choh is Parliamentary Secretary to the Ministry for Home Affairs.

In a Press statement accompanying their letter, the eight members explained why they had released its contents, though it was a "confidential" communication.

"They said they took objection to the utterances of Mr. C.V. Devan Nair, a leading trade unionist, on matters which had been raised in the letter to Dr. Toh.

Mr. Nair, they said, had ostensibly raised these matters on the instruction of the party leadership.

While Dr. Toh had replied to them saying that the party's central executive committee would call a meeting at some future suitable date, Mr. Nair had committed the party "in a most irregular manner" at a forum organised by the Uni-

★ See Back Page—Column Five

366

366
The Tunku's public suggestion of a new federation which would include Singapore, and Lee Kuan Yew's quick favourable response, led the Malayan Communist Party and the pro-communists in the PAP to believe that merger with Malaya had already been secretly agreed upon by the British, the Malayans and the PAP leadership. The communists viewed this with great concern.

Pro-communist leaders in the PAP, using trade unions, now openly pressurised the non-communist leadership of the party to change its policies, in particular to abandon the idea of merger with Malaya. There were calls for the abolition of the Internal Security Council and for the release of all political detainees. On 13 July, eight PAP Assemblymen issued a statement supporting the pro-communist leaders. When Lee Kuan Yew and his non-communist colleagues stood firm, the communists threw their support behind David Marshall in the Anson by-election.

367

367
The PAP candidate for Anson, Mahmud Awang (wearing garland) with party chairman Dr Toh Chin Chye and other officials.

The burning electoral issue at the Anson by-election was merger. Mahmud lost to David Marshall by a narrow margin of 546 votes.

The open challenge to the party's policies by its pro-communist leaders and their support for David Marshall, instead of the PAP candidate, prompted Lee Kuan Yew to ask for a vote of confidence in his government from the Legislative Assembly. The Prime Minister felt that the lines of battle had been drawn and it was necessary for PAP Assemblymen to make clear which side they were on in relation to the party's long established position on a non-communist society and on merger with Malaya.

368

Meanwhile, believing that they would be able to win a majority of Assemblymen to their side and form the government, the pro-communists within the PAP met the British Commissioner-General for Southeast Asia, Lord Selkirk, at his residence at Eden Hall (left). Their object was to seek assurance that the Constitution would not be suspended should they take over the government.

The debate on the confidence motion began on 20 July and raged all night. When the final division was called at 4.00 am on 21 July, 27 voted for the government, eight against, while 13 of the PAP dissidents abstained.

On the same day the dissidents were expelled from the PAP.

369

370

369/370

Dr Lee Siew Choh addressing a rally held to announce the formation of a new party, Barisan Sosialis (Socialist Front). The party was registered on 13 August by pro-communists who had been expelled from the PAP.

The 13 former PAP Assemblymen who had joined the Barisan Sosialis continued to sit in the Assembly till the next general election in 1963.

The split cost the PAP dearly. Thirty-five PAP branch committees defected to the Barisan Sosialis. The People's Association had been infiltrated and was now in rebellion. So was the Work Brigade.

371

371
Defiant People's Association staff at the headquarters in Kallang on 23 September 1961.

In late September, the procommunists engineered a strike in the People's Association to protest against the government's dismissal of 17 employees who were considered to be troublemakers. The illegal strike was called off by its organisers only 10 months later.

372/373
Security forces push their way into a Work Brigade camp (right); and (far right) a member of the Singapore Infantry Regiment breaks open a locked door to gain entry to the Jurong Work Brigade Camp.

372

374

373

374

The trade unions also split into two camps. The pro-communists took over the Trade Union Congress (TUC), while the non-communist unions formed a new body, the National Trades Union Congress, which aligned itself with the PAP. The TUC lost no time in fomenting strikes.

An example was the strike at Robinson's Departmental Store in Raffles Place on 11 September 1961 (above). When the strikers refused to disperse, police troopers were called in but many workers resisted by interlocking their arms.

7

BATTLE FOR MERGER

375

375
The crowd that turned up
at the Padang to enjoy
"Malam Malaysia", a cultural
event held as part of Malaysia
Week from 29 January to

7 February 1962. Artistes from
the proposed component states
of Malaysia participated in the
event.

1961~1963

It had been the declared objective of the PAP to seek independence through re-unification with Malaya. Apart from the economic and security reasons for merger, the PAP leadership believed that the British would not give independence to Singapore on its own.

Malaya had attained independence on 31 August 1957. However, the government of Malaya had not favoured merger with Singapore because the inclusion of a million Singapore Chinese would have upset the delicate racial balance in Malaya. It was only the fear of a possible communist takeover in Singapore following the Hong Lim by-election that prompted re-thinking in Kuala Lumpur. Tunku Abdul Rahman's proposal on 27 May 1961 envisaged a "Malaysia" embracing not just Singapore but also British North Borneo (Sabah), Sarawak and Brunei, precisely in order to provide a racial counterpoise to the population of the island.

In July 1961, the leaders of Malaya, Singapore, British North Borneo, Sarawak and Brunei met in Singapore to discuss the terms of the proposed federation. On 24 August, and then again on 14 September, Lee Kuan Yew met Tunku Abdul Rahman to discuss

the terms of Singapore's inclusion. Then, in February 1962, Lord Cobbold headed a Commission of Inquiry to find out whether the people of British North Borneo and Sarawak wanted to join Malaysia. The Commission found that the majority were in favour.

In their talks, Tunku Abdul Rahman and Lee Kuan Yew agreed that Singapore should have a special status within the federation and enjoy greater powers of self-rule than the Borneo territories. In return Singapore would have a reduced representation in the Federal Parliament, and Singapore citizens would not automatically become Malaysian citizens. They would, however, keep their Singapore citizenship and become Federal nationals holding Federal passports.

These points were spelt out in a Singapore Government White Paper issued on 16 November 1961. The White Paper also stated that Singapore would retain control of its education and labour policies, and most of its revenue (part of it would go to the Central Government to cover the cost of Federal services such as telecommunications, defence and security). It would have 15 seats in the Federal Parliament, its own Head of State, a Cabinet headed by a Prime Minister, a legislative assembly, and its own civil service (excluding pan-Malaysian departments). The British agreed to these terms. But the communists were unhappy with merger and Malaysia.

In September and October 1961, the Prime Minister gave a total of 36 radio talks in three languages to

explain to the people of Singapore the history of the anti-colonial united front of the PAP and the communists, the *modus operandi* and goals of the communists, why the front broke up, and why the communists really opposed merger.

The communists had always regarded Singapore and the Peninsula as one entity. The Malayan Communist Party had been a pan-Malayan party from the beginning and its policies and goals were pan-Malayan. However, the communists did not want merger so long as there was an anti-communist government in power in Kuala Lumpur which would take firm security action against them. That would frustrate their plans to extend their power progressively in Singapore, and eventually in Malaya. It also suited the communists to have the British continue as colonial rulers of the island so that they could expand their influence under the pretext of carrying out an anti-colonial struggle. However, it was not in their interest to express opposition to the idea of merger, for in those days it was taken for granted by many of the people and by the political parties that Singapore could only survive and prosper if it were part of Malaya. So the Barisan Sosialis took the public position that they were in favour of the merger, but that it was the *form* of the merger proposed that they were against.

The Barisan Sosialis line was that the merger conditions for Singapore should be the same as those for Malacca or Penang, with automatic Federal citizenship for all Singapore citizens and proportional representation in the Federal Parliament. Anything less than this would be "a sell-out", they claimed.

However, the government was able to point out that under the laws of the Federation, only those born locally in Malacca and Penang were automatically Federal citizens. Merger on the same terms as Penang or Malacca, therefore, would deprive nearly half of Singapore's citizens of their rights as they had not been born on the island. Singapore would also lose control of education, labour and the civil service, and

local Malays would have special privileges as they did in Malaya, including a claim on four out of five posts in the civil service. Chinese education would receive unfavourable treatment.

The government had already announced its intention of submitting the terms for merger to a referendum; it was assumed that most people wanted union with Malaya, so they were merely to be asked what sort of merger they wanted. The PAP leaders were prompted by a desire not only to obtain a mandate for "PAP merger", but to engage the Barisan Sosialis and the communists in open battle on the issue.

Despite the fact that the Barisan Sosialis position on merger was flawed, the government initially found itself on the defensive, for its opponents were able to whip up anti-merger agitation through their mass organisations and peddle the line that Malaysian nationality would be tantamount to second-class citizenship.

In November 1961 the pro-communists seized an opportunity to incite students to mount agitation against the government when secondary four students of Chinese schools were obliged to sit for examinations under a new policy. The new system was designed to standardise education in the four language streams. Instead of having three years of junior middle and three years of senior middle education, Chinese-stream schools (like English-stream schools) would now have four years of secondary and (after taking an examination) two years of pre-university education – and the examinations would be conducted by the Education Ministry, not the individual schools.

The pro-communists presented the new system as part of a plan to destroy Chinese education and culture, and incited students in three leading Chinese schools to boycott the examinations. Wearing masks to prevent easy identification, students picketed the examination centres. However, many parents who were anxious to see their children take the examinations escorted them past the picket lines. Nearly two-thirds of the 3,150 students sat for the examinations and the boycott failed.

As in 1955 and 1956, the pro-communist leaders had hoped to provoke police action against students in order to discredit the government in the eyes of the

people. However, instead of using the police, the government had appealed to the parents to ensure that their children took the examinations, with the result that student agitators found themselves in conflict with the parents rather than the police.

The Legislative Assembly provided another battlefield. The defection of PAP Assemblymen to the Barisan Sosialis had reduced the government majority in the Assembly from 17 to just one. The Barisan Sosialis lobbied determinedly to rob the PAP Government of its slim majority, and finally succeeded on 3 July 1962 when the Assembly was debating the Referendum Bill: in the middle of the heated debate, Hoe Puay Choo announced her resignation from the PAP and subsequently joined the Barisan Sosialis. But the government was determined to stay on and see merger through, and the opposition could not outvote the PAP because the Singapore Alliance stood with the government on the merger issue.

In addition to strife on the home front, the battle for merger was also fought on the regional and international plane. As plans for Malaysia gathered momentum, the Barisan Sosialis began to coordinate its anti-merger activities with left-wing political groups in Malaya, Borneo and Brunei, as well as with Partai Kommunis Indonesia (PKI). In December 1961 Barisan Sosialis leaders attended a PKI meeting in Jakarta at which an anti-Malaysia stand was adopted. In January 1962 there was a conference in Kuala Lumpur at which the Socialist Front of Malaya, the Barisan Sosialis, the Sarawak

United People's Party and the Partai Ra'ayat Brunei jointly opposed the plan for merger. The anti-merger and anti-Malaysia propaganda spread by the communists, both in Singapore and outside, as well as by international communist front organisations, began to influence opinion in Third World and non-aligned countries.

The Singapore Government's position on merger needed to be clarified abroad. On 20 April 1962 Lee Kuan Yew led a four-member team on a six-week tour of several Afro-Asian countries to present the issues at stake and to counter the propaganda that Malaysia was a neo-colonialist plot. This tour included meetings with Pandit Nehru, President Nasser and President Tito.

The parties which opposed the "PAP merger" – the Barisan Sosialis, the Workers' Party and the United People's Party – decided to bring their case to the United Nations. In July 1962, 19 Assemblymen sent a memorandum to the United Nations Committee on Colonialism against the form the proposed merger was to take, and a "Council of Joint Action" was then formed to ask for a UN hearing. But when in consequence Lee Kuan Yew put the case for merger and Malaysia to the Committee in New York in late July 1962, the opposition's objection was thrown out.

The debates on the Referendum Bill, first introduced on 13 March 1962, resumed in the Legislative Assembly in June. After stormy sessions which continued late into the night, the Bill was finally passed on 6 July 1962. It contained three options for merger:

(A) Merger under the terms of the Government White Paper ("PAP Merger");

(B) A complete and unconditional merger as a state on an equal basis with the other 11 states "in accordance with the Constitutional documents" of the Federation of Malaya (the

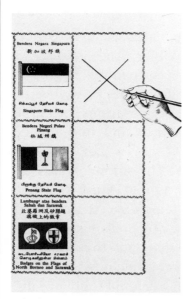

"Penang Merger" of the Barisan Sosialis); and

(C) Entry into Malaysia "on terms no less favourable than the terms for the Borneo territories."

The Barisan Sosialis said Option B was a misrepresentation of their position. They asked the people to cast blank votes in protest. But the government amended the Referendum Bill so that blank votes would be counted with the majority vote. The reasoning for this was that a blank vote would indicate that the voter could not make up his mind and would therefore be prepared to go along with the decision of the Legislative Assembly.

Meanwhile the Barisan Sosialis propaganda continued to assert that Federal nationals would only be second-class citizens, thus causing some confusion and concern among the public. Taking advantage of recommendations that the people of North Borneo should be Malaysian citizens, the Prime Minister raised this issue again with the Tunku, and on 14 August he was able to announce that all Singapore citizens, whether they were born in Singapore or not, would automatically become Malaysian citizens. This announcement deprived the Barisan Sosialis of its main propaganda line. The Referendum was fixed for 1 September 1962.

One week before the Referendum the Prime Minister warned the people that if the majority cast blank votes, the Legislative Assembly might well conclude that most people supported the Barisan Sosialis. This would mean that they supported Option B, which would entail the loss of citizenship for all those not born in Singapore.

The campaign leading up to the Referendum had all the fervour and verve of a general election. Voting was compulsory and 90 percent or 561,559 of the 624,000 registered citizens voted. When the results were announced in the early hours of 2 September, 397,626 (70.8 percent) had voted for Option A. Option B had attracted only 9,422 votes (1.67 percent), and

Option C, 7,911 votes (1.40 percent). Blank votes totalled 144,077 (25.65 percent). The rest were spoilt votes.

The Referendum was a turning point in the struggle for the hearts and minds of the people between the PAP Government and the communists and pro-communists. The government demonstrated convincingly that the communists were not invincible and that the PAP would not crumble without communist support.

After the Referendum the PAP turned its attention to rebuilding grassroots support. A major effort was made by the Prime Minister himself through his tour of all 51 constituencies.

The Prime Minister went first to the rural constituencies where the left-wing had built up strong support. These were the areas which had cast the most blank votes in the Referendum. He started out on 24 November 1962 when he went to Jurong and by September 1963 he had covered the whole island, ward by ward.

In the course of these tours, he talked to the people in three languages, sometimes making as many as 30 speeches in a day as he moved from place to place. He

was thus able to identify respected local community leaders who were willing to come forward to be counted on the side of the government, despite communist intimidation. He also heard public grievances over shortcomings in government services which the government agencies could then put right. His visits were thus followed by the construction of rural roads and drains, the lighting of streets and the building of community centres which, with basketball courts, ping-pong tables and TV sets, soon became popular recreational centres.

Television, launched on 15 February 1963, enabled the government to carry its message to wider audiences in homes and community centres, and to wean the population away from the communists. The people were able to observe the response of the crowds to the Prime Minister's tours and the willingness of community leaders to come forward and be identified with the government.

Defeated and rejected by the people on the merger issue, the Barisan Sosialis now hoped that external forces would prevent the formation of Malaysia. They pinned their hopes on the PKI and on the Indonesian Government.

Until late in 1962, the Indonesian Government had raised no objections to the formation of Malaysia. It had been pre-occupied with the absorption of West New Guinea (Irian Jaya) into Indonesia, which was achieved by August 1962. However, from December 1961, the PKI condemned Malaysia as a neo-colonialist plot, a line already taken by the Malayan Communist Party and the Chinese Communist Party. By 1962 the PKI's role and influence in Indonesian politics had increased. It was the third largest communist party in the world, claiming a membership of 2.5 million — and President Sukarno was becoming increasingly accommodating to its demands.

As early as 1945, Sukarno had had territorial dreams of a greater Indonesia encompassing Malaya and Borneo. If this dream had changed by 1962, Sukarno at least wanted Indonesia to be the predominant power in the region. Now that the British were planning to leave Borneo, he resented the fact that their dependencies would be joining Malaya, which he regarded as pro-British, rather than coming under Indonesian influence. He therefore came out in open opposition against Malaysia with the outbreak of a revolt in Brunei which provided him with a pretext for claiming that the people of the Borneo territories did not want to join Malaysia.

The Brunei Revolt broke out on 8 December 1962. It was led by A M Azahari, president of the Partai Ra'ayat Brunei. Azahari had long established connections with Indonesia and received discreet Indonesian support for launching the revolt. When he proclaimed a new and independent state of Kalimantan Utara (Brunei, North Borneo and Sarawak), Indonesia declared its support for the revolt, but denied playing any part in starting it.

The revolt was quickly put down by the British, but it was then revealed by the Singapore Government that Lim Chin Siong, Fong Swee Suan and a left-wing journalist, Said Zahari, had colluded with Azahari.

They had met secretly with Azahari before the uprising and allegedly discussed plans to organise violent demonstrations in Singapore to express support for the revolt and to pin down British troops. The readiness of the pro-communist leaders to conspire with foreign anti-Malaysia forces who resorted to violence prompted the Internal Security Council to take security action. On 2 February 1963, more than a hundred people, including Lim Chin Siong, Fong Swee Suan, Said Zahari, S Woodhull, Dominic Puthucheary and James Puthucheary were arrested. The pro-communist organisations in Singapore were virtually crippled.

Indonesia had announced on 20 January 1963 that it was launching a policy of "confrontation" (*konfrontasi*) against Malaysia. But until September 1963 "confrontation" mainly took the form of a war of words, harassment of Malayan fishing boats, and armed raids into the Borneo territories.

Indonesia was not alone in opposing the formation of Malaysia. The Philippines also opposed it because Manila had revived an old claim to British North Borneo (Sabah). Malaya was determined to go ahead with Malaysia, but in the hope of finding an amicable settlement to the dispute it agreed to hold discussions with Indonesia and the Philippines at the foreign ministers' level in Manila from 7 to 11 June 1963. The outcome of this meeting was an agreement to ascertain, through a survey by the UN Secretary-General or his representative, the will of the people of Borneo. However, Malaya made it clear that favourable UN findings would not be a condition for forming Malaysia.

Meanwhile, on 9 July 1963, the leaders of Malaya,

Singapore, Sabah and Sarawak signed the Malaysia Agreement in London. (The state of Brunei decided not to join the federation.) The Federation of Malaysia was scheduled to come into being on 31 August 1963.

As soon as the Malaysia Agreement was signed, Indonesia and the Barisan Sosialis denounced it, Sukarno objecting that the Agreement should have been deferred until the outcome of the UN survey was known.

The survey in Borneo began on 26 August. On 29 August the Government of Malaya issued a proclamation fixing 16 September as the new date for the inauguration of Malaysia instead of 31 August, to allow the UN team to complete its work, but reiterated that the UN findings would not affect the formation of Malaysia. Lee Kuan Yew declared Singapore independent on 31 August 1963, and the PAP Government acted "as trustees" for the Federal Government for 15 days until Malaysia was inaugurated on 16 September.

The UN mission reported on 14 September that the majority of people in the Borneo territories were in favour of joining Malaysia. However, Sukarno rejected the findings; relations between Malaysia and Indonesia were severed, and Indonesia announced suspension of its trade with Malaysia, including Singapore.

Confrontation now took a more ugly turn. Indonesian propaganda, psychological warfare and subversion intensified. Armed raids into Sarawak and Sabah were stepped up, and preparations were made to start an insurgency in Sarawak in cooperation with the local clandestine communist organisation. Sabotage operations were planned and launched in Singapore. A bomb blast at the Ambassador Hotel on 24 September marked the beginning of sabotage and terrorist actions.

Singapore had only two infantry battalions and the

Malayan armed forces were much smaller than those of Indonesia. The main task of dealing with Indonesian attacks and harassment was undertaken by the British forces, with some support from Malayan, Singapore, Australian and New Zealand forces. "Confrontation" was contained by the limited but skilful use of force.

The presence of the British military in strength (there were about 50,000 men at the height of "confrontation") successfully deterred aggression on a larger scale.

By the time Malaysia was officially promulgated on 16 September, Singapore was already caught up in an election campaign. The Prime Minister had decided to call a general election so that his government could obtain a fresh mandate from the people. The Legislative Assembly was dissolved on 3 September 1963 and polling scheduled for 21 September.

Four main parties took the field: the PAP, the Barisan Sosialis, Ong Eng Guan's United People's Party and the new Singapore Alliance which comprised the remnants of Lim Yew Hock's old Singapore People's Alliance, and the Singapore branches of UMNO and the MCA. The Singapore Alliance was therefore backed by the UMNO-MCA-MIC Alliance in the Peninsula. The real fight, however, was between the PAP and the Barisan Sosialis.

The election was bitterly contested. Ong Eng Guan depended largely on his personal appeal. The Singapore Alliance depended on UMNO's racial appeal to the Singapore Malays to support it. The Barisan Sosialis exploited communal issues and championed the cause of Chinese culture and Chinese education. It also attacked the PAP for detaining its leaders and for what it claimed to be a "sell-out" merger with Malaya. The PAP campaigned on its record — its achievements in housing and education, in industrialisation and employment, in improving social and health services, and in dealing effectively with corruption and secret societies. Above all it claimed credit for having brought about the merger with Malaya through Malaysia, with its expected economic benefits.

When the votes were counted the PAP emerged as clear winners, capturing 37 of the 51 seats. The Barisan Sosialis won only 13. Of the United People's Party candidates, only Ong Eng Guan won, retaining Hong Lim. The Singapore Alliance did not win a single seat, and Tunku Abdul Rahman personally visited Singapore to express his disappointment with the Singapore Malays for not supporting UMNO.

After the elections, the pro-communists continued to exploit trade union and student issues. By this time enrolment in Chinese schools was beginning to decline, partly because of their reputation for political unrest instead of serious study, but the pro-communists claimed that the PAP Government was killing Chinese language and culture. There were problems with undergraduates at Nanyang University, which had been infiltrated by the communists after its establishment. In late September the police moved in to arrest a number of known pro-communist student leaders at Nanyang University. Two students were injured during a scuffle and the students then mounted protests against "police brutality". Then from 3 to 5 October the undergraduates staged a boycott of classes and followed this up with a "Peace March" to City Hall in protest against a proposed reorganisation of Nanyang University.

The majority of the strikes by unions continued to be politically motivated. On 28 August, notices were served on seven unions to show cause why their registration should not be withdrawn. In response, the pro-communist Singapore Association of Trade Unions (SATU), which was yet to be registered, called for a two-day island-wide strike against the "show cause" notices. The strike however fizzled out in a day. The authorities had warned that the pro-communists, having failed to capture power in the general election, "were embarking on direct and more violent form of action" through pro-communist unions and students, and that firm action would be taken. On 30 October the seven unions were duly deregistered and on 12 November, SATU was informed that its application to be registered was rejected. Fourteen of its leaders, including three Assemblymen, were arrested. Pro-communist rural associations and hawkers' organisations were also dissolved.

During its first term in office, the PAP Government achieved significant results in housing and education and in fighting corruption and the secret society menace.

Following its establishment in 1960, the HDB built nearly 32,000 flats and shop units in three years. Expenditure on education rose from $60.9 million in 1960 to $107.8 million in 1963. Primary school enrolment increased from 284,702 to 335,656 between 1960 and 1963; secondary school enrolment from 59,244 to 84,425. There was an expansion of health services and sanitation, especially in the outlying areas.

Law and order improved with arrests of gangsters and secret society members. Kidnapping gangs were smashed. By 1963 the number of secret society incidents had fallen to less than half of the monthly average for 1959.

However, despite the preparation of Jurong, the building of an industrial infrastructure and the announcement of incentives for investors, Singapore's industrialisation programme did not make much headway. The political turmoil and politically motivated industrial strikes of the period 1961 to 1963 discouraged investors. The number of man-days lost in strikes was 152,005 in 1960; 410,889 in 1961; 165,124 in 1962; and 388,219 in 1963. As of December 1963 there were only two factories in production in Jurong – the National Iron and Steel Mills and Pelican Textiles, which between them employed only 90 workers. The National Iron and Steel Mills, set up in September 1962, was the first industrial project in Jurong, a joint venture between the government and the private sector.

Preparing for Malaysia

376
Members of the Cobbold Commission, (left to right): Sir Anthony Abell; Mohammed Ghazali bin Shafie (Malayan nominee); Lord Cobbold (chairman); Dato Wong Pow Nee (Malayan nominee); and Sir David Watherston. The Commission was appointed by the British and Malayan governments to ascertain the views of the people of the Borneo territories on their inclusion in the proposed federation of Malaysia. The Commission found that the majority were in favour of Malaysia and recommended its early formation.

376

377

378

378
Singapore's Deputy Prime Minister, Dr Toh Chin Chye, and Culture Minister, S Rajaratnam, at the Malaysia Exhibition, soon after its opening during Malaysia Week. The exhibits were on the culture and life of the people of Malaya, Sarawak, Sabah, Singapore and Brunei.

377
The Fourth Conference of the Malaysia Solidarity Consultative Committee meets at the Singapore Legislative Assembly Library in early February 1962, with Donald Stephens of Sabah as chairman. The committee was set up on 23 July 1961 to promote the speedy realisation of Malaysia. It held meetings in the capitals of the various states which were to be part of the federation.

A souvenir publication of Malaysia Week, Jan. 29 to Feb. 7, held in conjunction with the Fourth Conference of the Malaysia Solidarity Consultative Committee, Singapore, Feb. 1-3, 1962

379

379
In its publicity drive for Malaysia, the Singapore Government issued several publications. Two hundred and forty-five thousand copies of the publication, *Malaysian Heritage*, in four languages (English, Chinese, Malay and Tamil) were distributed in Singapore and Malaya.

380/381
Lee Kuan Yew and a beaming
Tunku Abdul Rahman are
enthusiastically greeted by a
large crowd which turned up at
Paya Lebar Airport on 15 July
1962 to see the Tunku off to
London for the first round of
talks on Malaysia.
   (Below) Lee Kuan Yew takes
to the rostrum after the Tunku
and expresses his support for
the formation of Malaysia.

380

381

382
8 August 1962: Tunku Abdul
Rahman returns from London
with the news that Britain has
agreed to the formation of
Malaysia.

In Singapore, the
government decided to go
ahead with the Referendum to
gauge the people's response to
the terms of merger with
Malaya.

382

Fight with Communists on Merger

383

384

383/384

Lee Kuan Yew at the microphone at Radio Singapore during one of the radio talks he gave in September and October 1961. In the 12 talks which the Prime Minister gave in each of the three main languages – Malay, Chinese and English – he explained to the people why the PAP had joined in an anti-colonial united front with the communists, why the front broke up, and why the communists were opposing merger.

The government followed this up with a White Paper on 16 November 1961, setting out the terms under which Singapore would be joining Malaysia.

385

Once again the communists resort to the use of students and left-wing unionists to stir up trouble, this time to prevent the merger of Singapore with Malaya.

Here, striking workers of the Sun Life Assurance Company protest against the management. The portrayal of employer-employee relations in terms of hostile confrontation and class conflict was a characteristic of the times.

386

386
Communist elements exploit the dissatisfaction of Chinese middle school students over the new examination system implemented in November 1961.

The student activists boycotted the examinations and barricaded the examination centres to prevent anyone from sitting for the examinations.

However, the boycott failed because many parents escorted their children to the examination centres and would not let them be intimidated by the agitators.

(Above) Faces masked by handkerchiefs, student activists picket the examination centres on the first day of the examinations.

387/388
On the examination day, students are helped by parents and others to climb over or crawl under fences to get into the examination centres.

387

388

389
Protesting students using force against parents.

390
Student activists render first aid to one of their comrades who was injured when some students broke through a barricade to take their examinations.

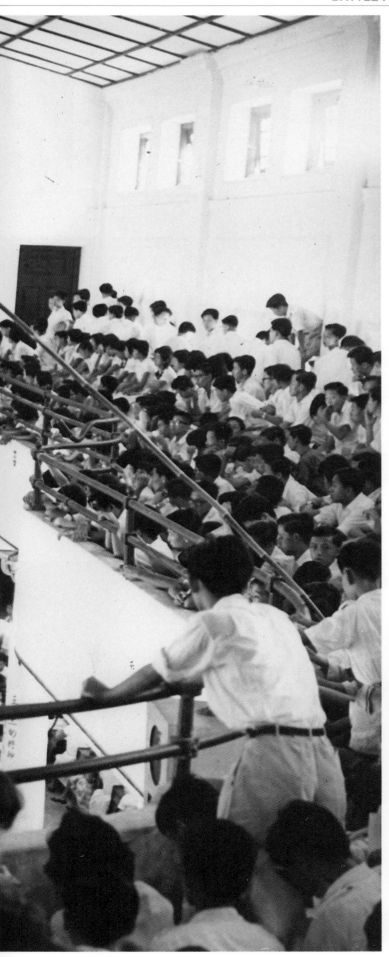

391
Student leaders addressing a rally at Chinese High School.

The rally was organised to protest against the Commission of Inquiry into the examination boycott of 1961.

The students claimed that the Commission represented another attempt to destroy Chinese education. The number 513 on the flag refers to 13 May, a reminder of the national service demonstration of 1954 and the Hock Lee bus riots of 1955.

On 21 May, student pickets, wearing black arm-bands to mourn the "death of Chinese education", intimidated students to prevent them from attending classes at six schools. At Chung Cheng High School, the pickets beat up two students. The boycott failed and 100 student activists were arrested.

392
A PAP branch vandalised by pro-communists. This happened to a number of PAP branches and community centres in 1962. Many centres were taken over by the Barisan Sosialis. The pro-communists were trying to intimidate PAP and government supporters.

392

393

393
The Prime Minister at Paya Lebar Airport on 20 April 1962 before starting a six-week Afro-Asian tour. The journey was undertaken to clear the doubts raised by the anti-Malaysia propaganda of the communists and their supporters. Lee Kuan Yew was accompanied by Devan Nair, Rahim Ishak and Jek Yeun Thong.

394
Among the places Lee Kuan Yew and his team visited were Rangoon, New Delhi, Cairo, Belgrade, Rome, Geneva and London.

The Prime Minister with President Nasser (in striped tie) of Egypt.

394

Assembly shock: PAP loses absolute majority
WE CARRY ON—LEE

Madam Hoe Puay Choo quits the party

SINGAPORE, Tuesday

THE Prime Minister, Mr. Lee Kuan Yew tonight pledged that the Peoples Action Party Government would carry on despite the shock resignation of Madam Hoe Puay Choo, the Assemblywoman for Bras Basah from the party.

Madam Hoe, 33, a founder member of the party, announced her resignation tonight as the Assembly was debating the Referendum Bill.

Though the PAP has now lost its one-vote absolute majority in the Assembly, Mr. Lee was smiling when he met reporters outside the Assembly to confirm the resignation.

'A pity'

The Premier issued his statement:

"It is the business of

MADAM HOE . . . . "A pity she lost her nerve at this late stage" — Premier Lee.

I WAS KEPT IN DARK ABOUT EVERYTHING, SHE SAYS

That is the primary duty of the Government and indeed the duty of all citizens who want to see racial peace and harmony prevail.

We are on the final phase towards our goal.

There is no question of our quitting and leaving the job unfinished.

lost her nerve at this late stage.

We went through the worst in July last year, and there are no troubles that can confront us now which can be worse than what has happened.

We shall see the referendum and merger through. There will be merger, there will be Malaysia on

Lingam is taken back by PAP

SINGAPORE, Thursday.

MR. S.V. Lingam, Assemblyman for Aljunied, returned to the ruling People's Action Party today to help in the fight against "anti-national elements."

The Government has now regained an absolute majority of one in the 51-man Legislative Assembly.

Re-admitting ...im, PAP's organising secretary, Mr. Ong Pang Boon, who is also Minister for Home Affairs, said today: "We all make mistakes, and so long as a person sees his error and makes amends, a political party, like a person, must be prepared to give a person another chance."

Full support

Ten days ago Mr. Lingam broke off with Mr. Ong Eng Guan and the United Peoples' Party which he had helped to found after their 1960 rebellion against the PAP.

In his application for re-admission, Mr. Lingam pledged complete support for PAP's policies and strategy for reunification with Malaya.

He said in his application, addressed to the party chairman, Dr. Toh Chin Chye, who is also the Deputy Premier: "I can

Cobbold report 'unbiased'

KUCHING, Thurs. — The chairman of the Sarawak National Party, Mr. J. S. Tinker, today said that the Cobbold Report was "an unbiased masterpiece of views." He agreed with recommendations almost in toto but added that heads of state should be eligible to become head of the Malaysian Federation or this high position should be held

MR. LINGAM

Minister Ahmad Ibrahim dies, 35

By
JACKIE SAM SINGAPORE, Tues.

INCHE AHMAD IBRAHIM, Minister for Labour, died in the General Hospital here today. He was 35 and had been in poor health since 1958.

He died at 3.15 p.m. — shortly after whispering "ma'af" ("pardon") to his father and wife, Chè puteh.

A State funeral for him has been ordered by the Yang di-Pertuan Negara, Inche Yusof bin Ishak. The cortege will leave Inche Ahmad's home in Nassim Road at 3 p.m. for the Bidadari Muslim cemetery.

Inche Ahmad underwent a major operation on his liver in January 1958. In December 1961, he was flown to London for another operation.

INCHE AHMAD

395

395

The PAP's position in the Legislative Assembly remained precarious. In the months leading up to Referendum Day, 1 September 1962, the Barisan Sosialis sought to undermine the PAP's slim majority of one in the Assembly by coaxing

PAP Assemblymen to defect. On 3 July, PAP Assemblywoman Hoe Puay Choo resigned, making the PAP a minority government (PAP 25 vs opposition 26). She remained in the Assembly as an independent until she joined

the Barisan Sosialis on 11 August.

On 16 August the PAP regained its majority of one when S V Lingam, who had left the PAP to join the United People's Party (UPP), was readmitted into the PAP

following his resignation from the UPP on 4 August. However, the death of PAP's Ahmad Ibrahim on 21 August brought the strength of the government and the opposition in the Assembly to 25-25.

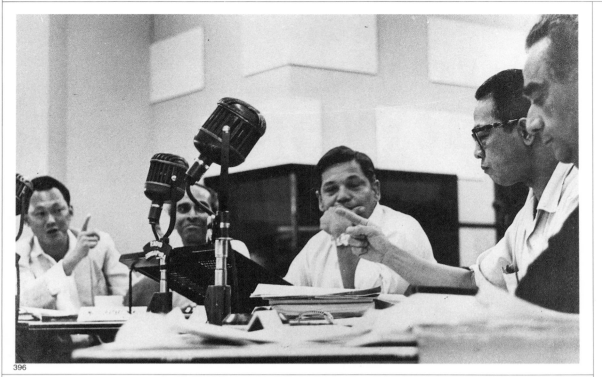

396

397

398

396
Prime Minister Lee Kuan Yew and Culture Minister Rajaratnam with opposition leaders Dr Lee Siew Choh and David Marshall at a radio forum held on 18 August 1962 to debate the controversial citizenship clause in the Malaysia Agreement. In the centre is John Duclos, the director of Radio Singapore.

Under the citizenship clause, Singapore citizens would be nationals of Malaysia but not Malaysian citizens. The anti-merger elements made the citizenship clause one of the burning issues of the Referendum. There were a number of radio forums on the issue of merger.

397
A section of the large crowd of students listening to a forum on "Merger and Malaysia", organised by the University of Singapore Students' Union.

398
Speakers at the forum included Lee Kuan Yew, David Marshall of the Workers' Party and S Woodhull (at the microphone) of the Barisan Sosialis.

The Referendum

399/400
The three options on merger open to the electorate of 624,000. Two senior citizens (below) study the options.

399

400

401
The Referendum was preceded by intense campaigning. Rallies became more frequent as Referendum Day, 1 September 1962, drew nearer, with the PAP Government urging the public to vote for Option A and the Barisan Sosialis calling on voters to cast blank votes to register their opposition to merger. An attempt by the Barisan Sosialis on the eve of the poll to get a Supreme Court injunction to halt the Referendum failed.

401

402
Voters on Referendum Day.
403
People keeping vigil outside the Badminton Stadium where the votes were being counted. The results were known only in the early hours of 2 September 1962 as the Barisan Sosialis had insisted on a recount. The majority, 70.8 percent, voted for Option A; 1.67 percent for Option B; and 1.4 percent for Option C. Blank votes totalled 25.65 percent. The rest were spoilt votes.

402

403

Re-building Grassroots Support

404
Prime Minister Lee Kuan Yew tours the Jurong constituency, a pro-communist stronghold, on 24 November 1962. In the Referendum, nearly 50 percent of Jurong's constituents had cast blank votes. The Prime Minister undertook the constituency tours to re-build grassroots support. He began the tours in rural areas where the communists exerted a strong influence.

405
Lee Kuan Yew on a tour of Yio Chu Kang. During such constituency tours, the Prime Minister was usually accompanied by community leaders who later formed the core of the Citizens' Consultative Committees.

404

405

406
The pro-communists and Barisan Sosialis members continued to dog the Prime Minister's footsteps, employing "boo-boo" girls and boys in an attempt to disrupt the tours. Pro-communist elements often shouted abuse or incited others to tear down banners and flags put up for the tours.

407

407
On 8 September 1963, as the Prime Minister was passing the premises of the Singapore School Canteen Vendors' Union at Towner Road (now called Whampoa Drive), during his tour of Kallang constituency, the pro-communists started booing, jeering, and jostling him. They nearly pushed him into a monsoon drain.

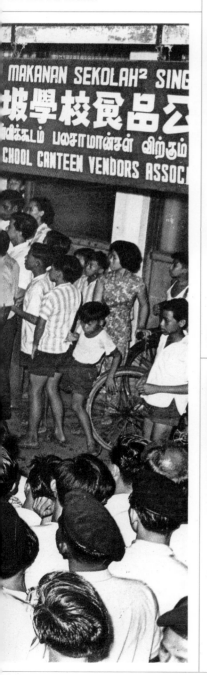

408
"Blackboard News" employed by the Barisan Sosialis to attack and discredit the government. These two boards were prominently displayed in front of the Barisan Sosialis branch during Lee Kuan Yew's tour of Nee Soon constituency on 10 March 1963.

409
Lee Kuan Yew chats with a senior resident over a cup of coffee during his tour of Bukit Panjang on 3 March 1963.

The constituency tours were punctuated by stops to attend functions or simply to have informal chats. It was at such stops that constituents made their requests for amenities such as roads, electricity and piped water. Follow-up action was swift. Public Works Department workers, supported by Work Brigade members, would build rural roads and drains, light up streets and provide piped water by constructing public stand-pipes.

410

411

410/411

The Prime Minister wades in knee-high water to board a boat for the ride to the Southern Islands where (left) the islanders turn up to welcome him.

What began as fortnightly tours soon became weekly ones. In July they were taking place three times a week, and by August five times a week. Lee Kuan Yew completed touring all 51 constituencies before the general election, scheduled for 21 September 1963.

The tour of the last of the 51 constituencies, Mountbatten, was completed at 6.15 am on 12 September 1963, the morning of Nomination Day for the general election.

The Brunei Revolt

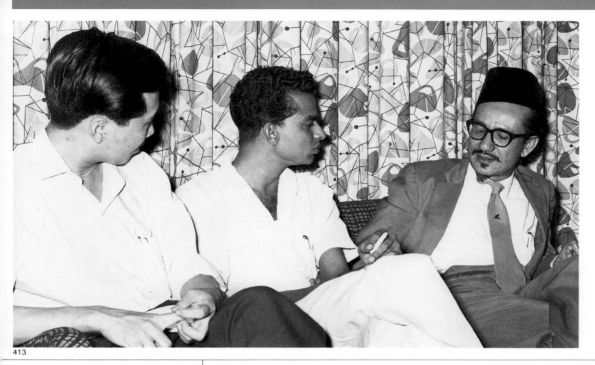

413

413
A M Azahari (with tie), the leader of the Brunei Revolt of December 1962, talking to Barisan Sosialis leaders, Dominic Puthucheary (centre) and Lim Chin Siong at the Singapore airport.

The revolt was quickly crushed by the British; however, the Singapore Government revealed that Lim Chin Siong, Fong Swee Suan and Said Zahari had colluded with Azahari to plan violent demonstrations in Singapore as a show of support.

412

412
Aidit, secretary-general of Partai Kommunis Indonesia (PKI) addressing a party congress. Aidit's anti-Malaysia line, echoing the line of the Malayan Communist Party, was endorsed by Sukarno and his government.

The local communists and the Barisan Sosialis, having been rejected by the people on the merger issue, now pinned their hopes on the PKI, Sukarno and the Brunei Revolt. They began to work more in concert with such "anti-colonial left-wing" forces to prevent merger and Malaysia.

414

414
Partai Ra'ayat Brunei staged the revolt on 8 December 1962 and declared the establishment of an independent State of Kalimantan Utara (Brunei, North Borneo and Sarawak). The Partai Kommunis Indonesia, the communists and pro-communists in Singapore, as well as Sukarno's government, expressed their support for the Brunei Revolt.

About 2,000 members of the secret wing of Partai Ra'ayat Brunei took part in the revolt. One thousand of them had shotguns but others had only axes or spears. They captured some towns and oilfields but the quick action by the British forces put down the revolt within days.

(Left) Men of the 1st Battalion Queen's Own Highlanders surround a village near the oil town of Seria in Brunei to round up the rebels.

NO. 1,427. SUNDAY, FEBRUARY 3, 1963. ★ 20 CENTS. KDN 355 Tel: 94057.

A 'Cuba' threat

SECURITY COUNCIL WAS UNANIMOUS

DATO ISMAIL

THE Communists have always intended to dominate and rule the whole of Malaya and Singapore. But the success of the merger proposals has driven them to oppose Malaysia and to try and set up a Communist Cuba in Singapore. The arrests are directly aimed at individuals—not political parties.

AT least 107 left-wing politicians and trade unionists in Singapore were arrested today in the biggest and "most important" security operation since the Emergency. The operation is continuing.

The swoop, aimed at preventing subversives from establishing a "Communist Cuba" in Singapore and mounting violence just before Malaysia, was carried out by the Singapore police assisted by men from the Federation.

Those picked up include the names in the Barisan Sosialis and other politicians like:

● LIM CHIN SIONG, secretary-general, Barisan Sosialis;

● S. WOODHULL, vice-chairman, Barisan Sosialis;

● FONG SWEE SUAN, secretary-general SATU and executive committee member, Barisan Sosialis;

● DOMINIC PUTHUCHEARY, committee member

107 HELD IN SINGAPORE DAWN DRIVE

By FELIX ABISHEGANADEN: Kuala Lumpur, Saturday

The swoop began at 3 a.m.

LAWYER Mr. T. T. Rajah is stopped by police from entering the Singapore General Employees Union.

SATU and Barisan Sosialis; vice-president Singapore General Employees' Union;

● TAN TECK WAH, president Singapore General Employees' Union; vice-president, SATU and

● A. WAHAB SHAH, chairman, Party Rakyat.

Also included in this big anti-Red round-up were a group of Nanyang University students. But no confirmation of their identities was available tonight.

Today's swoop was the result of a meeting of the Singapore Internal Security

LIM CHIN SIONG

COUNT

Wh

by
EE BOON LEE
and
LIM BENG TEE

SINGAPORE, Tue — T h e Specia Branch today de lined to give a brea down of the 113 d tainees who were a rested in "Operatio Cold Store" and the political or uni connections.

As far as is kno the Barisan Sosi suffered the heav casualties in the ope tion aimed at crippl Communist open fo organisations.

In several cases, th tainees had links with than one organisation Here is a list compi the Straits Times

BARISAN SOSIAN
Lim Chin Siong 's ary-general;
S. Woodhull (vice mani; Puthucheary visers;
Dr. Lim Hock Sie ant secretary genera Tan Yam Seng tive committee mem Wong See Kew all mittee member;
Yap Ser Jin (e committee member D. Puthucheary tive committee man

Estd. 1845.

WEDNESDAY, FEBRUARY 6, 1963.

KEY MAN IN SINGA

He knew of Brunei revolt in advance, arrang meeting between Azahari and Chin Siong

ZAHARI THE

KUALA LUMPUR Tuesday

THE Brunei re

DETAINEES TO GO TO

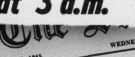

e big swoop

FULL LIST OF THE SINGAPORE ARRESTS

FROM LEFT: Wahab Shah, Tan Siew Chwee, Chua Chin Keat, Hussein Jahidin and S. Ghouse.

Dr. Poh Soo Kai,

Dr. Lim Hock Siew, Peter Pang and Chan Chiaw Thor.

Also held: Linda Chen and sister

guests of honour at the inauguration ceremony of the Barisan Sosialis in Singapore in September 1961.

On that occasion, in spite of the divergence between their ultimate objectives, Azahari and the Barisan Sosialis leaders preached opposition to Malaysia from the same platform and declared their common aim as Socialism.

Subsequently Azahari and Lim Chin Siong, identified as companions by other Barisan leaders, met on several occasions when Azahari visited Singapore during 1962.

In spite of their mutual distrust they are known to have discussed plans for the defeat of Malaysia by action in the five territories of the future Federation.

These meetings were held in clandestine circumstances. They were arranged by Said Zahari, one of Lim's closest Malay associates and Azahari's closest companion during his final visit to Singapore in December 1962 before the Brunei revolt.

Said Zahari also accommodated Azahari in his hotel in October 1962. Zahari had a meeting with Azahari four days before the outbreak of the Brunei rebellion.

SETBACK

The whole Communist United Front quickly demonstrated their approval of armed struggle in Brunei. In spite of the disruption of normal communications and the obscurity of the situation, within 24 hours of the outbreak the Barisan Sosialis and their friends in the Partai Rakyat Singapore, simultaneously declared their support for "a popular nationalist movement for independence and liberation from British colonialism"

The same elements have subsequently done their utmost

Ah Kow Lee Kim Yong alias Lee Kim Leong, Lim Seck Kian, Ng Cheng Siong alias Ng Mang, Mohd.

Beng, Tan Say Khai alias Chan Say Jame, Tan Hai, Tan Yam Seng
Wong See Kew alias Wang Chia Mong
Nyuk See, Puah Koon, Yeh Kim alias Yuen Poh alias Yeh Kim Ch.

415

248

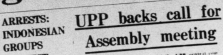

RISAN SUFFERED THE HEAVIEST CASUALTIES

who in the big round-up

LIM BECK KIAN
Former president of Chinese School Teachers' Union.

CHAN CHIAW THOR
Deputy secretary of Barisan's publicity and education committee.

TAN TECK WAH
Chairman of General Employees' Union.

DR. LIM HOCK SIEW
Barisan executive committee member.

D. PUTHUCHEARY
Barisan executive committee member and vice-chairman of General Employees' Union.

...ties and unions

central or- e mem- ... (deputy ...ity and ...el): ...(secre- ... d educa-	**SINGAPORE RURAL RESIDENTS' ASSN.** Chew Hwee (branch executive committee member and Chinese School teacher); Lim Woon Chye (paid

SINGAPORE BUS WORKERS' UNION
Tan Say Khai alias Chen Say Jame.

BUSINESS HOUSES EMPLOYEES' UNION

ARRESTS: INDONESIAN GROUPS PROTEST

JAKARTA, Tues. — The big Communist-controlled Sobsi Trade Union Federation has cabled a protest to the Singapore Government for its mass arrests of leftwing elements on the island last weekend.

The cable read in part "on behalf of three million Indonesian labourers we condemn strongly the arrests and demand the immediate release of the detainees."

The extreme leftwing Partindo (Indonesia Party) and the Gerwani Women's Movement have also protested against the arrests. — Reuter.

HAWKERS' UNION
Chan Kwang Yeng alias Chan Kong Yeng alias Chan Kong Ying.

WOOD WORKERS' UNION
Chang Show Jen alias Chong Saw Jen.

METAL BOX WORKERS' UNION
Chia Check Sam alias Seah Chong Wah (former secretary).

MOTOR WORKSHOPS EMPLOYEES' UNION
Low Jwee Peng alias Low Peng (paid secretary).

SPINNING WORKERS' UNION
Hong Ah Mee alias Fang Loo Khung (paid secretary).

CHINESE SCHOOL TEACHERS' UNION
Lim Beck Kian (former president).

ASSOCIATION OF SINGAPORE DENTAL

UPP backs call for Assembly meeting

SINGAPORE, Tues. — The United People's Party today supported two Opposition parties — the Barisan Sosialis and the Singapore People's Alliance — in calling on the Government to convene an emergency session of the Legislative Assembly for a full debate on last Saturday's mass arrests.

The UPP also demanded that the Government should give reasons for detaining three of its "important members."

The UPP secretary general, Mr. Ong Eng Guan, issued a statement saying: "A member of the UPP central committee was detained. Why? Is the Government anxious to know the deliberations

of the UPP central committee?

"An official of UPP headquarters is detained. Why? Is the Government anxious to know strength of our membership and details of UPP?"

Ng Ho secretary of the party's Tanjong Pagar branch who was detained "was personally known to the PAP leadership as an effective organiser," Mr. Ong added.

He asked "Is the Government about Tanjong coming...."

Tanjong Pagar is the Prime Minister's constituency.

Children's Britannica

'NK'

...ED BY ...ND ...IANS'	**Malaysia:** Red bid to

...kirk and Ministers are back after
...the internal security meeting

The Sunday Times, February 3, 1963

...n S'pore: This is not the end of Communists

...san HQ at
...Victoria
...eet sealed
...by Police

SINGAPORE, Saturday.

LORD SELKIRK, who chaired the Internal Security Council meeting in Kuala Lumpur, and two Singapore members of the council, Dr. Goh Keng Swee, the Finance Minister, and Mr. Ong Pang Boon, the Minister for Home Affairs, flew back here this evening.

Lord Selkirk arrived in a Malayan Airways Comet jetliner at 4.15 p.m. To the large throng of reporters and foreign correspondents he said: "I have nothing more to say."

Just before boarding his car, Lord Selkirk smiled at a reporter's question on whether British Army units in Singapore have been put on special alert, and said: "I don't think so."

Dr. Goh and Mr. Ong were accompanied by the Minister for National Development, Mr. Tan Kia Gan, the Ministry's acting Permanent Secretary Mr. Sim Kee Boon, and the

...ge One

younger brother has been under detention for several years.

Two other Barisan leaders — Dr. Lim Hock Siew and S. Woodhull — were arrested together in the doctor's home in the Upper Serangoon area.

Dr. Lim and Dr. Poh were in the top hierarchy of the PAP before they quit to throw in their lot with the breakaway group which formed the Barisan Sosialis.

The two doctors, who share a practice in Balestier Road, have been very active "backroom boys" in the party.

The police party who arrested them had earlier called at the MacPherson Road home of Mahadeva, secretary-general of the Singapore National Union of Journalists, and a staff reporter of the Straits Times.

Only six hours later, Mahadeva was due to leave with Said Zahari for Jakarta.

CALL TO REJOICE ON TENGKU'S 60TH BIRTHDAY

KUALA LUMPUR, Sat. — The national president of the Malayan Indian Congress, Dato V. T. Sambanthan, today called on members of its central working committee, state and local branches to celebrate the 60th

415
These newspaper clippings tell the story behind "Operation Cold Store", the massive security operation that led to the detention of more than 100 pro-communist trade union and student leaders. "Operation Cold Store" had been ordered by the Internal Security Council after it was discovered that the pro-communists were working with external anti-Malaysia forces to create tension and disorder in Singapore.

Birth of Malaysia and Confrontation

416

Tunku Abdul Rahman and President Sukarno pictured in the gardens of the residence of the Japanese Foreign Minister, Ohira. The Tunku and Sukarno met in Tokyo on 31 May and 1 June 1963 to discuss Indonesia's objections to the formation of Malaysia. Soon after this, a meeting in Manila of the foreign ministers of Malaya, Indonesia and the Philippines agreed that a UN team ascertain the wishes of the people of Borneo. The Malayan Government was doing its best to accommodate Indonesia and the Philippines without abandoning the movement towards Malaysia.

416

417/418

Prime Minister Lee Kuan Yew leaves for London on 25 June 1963 to sign the Malaysia Agreement. Thousands of well-wishers were at the airport to see him off.

417

418

419

420

421

419
The leaders of the Federation of Malaya, Sabah, Sarawak and Singapore at Marlborough House in London for the signing of the Malaysia Agreement on 9 July 1963. Brunei, the other proposed member of the new nation, decided against joining it at the last minute.

The Singapore Legislative Assembly approved the Malaysia Agreement on 2 August. Malaysia was scheduled to come into being on 31 August. However on 29 August, the Yang di-Pertuan Agung signed a Proclamation fixing 16 September as Malaysia Day, so as to give the UN fact-finding mission sufficient time to ascertain the views of the people of British North Borneo and Sarawak.

420
Lee Kuan Yew, moments after he had signed the Malaysia Agreement.

421
Prime Minister Lee Kuan Yew declares *de facto* independence for Singapore at a mass rally and march-past held at the Padang on 31 August 1963 to mark Malaysia Solidarity Day. He said that in the 15 days to Malaysia Day on 16 September, "we look upon ourselves as trustees for the Central Government of Malaysia..."

422
(Right) The facade of City Hall is brightened by illuminated billboards depicting the Malaysian flag and the multi-racial people of Malaysia linking their arms in harmony.

423

424

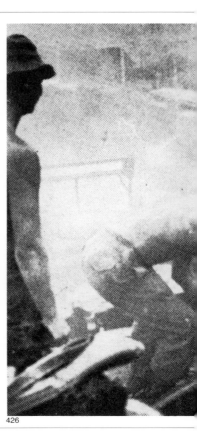

423
The UN survey mission to Borneo was headed by L Michel More (second from left). The deputy leader of the team, George Janacek, is on his left. The mission confirmed that the formation of Malaysia was in accordance with the wishes of the people of British North Borneo and Sarawak. However, Sukarno rejected the mission's findings and refused to accept Malaysia as a reality.

424
Indonesian rioters vent their anti-Malaysia anger on the British Embassy in Jakarta. They wrecked the building and made a bonfire of its furniture. The Malayan Embassy in Jakarta was also sacked.

Owing to "confrontation", diplomatic relations between Kuala Lumpur and Jakarta were severed. Trade links were cut, a development which caused considerable economic difficulty to Singapore. "Confrontation" took a more ugly turn.

426

425

427/426/427
British military forces, supported by Malaysian, Australian and New Zealand forces, played a crucial role in containing "confrontation". Apart from ground troops, sizeable British naval and air force units were deployed in the region to deal with the threat.

(Left) Men of the Royal Ulster Rifles prepare for a river patrol; and (below) they seek out the enemy in a deep swamp.

(Below centre) A Royal Artillery detachment's 105 mm Howitzer in action from a forward base in East Malaysia.

427

428
On 16 September 1963, the Padang is again the scene of pomp and splendour as the people of Singapore gather to celebrate Malaysia Day.

Prime Minister Lee Kuan Yew read the Malaysia Proclamation from City Hall steps. Those present at the ceremony included the Yang di-Pertuan Negara, Yusof bin Ishak; the Federal Minister for Internal Security, Dato Dr Ismail bin Dato Abdul Rahman; and the British Secretary for Commonwealth Relations, Duncan Sandys.

Dr Ismail is seen here reading a message from the Malaysian Prime Minister, Tunku Abdul Rahman.

429
The Malaysian King receives the Malaysia Proclamation from Tunku Abdul Rahman at a ceremony held at Kuala Lumpur's Merdeka Stadium on 17 September 1963. Leaders of the constituent states, including Singapore's Yang di-Pertuan Negara, Yusof bin Ishak, and Prime Minister Lee Kuan Yew were present at the ceremony.

On joining Malaysia, Singapore entered a new political environment. The Peninsula and Singapore had different political and social systems and the two ruling parties had different political philosophies. Some element of friction had already developed in the course of negotiations on Singapore's entry terms. Soon communal forces were to give an ugly communal character to differences and discord over economic and political issues.

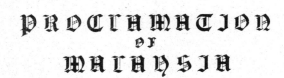

PROCLAMATION OF MALAYSIA

In the name of God, the Compassionate, the Merciful.

Praise be to God, the Lord of the Universe, and may the benediction and peace of God be upon Our Leader Muhammad and upon all His Relations and Friends.

WHEREAS by an Agreement made on the Ninth day of July in the year one thousand nine hundred and sixty-three between the Federation of Malaya, the United Kingdom, North Borneo, Sarawak and Singapore it was agreed that there shall be federated the States of Sabah, Sarawak and Singapore with the Federation of Malaya comprising the States of Pahang, Trengganu, Kedah, Johore, Negri Sembilan, Kelantan, Selangor, Perak, Perlis, Penang and Malacca, and that the Federation shall thereafter be called "Malaysia":

AND WHEREAS it has been agreed by the parties to the said Agreement that as from the establishment of Malaysia the States of Sabah, Sarawak and Singapore shall cease to be colonies of Her Majesty the Queen and Her Majesty the Queen shall relinquish Her sovereignty and jurisdiction in respect of the three States:

AND WHEREAS there has been promulgated a Constitution for Malaysia which shall be the supreme law therein:

AND WHEREAS by the Constitution aforesaid provision has been made for the safeguarding of the rights and prerogatives of Their Highnesses the Rulers and the fundamental rights and liberties of subjects and for the promotion of peace and harmony in Malaysia as a constitutional monarchy based upon parliamentary democracy:

AND WHEREAS the Constitution aforesaid having been approved by a law passed by the Parliaments of the Federation of Malaya and of the United Kingdom has come into force on the Sixteenth day of September in the year one thousand nine hundred and sixty-three:

NOW in the name of God the Compassionate, the Merciful, I, TUNKU ABDUL RAHMAN PUTRA AL-HAJ IBNI ALMARHUM SULTAN ABDUL HAMID HALIM SHAH, Prime Minister of Malaysia, with the concurrence and approval of His Majesty the Yang di-Pertuan Agong of the Federation of Malaya, His Excellency the Yang di-Pertuan Negara of Singapore, His Excellency the Yang di-Pertua Negara of Sabah and His Excellency the Governor of Sarawak DO HEREBY DECLARE AND PROCLAIM on behalf of the peoples of Malaysia that as from the Sixteenth day of September in the year one thousand nine hundred and sixty-three, corresponding to the Twentyeighth day of Rabi'ul Akhir in the year of the Hijrah one thousand three hundred and eighty-three, that MALAYSIA comprising the States of Pahang, Trengganu, Kedah, Johore, Negri Sembilan, Kelantan, Selangor, Perak, Perlis, Penang, Malacca, Singapore, Sabah and Sarawak shall by the Grace of God, the Lord of the Universe, forever be an independent and sovereign democratic State founded upon liberty and justice, ever seeking to defend and uphold peace and harmony among its peoples and to perpetuate peace among nations.

Kuala Lumpur,
Sixteenth day of September, 1963.

Prime Minister.

430

The Malaysia Proclamation.

General Election 1963

431

431
A Barisan Sosialis member addressing a rally at Fullerton Square during the 1963 general election campaign. The main contenders in the 1963 general election, held on 21 September, were the People's Action Party (PAP), the Barisan Sosialis and a new Singapore Alliance comprising the remnants of the Singapore People's Alliance and the Singapore branches of the Malayan parties, UMNO and MCA.

It was obvious from the beginning that the main battle was going to be between the PAP and the Barisan Sosialis.

A number of Barisan Sosialis candidates were Nanyang University graduates. The election rallies provided them with the platform to whip up Chinese chauvinism by claiming that the government was killing Chinese language and culture.

432

433

432
Cheering supporters chair Lee Kuan Yew after the PAP's election victory in the 1963 general election. The PAP won 37 of the 51 seats and obtained 47.4 percent of the votes cast. The Barisan Sosialis mustered 32.1 percent of the votes, winning 13 seats. The remaining seat was won by Ong Eng Guan of the United People's Party. The Alliance obtained only eight percent of the votes cast and did not win any seat.

433
Three garlanded and obviously jubilant PAP victors. From left: Dr Toh Chin Chye (Rochore), Fong Sip Chee (Stamford), and Ho See Beng (Bras Basah).

The election was keenly fought. It was the first time that the PAP had taken on the pro-communists in a general election. Ninety-three percent of the electorate voted. In many constituencies there were four to five candidates. Ninety-two of the 149 defeated candidates lost their deposits.

In a few constituencies the defeated candidates lost by a narrow margin. The PAP chairman, Dr Toh Chin Chye, defeated Dr Lee Siew Choh (Barisan) in Rochore by 89 votes; K M Byrne (PAP) lost to S T Bani (Barisan) by 110 votes; and Madam Chan Choy Siong (PAP) beat the Barisan Sosialis candidate by 63 votes.

David Marshall, who stood as an independent in Anson constituency, lost to PAP's P Govindasamy. Six candidates had fought for this seat.

259

Further Action Against Pro-communists

434

434
In late September 1963, the police arrested a number of Nanyang University student leaders at the campus for pro-communist activities. Egged on by the pro-communists, the students boycotted classes. A few weeks later, in October, they staged a "Peace March" to City Hall to present a petition to the Prime Minister against a proposed reorganisation of their university.

They are seen here leaving the Padang. The placards and banners read "Nantah students petition for peace".

435

The day after the "Peace March", the pro-communist Singapore Association of Trade Unions (SATU) called for a two-day island-wide strike in protest against the "show-cause" notices issued to seven of its affiliated unions. When the notices were issued it had become clear that the SATU unions had channelled funds to support political and other causes not in keeping with trade union regulations. The strikes called by SATU failed and the seven unions were deregistered on 30 October. Two weeks later, on 12 November, SATU's application to be registered was rejected and several of its leaders were jailed.

SATU had actively championed strikes, many in support of communist united front activities. Between 1961 and 1963, 964,232 man-days were lost in strikes.

Towards a Better Life

436
The National Theatre, built as a memorial to mark the attainment of self-government and as a symbol affirming the people's faith in their ability to create a Malayan nation and culture. Citizens from all walks of life gave donations towards its building under a "dollar-a-brick" scheme. A total of $850,000 was raised from the public for the $2.2-million building.

436

438

437

437
A presentation of the Royal Ballet of Cambodia at the Southeast Asia Cultural Festival held to mark the opening of the National Theatre. At the centre of the stage is Princess Bupphadevi, daughter of Prince Norodom Sihanouk.

Apart from Malaysia, eight other countries — Cambodia, Hongkong, India, Laos, Pakistan, the Philippines, Vietnam and Thailand — presented items at the week-long festival held from 8 August 1963.

439

438

Tanglin Halt, one of the earliest housing estates developed by the Housing and Development Board.

By 1963, the Housing and Development Board had built about 32,000 low-cost flats and re-housed many slum dwellers.

440

441

439/440/441

An aerial view of the Pasir Panjang Power Station (left). In 1963 the Public Utilities Board was set up to coordinate the supply of water, electricity and gas to the increasing number of houses, shops, factories and schools.

The expansion of utilities saw street lighting (top) introduced in many rural areas and standpipes (above) installed in outlying villages for the use of residents who had no running water.

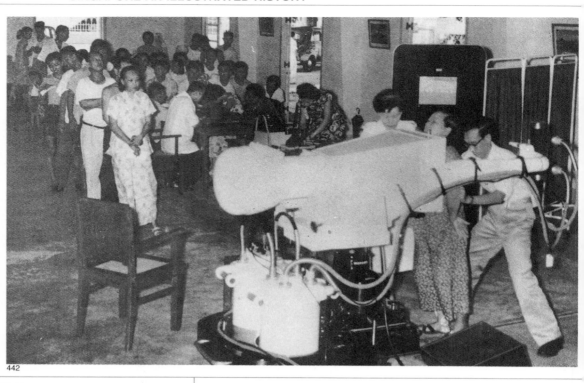

442
To control tuberculosis, the number one killer disease at the time, a mass X-ray campaign was launched. Between June 1959 and 1963, 381,724 people were given free X-rays.

443
Meet-the-People sessions, introduced by the PAP soon after it came to power in 1959, enabled the people to bring their problems and grouses to their Legislative Assemblymen. The regular weekly sessions helped the government to keep in close touch with the people.

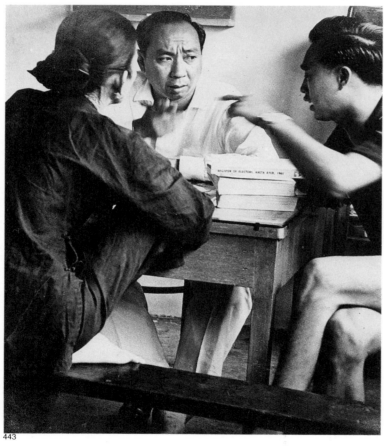

443

444

445

444

446

445
Members of the Tanglin Citizens' Consultative Committee with their Legislative Assemblyman and Minister for Law, E W Barker.

Soon after its re-election for a second term, the PAP Government set out to strengthen its ties with people at the grassroots level.

Lee Kuan Yew announced in the Legislative Assembly on 9 December 1963 the government's intention to establish a Citizens' Consultative Committee (CCC) of community leaders in each constituency. The committees were to serve as a bridge between the public and the government by bringing the needs and aspirations of the people to the attention of the government.

444
Lam Soon Village Community Centre (CC), one of the CCs built in the early 1960s. CCs functioned as multi-purpose institutions, providing both leisure activities and education, and drawing people from all walks of life to a common meeting place.

During the 14 months from November 1962 to December 1963, 121 community centres were built, 102 of them in rural areas. Centres in the rural areas were built of plank and zinc, but they provided the same recreational and educational amenities as the urban centres — vocational classes, basketball and badminton courts, ping-pong tables and television sets.

446
Children at play at one of the kindergarten classes run by the People's Association in its community centres.

265

8

STORMY YEARS IN MALAYSIA

447
The Malaysian Solidarity
Convention's mass rally at the
National Theatre on 6 June

1965. The Convention aimed to
achieve a non-communal
"Malaysian Malaysia".

1963~1965

When Singapore joined Malaysia it entered a new political setting and environment. Peninsular Malaysia was ruled by the United Malays National Organisation (UMNO) in partnership with the Malayan Chinese Association (MCA) and the Malayan Indian Congress (MIC). Political power was in the hands of the Malays and they were determined to keep it. At the apex of the federal system was the Agung, who was a constitutional monarch, while most of the states in Peninsular Malaysia had Sultans as titular heads. It was a more conservative political system than the one in Singapore.

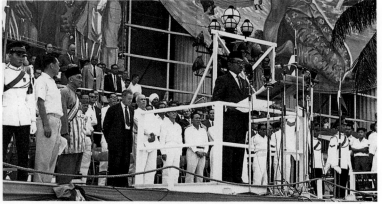

There were underlying racial sensitivities in the new federation. As the indigenous community, the Malays enjoyed special privileges in the Peninsula. But they were worried by the sympathy and support that sections of the Chinese community gave to left-wing political parties, including the Malayan Communist Party, and resentful of Chinese domination of the economy.

Singapore had a large Chinese majority, and a pre-dominantly ethnic Chinese government with proclaimed socialist goals and a commitment to rapid social change. The differences in the social and political systems and the ethnic character of the two territories therefore offered considerable potential for mutual suspicion and conflict. Singapore therefore had to assure the Malayan leaders that the Chinese majority in Singapore posed no threat to Malay rule in the federation.

Accordingly, Singapore acknowledged the special position of the Malays in the Peninsula. But the Central and Singapore governments still held divergent views on Malaysia's political and economic development.

Despite the signing of the Malaysia Agreement, the negotiations that preceded it had already introduced an element of friction between the leaders of both governments. Two major areas of discord had been the sharing of revenue and the common market issue. Singapore had pressed for a common market, but Malaya had tried to leave it out of the merger agreement. Malaya finally accepted its establishment in stages after Singapore reluctantly consented to contribute 40 percent instead of 30 percent of its revenue to the Central Government, and to provide a loan of $150 million for the development of Sabah and Sarawak, repayable over 15 years.

The negotiations leading up to the Malaysia Agreement had therefore been trying for both sides. Singapore's move in declaring *de facto* independence on 31 August 1963 instead of waiting for 16 September, the date to which Malaysia's formation had been postponed by Tunku Abdul Rahman, had also irked the Central Government.

The first open clash in the Malaysian Parliament came on 21 December 1963, when Lee Kuan Yew criticised the Malaysian budget, arguing that instead of improving social conditions, its tax provisions would create a more unequal distribution of wealth.

Singapore had expected merger to result in a common market and an increase of trade. Instead, Singapore's trade was badly affected by Indonesia's economic boycott against Malaysia, which cut off the island's barter trade with Indonesia; meanwhile, no progress was made towards forming the common market. Singapore therefore with-held the development loan to Sabah and Sarawak, declaring that it had agreed to the loan only on condition that the common market would be set up. Each side was soon accusing the other of dragging its feet, and Singapore industrialists began to complain that Kuala Lumpur was discriminating against Singapore in granting pioneer status certificates and allotting textile export quotas.

Economic tension heightened in December 1964 when the Central Government demanded a larger proportion of Singapore's revenue in order to meet the increased defence expenditure imposed by "confrontation". That same month, Kuala Lumpur also announced that it intended to close the Bank of China in Singapore. The bank played an important role in Singapore's trade with China, and also served as a channel for sending remittances to relatives in China. Despite Singapore's objections, the Central Government ordered the bank's closure in July 1965.

As the economic wrangling became more acrimonious, the political tensions increased. Soon after the 1963 Singapore general election, Singapore UMNO set out to reorganise its strength with the backing of Kuala Lumpur. The defeat of the UMNO/Alliance candidates in the two traditional Malay areas of Geylang Serai and Kampung Kembangan had shocked the Alliance in Peninsular Malaysia. They had expected the Singapore Malays to vote for the UMNO rather than the PAP candidates, and they openly showed displeasure.

The Alliance Government was further piqued when the PAP decided to put up a token number of candidates in the Malaysian general election scheduled for April 1964. The Alliance was a pan-Malayan organisation and it had contested the Singapore state elections in 1963 on that basis. The PAP therefore felt that it, too, should have a pan-Malayan character and a say in peninsular politics. However, from the outset the PAP made it clear that it was challenging the MCA, not UMNO. In fact, two of its candidates did not campaign in Johor when they found themselves in straight fights with UMNO candidates. The PAP claimed that it would be a more effective partner of UMNO within the Alliance than the MCA, because it would be better able to enlist the support of the Chinese population, which, it believed, needed a progressive, dynamic political leadership committed to rapid social change if it was not to turn increasingly to the left-wing Socialist Front or the communists. In its manifesto for the Malaysian general election, the PAP stated that it wanted to help the Central Government to build a united, democratic and socialist Malaysia, based on principles of social justice and non-communalism.

UMNO, however, read the PAP's participation in the April 1964 general election as a direct challenge to its Malay-based political system, while the MCA regarded the PAP as a threat to its position in the Alliance. The large crowds which attended the PAP rallies did little to allay these fears. And despite the PAP's conscious efforts to stress its non-communal stand, certain UMNO leaders — and Jaafar Albar, the secretary-general of UMNO, in particular – began to present the PAP challenge along communal lines.

On polling day, 25 April 1964, the PAP won only one of the 11 seats it contested. This was the constituency of Bungsar, which elected Devan Nair as its MP. The PAP had gone into the election in a hurry,

with little back-up organisation. It found that the non-Malay electorate in the Peninsula was not yet ready to switch its traditional support for the MCA and MIC to the PAP, nor was it at home with the PAP's style of politics. The ruling Alliance won 125 of the 159 seats in the lower house of Parliament, the *Dewan Rakyat*. As the PAP already had 12 representatives of the Singapore Legislative Assembly in the federal legislature, the additional member for Bungsar made it the leading opposition party.

The PAP's poor electoral showing, however, did not reduce tensions, and its post-election announcement that it planned to open branches in all states where it had contested only worsened matters. In consequence, Lee Kuan Yew reiterated in the *Dewan Rakyat* in May 1964 that the PAP would remain a loyal opposition and help to create a harmonious, non-communal society in which prosperity would be more equally shared among all men regardless of race, language or religion. The extremists in UMNO regarded this as a criticism of the existing political order. Their attacks on Singapore leaders intensified and both sides began charging each other of communalism.

At a convention of representatives from a wide spectrum of Malay bodies held in Singapore in July 1964, the UMNO-sponsors — notably Jaafar Albar — attacked the Singapore Government for allegedly discriminating against the local Malays. The meeting adopted a resolution demanding that they be given special rights and privileges, as they were on the mainland. The Malay press, especially the *Utusan Melayu*, which often reflected the views of UMNO, took up the cry.

The tension created by all this agitation finally erupted into racial riots in Singapore on 21 July 1964 when fights broke out during a Muslim procession on Prophet Muhammad's birthday. As rioting spread, the whole island was put under curfew, but the disturbances continued for a week. By the time the curfew was completely lifted, 23 people had been killed and 454 injured. Goodwill committees were established in every constituency to normalise the situation, and the Singapore Prime Minister toured the island, emphasising that the communal riots had been the work of a few extre-

mists and urging the people of Singapore not to be manipulated by the demagogues. Tunku Abdul Rahman and his deputy, Tun Abdul Razak, also toured Singapore to help calm things down.

Lingering hostility and fear again led to communal violence in early September, this time provoked by Indonesian agents. Twelve people were killed and 109 injured, and although law and order was again restored within a week, tension persisted.

Distressed by these communal clashes, Tunku Abdul Rahman and Lee Kuan Yew agreed in late September 1964 to avoid for two years any public discussion of sensitive issues which could inflame communal feelings, and to stop public recriminations between the two governments. But the agreement failed to end the conflict and the acrimony continued. By the end of 1964, Lee Kuan Yew was being described by the extremists in UMNO as a communalist and an enemy of Malaysia. The PAP, on the other hand, was calling for a Malaysia that would be for all Malaysians, not for any one community.

In May 1965, the PAP took matters further when, together with four opposition parties from Peninsular Malaysia and Sarawak, it formed a Malaysian Solidarity Convention with the aim of achieving a non-communal, multi-racial "Malaysian Malaysia".

The Convention's formation in Singapore on 9 May 1965 exacerbated UMNO's animosity towards the PAP. The Central Government viewed the Convention as a conspiracy of opposition parties bent on unseating it.

When the *Dewan Rakyat* met on 27 May 1965, the dispute between the PAP and the Alliance had assumed explosive proportions. The Yang di-Pertuan Agung's address referred to an unspecified "enemy within" the state. Lee Kuan Yew's arguments for a Malaysian Malaysia were rejected, and in winding up the debate, Tun Abdul Razak said that the "gulf that divides the PAP and us, the Alliance, is now wide and clear".

In the middle of all this, Ong Eng Guan suddenly

resigned from the Singapore Legislative Assembly. The by-election in July for his Hong Lim seat was a straight fight between the PAP and the Barisan Sosialis. The PAP candidate, Lee Khoon Choy, won the seat with an impressive majority. But the fast deteriorating relations between the Alliance in Malaysia and the PAP worsened further because the *Utusan Melayu*, which generally reflected UMNO's views, had come out in open support of the Barisan Sosialis candidate.

By this time Tunku Abdul Rahman, in London for the Commonwealth Prime Ministers' Conference and kept there by illness, had received reports from his Cabinet which indicated that the dangerous build-up of pressures could lead to communal clashes. Faced with demands for the arrest of Lee Kuan Yew and other PAP ministers, Tunku Abdul Rahman felt that the only way to prevent unnecessary bloodshed was to separate Singapore from Malaysia.

Tunku Abdul Rahman's return to Malaysia on 5 August set in motion the rapid chain of events leading to the break-up. On 6 August, Lee Kuan Yew and a few of his ministers were told that Singapore must leave Malaysia immediately. The Singapore Prime Minister tried unsuccessfully to persuade Tunku Abdul Rahman to modify this drastic decision, and suggested other solutions, even a looser federation. Finally, however, he agreed to the separation. Two Singapore ministers, Dr Toh Chin Chye and S Rajaratnam, at first refused to sign the Separation Agreement. Tunku Abdul Rahman wrote to Dr Toh Chin Chye, Singapore's Deputy Prime Minister, in order to convince him that the "amicable settlement of our differences in this way is the only possible way out".

On 9 August the *Dewan Rakyat* passed the Bill approving separation with 126 in favour and none against. All the Singapore representatives were absent from the *Dewan Rakyat*. That same day, the Singapore Prime Minister proclaimed the island a sovereign, democratic and independent state.

At a TV press conference that afternoon, the Prime Minister stated that Tunku Abdul Rahman had told him that if there was no break there would be serious communal conflict. For he could no longer keep the situation under control. After this, Lee Kuan Yew had agreed that there was nothing for it but to separate. The

Prime Minister added that when Singapore was in Malaysia his government had had to take a firm stand against communal politics and pressures — "any other kind of Malaysia than a Malaysian Malaysia (was) unacceptable". He also stressed that after separation it was his desire to see close cooperation between the two countries on a fair and equal basis.

Singapore's sudden eviction came as a shock, but the people accepted the news calmly. The general mood of anxiety over Singapore's future was mixed with a sense of relief at being free from all the communal bickering that had soured relations between Kuala Lumpur and Singapore.

Indonesian "confrontation" had continued throughout the period that Singapore was part of Malaysia. Trained saboteurs were sent to attack military installations and public utilities and to mount a campaign of terrorism to wreck the economy and to weaken the will of the people. Despite the British naval patrols and the efforts of the Singapore police, small groups of saboteurs managed to infiltrate the island to plant bombs. The most serious bomb explosion at MacDonald House, in Orchard Road, killed three people and injured 33. Indonesian propaganda and Indonesian agents also tried to incite communal conflict in an atmosphere which was already charged with tension because of the deteriorating relations between the Singapore Government and the Malaysian Central Government.

During the years in Malaysia the people of Singapore learned what communal politics and communal conflict meant: communalism had proved to be not only as dangerous a threat as communism, but more irrational and unpredictable. In Indonesian "confrontation" they also experienced the threat of external aggression against which they had no defence of their own.

Explaining Malaysia Overseas

448

450

449

448
In late January 1964, Lee Kuan Yew, on behalf of the Malaysian Government, headed a 12-member Malaysian Goodwill Mission to 17 African states and India to counter Indonesian propaganda against Malaysia. The mission's first stop was the United Arab Republic (Egypt). In Kenya, Lee Kuan Yew met Jomo Kenyatta, the Prime Minister (above).

449
(Below)Members of the mission with President Nyerere of Tanganyika (Tanzania) and his ministers. President Nyerere (in checked shirt) is seen here with Lee Kuan Yew (left) and Stephen Kalong Ningkan, Sarawak's Chief Minister (third from left). Dato Ganie Gilong, an MP from Sabah, is on the extreme right (nearest camera).

450
On the way home, the mission stopped at New Delhi. Lee Kuan Yew is seen with India's Prime Minister, Jawaharlal Nehru.

449

PAP Contests Malaysian Elections

451

451

Six of the PAP candidates who contested the Malaysian parliamentary and state assembly elections in April 1964. The PAP put up a token 11 candidates in urban areas in the parliamentary constituencies.

The Alliance had contested the Singapore state elections in 1963, and after the elections, UMNO and MCA had moved to strengthen their organisations in Singapore. The PAP now felt that it too should have a pan-Malayan character and a say in peninsular politics. It made clear that its intention was not to challenge Malay/UMNO supremacy in Malayan politics.

452

452

Lee Kuan Yew is mobbed by enthusiastic crowds at one of the PAP rallies in West Malaysia during the election campaign, which lasted from 21 March to 24 April 1964.

453

453
Devan Nair, the only PAP candidate to win, is chaired by jubilant supporters. He won in Bungsar constituency.

The PAP's participation in the elections in the Peninsula was viewed by Alliance leaders as a challenge not only to the MCA but to the Malay-based political system. This placed further strains on Singapore-Kuala Lumpur relations. The situation was aggravated by communalists who portrayed the PAP as a Chinese communal party threatening Malay interests.

Charges of communalism continued to be exchanged between Singapore leaders and certain leaders in UMNO who also started calling for special rights and privileges for Singapore Malays.

Communal Riots

454

455

456

454
The atmosphere of communal distrust and suspicion was soon to lead to an outbreak of racial violence in Singapore. During a Muslim procession (above) on 21 July 1964 to celebrate Prophet Muhammad's birthday, a scuffle broke out between some Malays and Chinese which led to rioting.

455/456
Word of the fighting spread and riots soon broke out in other parts of the island. Vehicles were burnt, houses set on fire, and innocent people attacked.

457

457
The whole island was immediately placed under a curfew and barricades, like this one in New Bridge Road, appeared on the roads. By the time the curfew ended on 2 August, 23 people were dead and 454 injured.

458
The curfew was lifted for a few hours daily to enable the people to buy food and other necessities. Armed troops were around to prevent any outbreak of incidents.

458

459
The Malaysian Deputy Prime Minister, Tun Abdul Razak (with walking stick) and a few of his Cabinet colleagues visited Singapore to help calm the people. Together with several Singapore ministers, he visited the injured in the hospitals and toured the troubled areas.

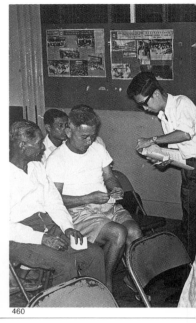

459

460
Minister for Social Affairs, Othman Wok, and P Govindasamy, a Legislative Assemblyman, at one of the relief centres set up for the riot victims.

461
Prime Minister Lee Kuan Yew and other Singapore ministers toured all 51 constituencies. They urged the people not to be manipulated by demagogues bent on creating discord between the different races.

461

462

462
Goodwill committees comprising leaders of the major ethnic communities were also established in every constituency. Committee members moved among the residents allaying fears and doubts. The government distributed food parcels to affected people.

Jek Yeun Thong, Minister for Labour, distributes food parcels during one such visit.

463

463
Tunku Abdul Rahman, who had been away in the United States when the riots took place, toured the affected areas with Lee Kuan Yew on his return in August.

464

464
As normalcy was slowly returning, Indonesian agents exploited the lingering tension to incite fresh communal violence on 3 September 1964. Another senseless and bloody riot followed and curfew was imposed again. The violence was checked before it became widespread, but not before 12 people were killed and 109 injured. The Minister for Social Affairs, Othman Wok, and several other Assemblymen tour one of the affected areas.

Indonesian Confrontation

465

Indonesia had stepped up its "confrontation" against Malaysia. Indonesian troops made incursions into Sabah and Sarawak. There were landings in Johor and more sabotage incidents in Singapore. Sukarno called for volunteers to fight Malaysia.

(Below) Some youths at an anti-Malaysia rally in Jakarta on 24 March 1964 carry "Crush Malaysia" banners.

465

466

466/467

In Singapore, as Indonesian terrorist activities continued, men between 21 and 29 years of age were called up for national service. A voluntary Vigilante Corps was also set up on 22 April 1964. By the end of June, more than 10,000 people, both young and old, had volunteered for the Corps. By mid-May, about 75,000 out of an estimated 82,000 eligible persons had registered for national service.

467

278

468

468
Members of the Vigilante Corps, identified by dark blue armbands stamped with the letters "VC", on patrol.

469
Men of the Second Battalion, Singapore Infantry Regiment (SIR), in the jungles of Johor, Malaysia. The SIR was deployed to combat armed Indonesian infiltrators in Malaysia.

469

470

471

470/471/472
By mid-1964, as bomb explosions became frequent, students underwent bomb drills, and Singaporeans were warned not to handle any suspicious-looking parcels in buildings or along streets. By March 1965, 29 bombs had been set off, causing damage to private and public property.

These pictures illustrate the damage caused by Indonesian saboteurs. The explosion at a block of HDB flats at Jalan Rebong on 12 April 1964 (right) killed two men.

473

473
The scene outside MacDonald House (below) moments after a powerful bomb exploded within the building on 10 March 1965, causing extensive damage and strewing glass splinters onto the street. Three people were killed and 33 others injured, seven of them seriously. Two Indonesian marines subsequently found guilty of the bombing were sentenced to death.

472

474

474
An ambush by the Indonesians at Kota Tinggi resulted in the death of eight SIR soldiers. Singapore's Deputy Prime Minister, Dr Toh Chin Chye (with coat, foreground), at the funeral of one of the soldiers.

475
Suspected Indonesian infiltrators are escorted from a mangrove swamp in Pasir Panjang on 29 December 1964.
   Local security forces, working in close cooperation with British forces, succeeded in rounding up many infiltrators and saboteurs and in keeping terrorism generally under control.

475

Singapore-Kuala Lumpur Rift Widens

476

476

The Malaysian Solidarity Convention was formed on 9 May 1965 by the PAP and four opposition parties in Malaysia. The Convention's aim was to create a democratic, non-communal "Malaysian Malaysia".

On 6 June, the Convention held its first mass rally at the National Theatre. Singapore's Deputy Prime Minister, Dr Toh Chin Chye, addresses the rally.

The Convention's symbol featured four interlocked arms signifying racial unity and solidarity.

477

Members of the Malaysian Solidarity Convention. The Convention comprised representatives from the PAP, the People's Progressive Party (PPP), United Democratic Party (UDP), Sarawak United People's Party (SUPP) and the Machinda Party. The heads of the component parties (seated, from left): Stephen Yong (SUPP); M Buma (Machinda); Dr Toh Chin Chye (PAP); Dr Lim Chong Eu (UDP); and D R Seenivasagam (PPP).

477

478

479

478
The Yang di-Pertuan Agung,
the Malaysian King, opens the
Malaysian Parliament on
27 May 1965. The Singapore
delegation is seated in the
opposition bench on the
right.

    In his opening address, the
Agung referred to an
unspecified "enemy within" the
state. But the UMNO
backbenchers were more
explicit in portraying the PAP
as a Chinese communal party.

479
Lee Kuan Yew and some of the
other Singapore representatives
in the Malaysian Parliament
during the sitting on 27 May
1965.

    The inauguration of the
Malaysian Solidarity
Convention had angered many
in UMNO. Lee Kuan Yew
became the target of sharp
criticism.

480

In Singapore, Ong Eng Guan suddenly resigned from the Assembly on 16 June 1965, forcing a by-election in Hong Lim. The by-election was a straight fight between Lee Khoon Choy of the PAP and Ong Chang Sam of the Barisan Sosialis. The Malaysian Malay press came out in open support of the Barisan Sosialis candidate.

(Left) The PAP candidate, Lee Khoon Choy (third from left) touring the Hong Lim constituency.

481

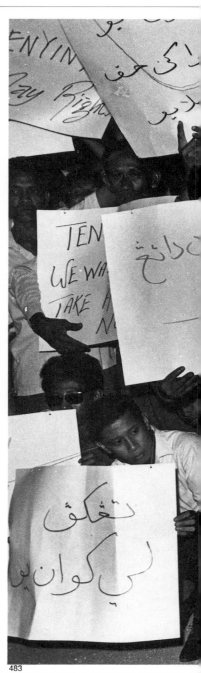

481
At the polls on 10 July, Lee Khoon Choy won the Hong Lim seat.

483

482

482/483
The political and communal atmosphere worsened. The Malaysian Prime Minister, who was away in London, was informed by his government that communal tensions were building up and could result in racial violence. He was soon faced with demands for strong action to deal with the PAP.

On his way back from London, Tunku Abdul Rahman stopped in Singapore on 5 August. At Paya Lebar Airport, he is greeted by some UMNO supporters carrying placards (left and below) denouncing Lee Kuan Yew.

The Separation

Telephone No. 4432

Prime Minister,
Federation of Malaya,
Kuala Lumpur

My dear Chin Chye,

I am writing to tell you that I have given the matter of our break with S'pore my utmost consideration and I find that in the interest of our friendship and the security and peace of Malaysia as a whole there is absolutely no other way out.

If I were strong enough and able to exercise complete control of the situation I might perhaps have delayed action, but I am not, and so while I am able to counsel tolerance and patience I think the amicable settlement of our differences in this way is the only possible way out.

I request you most earnestly to agree.

Kind regards

Yrs sincerely

Abdul Rahman

PM L—W 3639

Deputy PRIME MINISTER,
SINGAPORE.

8th August 1965

My dear Tunku,

I thank you for your undated letter which I received yesterday explaining your position and your solution to the present difficulties that have arisen between the Central government and the Singapore government. It is indeed sad that in your view our problems can be solved only by asking Singapore to quit Malaysia and this barely two years from the day Malaysia was inaugurated.

My colleagues and I would prefer that Singapore remain in Malaysia and we felt that there could be other solutions to the present impasse. However as you have indicated that the situation does not lend itself to any other workable settlement and as you have impressed upon me that Singapore remaining in Malaysia

PM L—W 3639

PRIME MINISTER,
SINGAPORE.

will lead to a situation you may not be able to control, we have no alternative but to be resigned to your wish that Singapore leaves the Federation of Malaysia.

I & my colleagues had rejoiced at the re-unification of Singapore with Malaya in September 1963. It has come as a blow to us that the peace and security of Malaysia can only be secured by the expulsion of Singapore from Malaysia. If this is the price for peace in Malaya and Singapore then we must accept it however agonising our inner feelings may be. Although lasting unification of Singapore and Malaya has not been achieved this time, nevertheless it is my profound belief that future generations will succeed where we have failed.

484
Tunku Abdul Rahman and his Cabinet decided to separate Singapore from Malaysia. On being informed of the decision on 6 August, Lee Kuan Yew discussed the matter with Dr Toh Chin Chye, Dr Goh Keng Swee and S Rajaratnam in Kuala Lumpur, and then tried to persuade Tunku Abdul Rahman to consider other alternatives to separation, such as a looser federation. However, the Malaysian Prime Minister remained firm. On 7 August he wrote to Dr Toh Chin Chye explaining his decision.

485
Dr Toh's reply to the Malaysian Prime Minister.

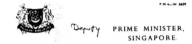

Deputy PRIME MINISTER, SINGAPORE

In order that my friends and political colleagues in the other states of Malaya and particularly those in the Malaysian Solidarity Convention may know my true feelings on this matter I may have at some future date to tell them of the true position

With kind regards

Yours Sincerely
Toh Chin Chye

Prime Minister's Office,
Singapore.

Proclamation of Singapore

WHEREAS it is the inalienable right of a people to be free and independent:

AND WHEREAS Malaysia was established on the 16th day of September, 1963, by a federation of existing states of the Federation of Malaya and the States of Sabah, Sarawak and Singapore into one independent and sovereign nation:

AND WHEREAS by an Agreement made on the seventh day of August in the year one thousand nine hundred and sixty-five between the Government of Malaysia of the one part and the Government of Singapore of the other part it was agreed that Singapore should cease to be a state of Malaysia and should thereupon become an independent and sovereign state and nation separate from and independent of Malaysia;

AND WHEREAS it was also agreed by the parties to the said Agreement that, upon the separation of Singapore from Malaysia, the Government of Malaysia shall relinquish its sovereignty and jurisdiction in respect of Singapore so that the said sovereignty and jurisdiction shall on such relinquishment vest in the Government of Singapore;

AND WHEREAS by a Proclamation dated the ninth day of August in the year one thousand nine hundred and sixty-five the Prime Minister of Malaysia Tunku Abdul Rahman Putra Al-Haj Ibni Almarhum Sultan Abdul Hamid Halim Shah did proclaim and declare that Singapore shall on the ninth day of August in the year one thousand nine hundred and sixty-five cease to be a state of Malaysia and shall become an independent and sovereign state and nation separate from and independent of Malaysia and recognised as such by the Government of Malaysia.

Now I LEE KUAN YEW Prime Minister of Singapore, DO HEREBY PROCLAIM AND DECLARE on behalf of the people and the Government of Singapore that as from today the ninth day of August in the year one thousand nine hundred and sixty-five Singapore shall be forever a sovereign democratic and independent nation, founded upon the principles of liberty and justice and ever seeking the welfare and happiness of her people in a more just and equal society.

Prime Minister, Singapore

Dated the 9th day of August, 1965.

486

486
On 9 August 1965, less than two years after Malaysia was formed, the Federal Parliament passed the Bill approving separation, with 126 in favour and none against. The Singapore representatives were absent. That same day, Lee Kuan Yew issued the Proclamation making Singapore a sovereign and independent nation.

487

488

487/488
On the afternoon of 9 August, in an emotion-charged TV press conference, Lee Kuan Yew explained why separation could not be avoided and appealed for calm among the people. Visibly moved, he told Singaporeans and the world:
   "For me, it is a moment of anguish. All my life, my whole adult life, I have believed in merger and unity of the two territories."

9

THE MAKING OF A NATION

489
The National Day Parade at the Padang in 1966, in which 23,000 people presented a rhythmic and colourful display. It was the first after separation from Malaysia.

1965~1970

Singapore, which had all along assumed that it could survive and prosper only in union with Malaya, found on 9 August 1965 that it had to work out its destiny and survival on its own.

There were many who thought that the small island, with nearly two million people and no natural resources, would not be viable as an independent nation. Industrialisation had not made any significant progress. Indonesian "confrontation" was still on. Singapore had no defence capability of its own.

Nevertheless, the people and leaders of Singapore were determined to succeed. The population was hard-working, adaptive and keen to learn. Politically, the tensions and constraints associated with being part of Malaysia were over and the destructive capacity of the local communists had been reduced. The world economy was booming and the giant industrial organisations of the developed countries were looking for attractive off-shore sites on which to set up manufacturing bases.

Singapore's strategy for survival and development was essentially to take advantage of the favourable factors in the world economy and of its own strategic location through sound policies and firm direction. To this end it was essential to ensure political stability and industrial peace and to develop human resources. Government policies sought to foster unity, discipline, hard work and the acquisition of technical skills, while at the same time nurturing a Singaporean identity. It was imperative that the communists and the communalists be kept in check.

Two days after separation from Malaysia, the government announced that Singapore was to become a Republic. Malay, Chinese, English and Tamil continued as the new Republic's official languages, while Malay was retained as the national language. The Legislative Assembly became Parliament. The Head of State became the President of the Republic, to be elected every four years by Parliament. August 9, the day of Singapore's independence, was designated National Day.

The government was determined that there be no discrimination against minorities. A 11-man Constitutional Commission on Minority Rights was formed in December 1965 to recommend ways of safeguarding the rights of minority groups. On the recommendations of the Commission, a Presidential Council was set up in May 1970 to ensure that no bills or subsidiary legislation would discriminate against them.

In the political arena, the Barisan Sosialis denounced Singapore's independence as "phoney" and a British ploy to retain their military bases on the island. In line with this stand, the Barisan Sosialis members boycotted Parliament when it convened in December 1965. Parliament passed, by a two-third majority, the Singapore Independence Bill and the Constitution Amendment

Bill. Of the 13 Barisan Sosialis members who had won their seats at the 1963 general election, three had already been detained in 1963, and two others had fled, presumably to Indonesia. In January 1966 four Barisan Sosialis MPs resigned and in October the remaining seven quit, stating that they would carry on their party's "struggle against imperialist aggression outside Parliament".

Though the capacity of the pro-communists to cause serious trouble had declined, they were still able to exploit discontent among students, especially at Nanyang University which had been a prime target of communist subversion for some time. In October 1965 Nanyang University students showed resentment with the Wang Gungwu Report, which recommended the raising of academic standards and a greater use of English as a medium of instruction. Condemning the Report as another attempt by the government to "destroy" Chinese education, students boycotted classes in October and November, threatened their lecturers with violence, and tried to set fire to their dormitories. The university expelled 85 student agitators, nearly half of them Malaysians. Despite this action, the students organised house-to-house campaigns and processions in city areas. Subsequently, 44 were arrested.

Student unrest over the government's Amendment Bill on Nanyang University and the Wang Gungwu Report surfaced again in October 1966. It coincided with agitation by Ngee Ann College Students' Union against the Thong Saw Pak Report which recommended a reorganisation of Ngee Ann College, including changes in its syllabus. Nanyang University and Ngee Ann College student militants supported each other in their campaign against alleged "destruction" of Chinese education, and in November 1966, 117 pro-communist students were expelled from Nanyang University. Ngee Ann students organised a protest march to City Hall that ended in a riot in which eight policemen and three civilians were injured. Ngee Ann students continued agitating and holding "sit-ins". This resulted in 81 students being expelled from the college.

In line with their "extra-parliamentary struggle" the Barisan Sosialis also mounted agitation against the National Service Bill and amendments made to the Trade Union Ordinance. They called for a general strike on 3 April 1967, and demonstrations, hunger strikes by pro-communist detainees, and a "sit-down" campaign outside Changi Prison followed. The government was compelled to take firm action if it was to make headway in attracting manufacturing investments to Singapore. Three trade unions which heeded the call for the illegal strike on 3 April 1967 were deregistered, and many demonstrators were sentenced to prison.

In the face of stern government action, the "extra-parliamentary struggle" failed. The Barisan Sosialis lost ground in the trade unions, and schisms developed within the party itself. Added to this, the Barisan Sosialis was also deprived of valuable allies abroad when the Sukarno Government was replaced by the anti-communist Suharto Government in Indonesia, and the PKI was destroyed. These factors, combined with their decision to boycott Parliament and the 1968 general election, resulted in a drastic reduction of Barisan Sosialis influence in national politics.

An immediate priority of the government after the separation from Malaysia was to gain international recognition as an independent state and to establish friendly relations with other countries. S Rajaratnam, hitherto Minister for Culture, became the Foreign Minister. Malaysia was the first country to recognise Singapore's independence, and by mid-September, 41 nations, including 21 from Asia and Africa, had followed suit. On 21 September 1965 Singapore was unanimously admitted to the United Nations as its 117th member. In October, Singapore became the 22nd member of the Commonwealth. In February 1967, it joined the Afro-Asian People's Solidarity Organisation.

As a small country situated in a turbulent part of the world and dependent on trade and commerce for its survival, Singapore adopted a pragmatic foreign policy of friendship with as many countries as possible, irrespective of their ideology, so long as they did not engage in hostile acts against Singapore. Special attention was paid to establishing good relations with neighbours. Singapore also declared that it would be non-aligned in relation to the conflicts and rivalries of the two main world power blocs.

Indonesian "confrontation" ended on 12 August 1966 following the assumption of power in Jakarta by the Suharto Government. On 8 August 1967 Singapore joined Indonesia, Malaysia, the Philippines and Thailand in forming ASEAN, the Association of Southeast Asian Nations, to promote regional cooperation.

An urgent priority after separation was to build up Singapore's own defence capability. Singapore's armed forces had to be created virtually from scratch. The government realised that, given a small population and the need for manpower for the civilian sector, it would be too costly to maintain a large standing army. It was therefore decided that Singapore's defence would be based upon a citizens' army backed by trained reserves. Compulsory national service for young men from all the different ethnic, cultural and social backgrounds would also help in nation building.

Since military service had traditionally been held in low esteem by the predominantly Chinese population of the island, it was necessary to educate the public about the need for national service. The people of Singapore, mainly descendants of migrants who had not considered Singapore as their permanent home, had been accustomed to regard the defence of the island as the responsibility of the colonial rulers. They had to be reminded that they themselves were now the owners of Singapore and hence had to discharge their obligation for its defence.

Soon after independence a Ministry of Interior and Defence was set up under Dr Goh Keng Swee.

On 23 December 1965, Parliament passed the Singapore Army Bill 1965. The Singapore Armed Forces Training Institute was established in 1966 to train officers and NCOs for the army. On 14 March 1967 the National Service Amendment Bill was passed, making registration for national service of all males who had reached the age of 18 compulsory. The first batch of national servicemen was drafted in July 1967. As the infantry expanded, supporting arms such as signals, artillery and combat engineers were also created.

When the defence build-up started the government assumed that it had eight to 10 years to develop a military capability before the British military forces withdrew from Singapore. However, in January 1968 the British Government announced that their military presence in Singapore would end in 1971, contradicting the assurances given six months earlier that only about half of their forces would be withdrawn by 1970/1971, and that complete withdrawal would take place only in the mid-1970s. Singapore now had less than four years in which to develop a military capability.

A Singapore Air Defence Command was established in 1968 and its first pilots were trained abroad. The Singapore Maritime Command was also established in

1968 and given the task of building up a small navy. In early 1969 army officers were sent abroad to be instructed in the use of the AMX-13 tank. In July 1970 the first battalion of the Tank Regiment was formed.

The British Government's sudden decision to bring forward the date of the withdrawal of their armed forces from Singapore threw into disarray not only the Republic's defence but also its economic development plans. In 1967 British military expenditure in Singapore amounted to $489.9 million annually or about 15 percent of Singapore's Gross National Product. About 40,000 people were working directly for the British forces and thousands of others were indirectly dependent on the British military presence for their employment and income. In 1967 there were already about 50,000 unemployed persons in Singapore while about 25,000 teenagers entered the job market each year. Industrial expansion since 1963, however, had resulted in an annual net increase of only 5,000 to 6,000 jobs.

After Singapore separated from Malaysia, it had launched a concerted industrialisation drive in order to solve its unemployment problem. The Jurong Industrial Estate was extended and more infrastructure facilities were built. Smaller industrial estates were created in Kallang Park, Tanjong Rhu, Redhill, Tiong Bahru and Tanglin Halt. Technical education to meet the needs of modern industry was expanded. As a result of these efforts, and because of the resumption of trade with Indonesia, the expansion of exports to Vietnam, and an increase in earnings from tourism, the Singapore economy was making good progress by 1967.

But now new policies were required to cope with the consequences of the accelerated British military withdrawal. In April 1968 the PAP went to the polls to seek a fresh mandate from the people. On Nomination Day, 17 February 1968, the PAP candidates were returned unopposed in 51 of the 58 constituencies. On election day the party won all the seven seats contested, obtaining 84.4 percent of the votes cast. For the first time, Singapore had a one-party Parliament. The Barisan Sosialis had boycotted the election, and the Singapore People's Alliance and the UMNO-

MCA Alliance had not contested. The PAP was challenged by only two Workers' Party candidates and five independents.

With the clear mandate from the people the government proceeded to implement a series of measures to deal with the problems posed by the British military withdrawal.

The Employment Act and the Industrial Relations (Amendment) Act which were enacted in August 1968 defined the rights and obligations of employers and employees, reduced the number of public holidays, restricted overtime and bonus payments which had been subjected to abuse, and gave employers more authority in hiring, promoting, transferring or dismissing employees. As a result the government was able to enforce discipline and industrial peace while providing avenues for workers to seek redress from unjust employers. The National Trades Union Congress, while initially expressing fears that labour might be exploited, accepted the curbs as necessary for Singapore's industrial development and thus for the long-term good of the workers.

The new labour laws helped to dispel the image of a strike-prone workforce created in the 1950s and 1960s

when there were numerous politically-motivated stoppages. 1969 became the first strike-free year. Labour disputes became so rare that in January 1970 the second Industrial Arbitration Court was closed for lack of business.

In mid-1968 the Economic Development Board was reorganised and in June 1968, the Jurong Town Corporation was formed to manage and develop Jurong and the other industrial estates. The Development Bank of Singapore, set up in 1968, took over development financing operations from the Economic Development Board, which was left to concentrate on investment promotion. Under the Economic Expansion Incentives Act of 1967, the government was able to offer a package of fiscal incentives ranging from tax relief of up to five years to unrestricted repatriation of profits and capital to investors willing to launch industries favoured by the government.

The atmosphere of industrial peace, together with investment promotion and supporting operations, attracted an influx of foreign investors. By the end of 1970, 271 factories were operating in Jurong, while another 103 were under construction. Direct foreign investments in fixed assets in manufacturing industries stood at $1,700 million.

Plans were drawn up and implemented to use the lands, buildings and other facilities of the British military bases for productive economic and commercial purposes and to retrain the workers for new jobs. In February 1968 a Bases Economic Conversion Department was set up for this purpose. In June, Sembawang Shipyard Ltd, a fully government-owned shipyard, was formed to take over the King George VI Dock at the Naval Base and to convert it for commercial use. Sembawang Shipyard, managed by the British Swan Hunter Group, began shiprepairing operations on 1 December 1968 with more than 3,000 workers retrenched by the Naval Base. By the 1970s Sembawang Shipyard was a highly successful and profitable company.

In August 1966 the Singapore and Malaysian governments decided to have separate currencies. Singapore opted for a fully convertible currency with 100 percent backing in reserves; the new currency was issued in June 1967. Policies to develop Singapore as a financial and banking centre were initiated in 1968 and foreign banks were encouraged to start operations on the island. Withholding tax on interest payable to non-resident depositors was abolished to pave the way for the establishment of the Asian Dollar Market from November 1968. Exchange controls were liberalised, and tax incentives introduced to promote the growth of banking activity and the expansion of financial expertise through the development of training facilities. In 1970 the Monetary Authority of Singapore was established to formulate and implement Singapore's monetary policies, and supervise and regulate the financial system.

Public housing remained high on the government's list of priorities. However, while the first five-year plan concentrated on "emergency" and "standard" one- and two-room units, the second five-year plan launched in 1966 saw the introduction of better quality one-room to three-room low-cost housing. The Home Ownership for the People scheme which had been launched in 1964 offered public housing units for sale well below market prices. To enable as many people as possible to own homes, buyers were allowed to use their Central Provident Fund savings for downpayments and monthly mortgage payments as from 1968.

Since the population growth was still too rapid, the government launched a family planning programme in 1966 and set up the Singapore Family Planning and Population Board to implement it. A combination of incentives and disincentives, coupled with professional advice on family planning and contraception, succeeded in reducing the crude birth rate from 29.9 births per 1,000 population in 1965 to 22.1 per 1,000 population by 1970.

In foreign affairs, two of Singapore's primary concerns during the first five years of independence were the continuation of security and stability in Southeast Asia, and the improvement of relations with Malaysia and Indonesia.

This improvement could take place only gradually. The memories of Indonesian "confrontation" and of conflicts while Singapore was in Malaysia were still fresh. They tended to be revived by the painful post-separation adjustments between Singapore and Malaysia as two independent nations, and by the residual effects of "confrontation".

Malaysia and Singapore still had a number of joint institutions and arrangements at the time of separation. In the next few years a number of them were to be dismantled. The initiatives to do so and the associated discussions inevitably produced some unhappiness and friction. In February 1966 the continued stationing of Malaysian troops in Singapore became a thorny problem until they were withdrawn on Singapore's insistence. In August 1966 the two governments decided to issue separate currencies. In April 1967 Malaysia imposed controls on Singaporeans travelling to Malaysia, and in June, Singapore did the same to Malaysians travelling to Singapore. Thus for the first time Singaporeans and Malaysians needed travel documents to visit each other's country. Slowly, however, the two neighbours began to get used to the idea that they were two separate, sovereign nations with interests which did not always coincide, but whose geography, economies and security dictated that there must be mutual understanding and co-operation.

Relations with Indonesia suffered a setback when the two Indonesian marines responsible for the bomb attack at MacDonald House in 1965 were executed in Singapore in October 1968 after due process of law. The desire to have close relations with Indonesia had earlier prompted the Singapore Government to view with compassion the cases of 45 other Indonesian nationals under detention for offences related to "confrontation". Forty-three had been released in December

1966, while two others, who had been sentenced to death for carrying into Singapore a time bomb which exploded but did not cause death, were freed in May 1967. On the day of the execution of the two marines in 1968 mobs sacked the Singapore Embassy in Jakarta, hauling down and trampling upon the Singapore flag. Jakarta accorded the executed marines a state funeral. These events cast a cloud over relations for some time.

The government had a number of regional security worries. In 1969 major racial riots broke out in Malaysia. Singapore was concerned whether its closest neighbour could preserve its stability with the new and strict policies implemented after the riots especially since the communists might well exploit the situation. However, the problem was eventually contained. There was also anxiety about the effects on non-communist Southeast Asia of a communist victory in Vietnam, once it became clear that American public opinion was turning against US participation in the war there. The decade nevertheless closed without any significant change in the military stalemate.

By 1970/1971 the basic problems of survival had been overcome and Singapore could look ahead and plan for a modern, prosperous nation. Gross Domestic Product (GDP) at current factor cost had increased from $2,707 million in 1965 to $5,320 million in 1970 and per capita GDP from $1,615 in 1965 to $2,689 in 1970 (at 1968 prices). Investment and industry had expanded rapidly, mopping up much of the chronic unemployment of previous decades. By the early 1970s it became necessary to import large numbers of workers from Malaysia to alleviate labour shortage. The structure of Singapore's economy had changed: in 1965 the manufacturing industry accounted for 15 percent of a relatively small GDP; in 1970 it accounted for 20 percent of a much larger GDP.

As a Separate Sovereign State

490

490
An immediate priority after separation from Malaysia was to gain international recognition as an independent state. Singapore's flag is raised at the United Nations Building soon after the Republic was admitted by the UN General Assembly as the UN's 117th member on 21 September 1965.

491
Deputy Prime Minister Dr Toh Chin Chye and Foreign Minister S Rajaratnam at the United Nations. Both had represented Singapore at the UN Security Council which had considered Singapore's application for membership, jointly sponsored by Malaysia, Jordan and the Ivory Coast.

491

492

492
President Yusof bin Ishak opens the first session of Parliament on 8 December 1965. Constitutional changes made necessary by Singapore's independent status were approved on 22 December when Parliament passed the Constitution Amendment Bill, and the Republic of Singapore Independence Bill, with retroactive effect to 9 August.

493
President Yusof bin Ishak discussing the report of the Constitutional Commission on Minority Rights with members of the Commission. On his right is the Commission's chairman, Chief Justice Wee Chong Jin.

The Commission was constituted on 22 December 1965 to recommend ways and means of safeguarding the rights of minority groups. A Presidential Council was set up on 2 May 1970 to ensure that no legislation discriminated against minorities.

493

494

495

494
Students assemble to pledge their loyalty to Singapore, before beginning the day's lessons.

In 1966 the flag-raising and -lowering ceremonies, including the loyalty pledge, were introduced in all Singapore schools as part of the nation building process.

495
Prime Minister Lee Kuan Yew with the Director of the Political Study Centre, G G Thompson, on 13 July 1966 when he spoke to civil servants of his vision and aspirations for Singapore.

Survival, the Prime Minister said, was not the question. "The question is – how well we can survive? What is required is a rugged, resolute, highly trained, highly disciplined community. You create such a community, and you will survive and prosper here for a thousand years. This is a lesson which other nations have learnt and which I hope we will learn in time."

496/497
May Day celebrations, 1966, the first after Singapore gained independence. Communist influence in the unions was on the decline. In 1968, when the Employment Act and the Industrial Relations (Amendment) Act were in force there were only four strikes.

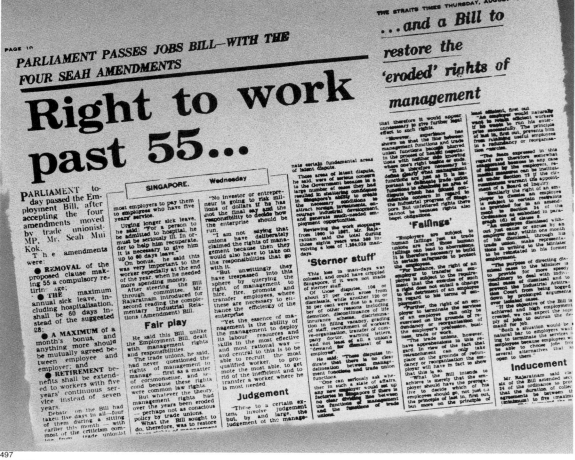

Extra-Parliamentary Struggle

498
The PAP's Lim Guan Hoo (in all white) raises his hand in victory after defeating independent candidate M P D Nair in the first by-election to Parliament held on 18 January 1966. The by-election in Bukit Merah was to fill the seat vacated by a Barisan Sosialis MP.

The Barisan Sosialis said that Singapore's independence was "phoney" and that the party's opposition to the government would thenceforth take the form of "extra-parliamentary struggle". By October 1966, the remaining Barisan Sosialis MPs had announced their decision to resign en masse.

498

499
Following their proposed resignation from Parliament, Barisan Sosialis MPs hold a protest march along High Street on 8 October 1966. The banner reads: "Parliamentary democracy is dead," and "Support Barisan Sosialis".

499

The "extra-parliamentary struggle" of the pro-communist forces which continued into the early 1970s, included arson and vandalism. The favourite targets were PAP branches, community centres and buses.

500
The PAP branch office in Old Kallang Airport Estate on 21 September 1967, after it was smeared with oil by a mob of about 100.

500

501

502

501/502
The burnt-out shells of a community centre and a Singapore Traction Company bus.

More Student Agitation

503

504

503
The pro-communists were still able to exploit discontent among students. In November 1966, there was agitation by Ngee Ann College students against the Thong Saw Pak Report on the future of the College. Again it was claimed that the recommendations of the Report were an attack on Chinese education.

On 4 November, the students organised a protest march to the Prime Minister's Office in City Hall. The protesters included students from Nanyang University.

(Above) Students sit on the City Hall steps and jeer and boo the police when they could not see the Prime Minister.

504
The students were soon involved in a scuffle with the police, attacking them with bottles and tin cans.

PROTEST AGAINST THONG SAW PAK REPORT ON THE FUTURE OF NGEE ANN COLLEGE

Students go on rampage: 30 hurt

By SIA CHEONG YEW

NGEE ANN College students, protesting against the Thong Saw Pak report on the future of their institution, this afternoon stormed City Hall and ended up in a series of scuffles with the police, culminating with a bloody clash.

About 30 students and policemen were injured, including two girl students.

About 10 policemen were taken to the General Hospital in two ambulances, including one constable who sustained a serious cut on the head from flying glass.

The injured students refused to go to the General Hospital, preferring to be treated at the Hill Street dispensary of Dr. Lee Siew Choh, chairman of the Barisan Sosialis.

A petition

In the three-hour demonstration, the 200 students — including a sprinkling of representatives from the University of Singapore, the Polytechnic and Nanyang University — stormed the City Hall about 1.45 p.m. after a meeting at their college in Tank Road.

Their intention was to present to the Prime Minister, Mr. Lee Kuan Yew, a petition which they had stained with blood from their fingers.

They suddenly broke through a police cordon outside the building and rushed up the wide concrete steps leading to the Prime Minister's office.

But before they could get into the building, police slammed three huge doors in their faces.

A 'sit-in'

Riot Squad police were unable to persuade the students to go to the padang in front of the City Hall, where their last demonstration on Oct. 25 was held.

The police were forced to allow them to stage a 'sit-in' in the corridors of the building.

At once, banners appeared, stretching from pillar to pillar of the vast building.

At this stage the police cordoned off the City Hall steps with orders not to allow anyone to pass.

For over an hour the students sang, jeered and booed until about 3.30 p.m. when the last traces erupted from an argument at the police cordon.

TWO students tackle a policeman whose beret has fallen off during the bloody clash between police and Ngee Ann College students outside City Hall yesterday. As the policeman pins down one student, another student is trying to choke him. **Straits Times picture by ALI YUSOF.**

(More pictures in pages 5 and 20).

505

506

505/506
About 30 students and policemen were injured in the scuffle.

CRACKDOWN ON STUDENTS

131 rebels in college are flushed out

PHOTONEWS
By WAN SENG YIP and HAN HAI FONG
... pictures on Pages Two and Three

By Philip Khoo, Sia Chong Yew and Jackie Sam

SINGAPORE, Sat.—The Ngee Ann student revolt was crushed today. An hour-long police siege and a barrage of tear-gas grenades ended their 26-day college rule.

Flushed out and detained were 131 people — 65 hardcore Ngee Ann agitators and 66 newly expelled Nanyang University undergrads

Heavy attack

This massive crackdown foiled plans for a big Communist-backed demonstration outside City Hall this afternoon.

No one was hurt during the operation although a Reserve Unit vanguard came under heavy attack in the opening minutes of the siege.

Resistance was expected and did not hold up "Operation Ro-

kam Dua" (Second phase of the Thorn). This was a double-pronged attack which entailed a broader sweep of the island by 10 other Internal Security squads.

But the main concentration of forces — almost 500 men and women — were deployed round Ngee Ann from 2.50 a.m.

House raids

This big force was assembled at the Police Training School in Thomson Road long before the crackdown.

The others fanned out from the I.S.D. headquarters in Robinson Road for surprise raids on homes of almost 50 former Nanyang students, mainly in the rural areas

The task force was expected by Ngee Ann rebel students, some of whom had viewed with concern the strong government measures taken over the past week to contain student unrest in the Republic.

FLUSHED OUT . . . two soaked student leaders who hid in water tanks during the police raid are escorted to a police car after their arrest. Expelled Nanyang University undergraduates were among the Ngee Ann students who for more than an hour defied a police order to come out peacefully. They shouted abuse as the police warned repeatedly in Mandarin. The siege ended when tear-gas grenades were tossed into hiding places.

507

507

The Ngee Ann students continued their agitation, organising "stay-ins" and disrupting classes in defiance of government orders. Finally, on 19 November, the police moved in and flushed out 65 student agitators of whom 52 were foreigners. By 22 November classes were back to normal.

Regional Security Scene Changes

508/509
Indonesian police and civilians inspect the hammer and sickle emblem on a flag found in the rubble of the ransacked headquarters of the Partai Kommunis Indonesia in Jakarta.

The building was destroyed during anti-communist demonstrations on 8 October 1965, following the abortive left-wing coup on 30 September 1965 to capture the Indonesian Government.

The abortive coup eventually resulted in the liquidation of the Partai Kommunis Indonesia. With Suharto taking charge of the government, Indonesia embarked on a new direction which emphasised economic development at home and friendly relations with neighbouring countries. The policy of "confrontation" initiated by Sukarno was soon brought to an end.

508

Soek 'rescued'

YANI KILLED, NASUTION WOUNDED IN REVOLT BY PRO-COMMUNIST OFFICERS

Coup crushed

KUALA LUMPUR, Friday

A COMMUNIST-inspired move to overthrow President Soekarno and capture power in Indonesia was crushed tonight by units of the armed forces under Brig. Gen. Suharto.

An announcement by Jakarta Radio, monitored here tonight by Radio Malaysia, said President Soekarno and Defence Minister General Nasution were rescued and were safe—after a day of bloodshed.

It made no mention of Dr. Subandrio (former First Deputy Prime Minister and Foreign Minister) who was included in the 45-strong Revolutionary Council under the coup leader, Lieut. Col. Untung, head of the presidential bodyguards.

Tengku waits for details

KUALA LUMPUR, Fri. — Tengku Abdul Rahman would not comment tonight on the coup d'etat in Jakarta.

"I have no details at all about what has happened," the Prime Minister said. "It may be the right coup, or it may be the wrong coup."

The Tengku was interviewed before Radio Jakarta announced that the coup had been crushed.

At least 12 Reds   **STOP PRESS**

509

510
Men of the 9th US marine expeditionary force scramble out of a landing barge onto the beach at Da Nang, South Vietnam on 8 March 1965. The marines were intended to bolster defence around the Da Nang air base against possible Vietcong attacks.

The direct American involvement in Vietnam with ground, air and naval forces meant that, at least for some time, communist expansion southwards from North Vietnam would be contained.

The consequence of the abortive Indonesian coup and the massive American involvement in South Vietnam were major setbacks to communist and pro-communist forces in Singapore and Malaysia enabling the non-communist governments in the region to concentrate on economic development and nation building.

510

Establishing External Relations

Good relations with Singapore's two nearest neighbours, Malaysia and Indonesia, were high on Singapore's foreign policy agenda. There were close contacts with Malaysia from the beginning, though, on both sides, it took time for the memories of the conflicts of 1963 to 1965 and the irritations of post-separation adjustments to fade.

With Indonesia, Singapore had to wait for the formal ending of *konfrontasi* on 12 August 1966. Full diplomatic relations between Singapore and Indonesia were resumed on 7 September 1967.

511
The first Malaysian High Commissioner to independent Singapore, Dato Jamal bin Abdul Latiff, presenting credentials to President Yusof bin Ishak. Malaysia was the first country to recognise Singapore's independence.

511

512
The Prime Minister of Malaysia, Tunku Abdul Rahman visited Singapore on 20 March 1966. He is seen at the airport press conference with Singapore Finance Minister Lim Kim San.

512

513

514

513
In May 1966, a Malaysian delegation followed up the Tunku's visit to discuss post-separation adjustments and cooperation. Members of the Singapore and Malaysian delegations are seen here during a meeting at the Economic Development Board on 19 May 1966.

514
Dr Adam Malik, Foreign Minister of Indonesia, was in Singapore from 17 to 19 March 1968. He is being shown some of Singapore's development projects by Hon Sui Sen, chairman of the Economic Development Board. Following Dr Malik's visit, a Singapore trade mission visited Indonesia on 3 May 1968 and signed a trade agreement.

ASEAN, the Association of Southeast Asian Nations, was formed by Indonesia, Malaysia, the Philippines, Thailand and Singapore on 8 August 1967 to promote regional cooperation.
515
The ministers of the five nations signing the Bangkok Declaration which set out the objectives of ASEAN.
516
The ministers soon after the signing ceremony. From left Narcisco Ramos (the Philippines); Dr Adam Malik (Indonesia); Thanat Khoman (Thailand); Tun Abdul Razak (Malaysia); and S Rajaratnam (Singapore).

515

516

517

518

519

Relations with communist countries were established, starting with trade agreements and exchange of trade representations. In 1966 the Prime Minister and the Minister for Foreign Affairs visited five East European countries – Poland, Czechoslovakia, Hungary, Yugoslavia and Rumania.

517/518/519
Some of the first trade missions to visit Singapore came from Bulgaria (top), the USSR (above left) and Poland (above).

520

520
The visit to Singapore of Eisaku Sato, Prime Minister of Japan, in September 1967 was the first by a Japanese prime minister after the war. Sato is seen here with President Yusof bin Ishak.

521
Singapore became a member of the Commonwealth and maintained close relations with its Commonwealth friends.

(Below) Lee Kuan Yew at the Commonwealth Prime Ministers' Conference held in London from 5 to 15 September 1966. He is flanked by Malaysian Prime Minister Tunku Abdul Rahman and the Indian Foreign Minister Swaran Singh.

521

522
With its foreign policy of non-alignment, Singapore sought to forge close ties with non-aligned states. Here Lee Kuan Yew is greeted by the Cambodian Head of State Prince Sihanouk during his visit to Phnom Penh in April 1966.

523
The ruling People's Action Party maintained links with world democratic socialist parties through its membership of the Socialist International.
 (Below) The Prime Minister addresses the Socialist International Conference held in Stockholm on 7 May 1966.

524

525

524/525/526

Relations with Indonesia suffered a setback when two Indonesian marines, after due process of law, were executed in Singapore on 17 October 1968 for the MacDonald House bomb attack in 1965 in which three persons died.

The Singapore Embassy (left and bottom left) after it was sacked by several hundred Indonesian youths protesting against the execution of the marines.

526

Building a Defence Force

527/528
After separation from Malaysia, a Singapore defence force had to be built almost from scratch.

(Right) Singapore youths sign up for national service at the Central Manpower Base when registration opened on 28 March 1967. The first batch of national servicemen was drafted in July 1967.

(Below) University of Singapore students register for national service in December 1967.

527

528

529

531

529
"Send-off" parties were organised in every constituency for the youths called up for national service. Ministers and community leaders turned up at such parties to meet the recruits and their parents, who were also invited to these functions.

530
There was no military tradition in the Singapore society; in fact, the bulk of the population had traditionally held military service in low esteem. An intense educational effort was required to overcome such attitudes. Ministers, Members of Parliament, senior civil servants and community leaders volunteered to serve in the People's Defence Force. In this way they set an example and drove home to citizens their responsibility to defend their nation.

(Right) The Minister of Interior and Defence, Dr Goh Keng Swee, in his uniform as colonel of the Singapore Artillery.

530

531/532

The Minister of Interior and Defence, Dr Goh Keng Swee, reviews the passing out parade of the first two training companies of 216 civil servants held on 18 June 1967, and (right) takes the salute at the passing out parade on 16 July 1967 of the first 117 officer cadets trained at the Singapore Armed Forces Training Institute.

532

British Pull-out Announcement

533/534
In January 1968, Britain announced its intention to withdraw all its military forces from Singapore by March 1971, a move with profound economic and security implications for Singapore. Only six months earlier Singapore had been told that complete withdrawal would take place only in 1975. Lee Kuan Yew flew to London to discuss the matter with the British Government. He was able to delay the withdrawal by only nine months – to 31 December 1971.

(Right) The Singapore Prime Minister with Harold Wilson, the British Prime Minister.

533

534

535/537/538
Britain's decision on the early withdrawal of its forces was also viewed with concern by Malaysia, which still had British troops on its territory and, like Singapore, was insured against external aggression by the Anglo-Malaysian Defence Agreement (AMDA). AMDA was to lapse with the withdrawal of all British forces.

The British decision also caused concern in Australia and New Zealand, which, over the years, had a military presence in Malaysia and Singapore as junior partners of the British.

A series of discussions on alternative security arrangements were now held between the leaders of all the countries involved.

These discussions led to the five-nation defence conference at ministerial level held in Kuala Lumpur on 9 and 10 June 1968.

Australian External Affairs Minister Haslauck (below) and New Zealand Prime Minister Keith Holyoake (bottom left) in Singapore in the first half of 1968.

(Bottom) Malaysia's Deputy Prime Minister Tun Abdul Razak golfing with Prime Minister Lee Kuan Yew during his visit to Singapore in March 1968 to discuss defence matters.

535
While in London, Lee Kuan Yew also met Edward Heath, leader of the opposition Conservative Party.

535

536

537

538

To Meet New Challenges

539

In April 1968, the PAP Government sought a new mandate from the people before implementing policies to meet the challenges posed by the accelerated withdrawal of the British forces. The PAP made a clean sweep of the polls gaining all 58 seats, only seven of which were contested. The Barisan Sosialis boycotted the election.

(Right) The PAP's Ya'acob Mohamed being chaired after he beat an independent candidate.

540

Woon Wah Siang, chairman of Jurong Town Corporation (JTC), introducing Dr Goh Keng Swee to officials and guests before the corporation's official opening ceremony.

The JTC was established in June 1968 to take over the development and management of Jurong and the industrial estates.

539

541

540

541
The Sembawang Shipyard. It is run by Sembawang Shipyard Ltd which was formed in June 1968 to convert the King George VI Dock at the Naval Base for commercial use. Much of the infrastructure of the British military bases handed over to the Singapore Government was similarly converted to economic and commercial use.

542

542
Trade unions kept pace with economic and industrial changes in Singapore. In 1969 the NTUC organised a national seminar on "Modernisation of the Labour Movement" to redefine the role of organised labour in nation building. The four-day seminar was opened by Lee Kuan Yew.

(Above) NTUC secretary-general C V Devan Nair welcomes the Prime Minister. Others in the photograph are (from left) Gerald de Cruz, Professor Tom Elliot and S R Nathan.

543
The Prime Minister addresses over 260 trade unionists at the seminar.

Arising from the seminar recommendations, INCOME, NTUC's Insurance Commercial Enterprise, and COMFORT, Corporative Commonwealth for Transport Ltd, were launched in 1970.

543

544

545

544
In 1969, Singapore celebrated the 150th Anniversary of its founding.

545
Prime Minister Lee Kuan Yew at a commemorative dinner given by the International Chamber of Commerce to mark the occasion.

He described the 150th anniversary as a "significant and formal moment, for a brief pause to study and scrutinise the record of the last 150 years, learn lessons therefrom and with confidence renewed, surge forward to improve upon the past".

546

547

548

546/547

The highlight of the 150th Anniversary celebrations was the National Day Parade held at the Padang. Many foreign dignitaries, including Princess Alexandra and her husband, Angus Ogilvy, and the Deputy Prime Minister of Malaysia, Tun Abdul Razak, were among the distinguished guests.

548

Among the parade's attractions were AMX-13 tanks, which were making their first public appearance.

549

The Family Planning and Population Board was set up on 12 January 1966. The Minister for Health, Yong Nyuk Lin, speaks at the inauguration of the Board.

Successful family planning programmes reduced the birth rate from 29.9 births per thousand population in 1965 to 22.1 per thousand population by 1970.

550

Eric Cheong, Member of Parliament for Toa Payoh, officiating at a public balloting ceremony in his constituency in 1968, under the Home Ownership for the People scheme, launched in 1964.

From 1968, Central Provident Fund savings could be used for the purchase of HDB flats. This enabled more people to own their homes. By the end of 1970, the HDB had completed more than 120,000 units and about 35 percent of the population were living in HDB flats.

At 1970 prices, flats sold ranged from $3,300 for a one-room (Improved) flat to $12,500 for a four-room flat.

549

550

551

The Sultan of Johor, Sultan Ismail Ibni Al-Marhum Sultan Ibrahim, opens the Johor River Waterworks built by the Singapore Public Utilities Board at an initial cost of $30 million at Kota Tinggi.

With its opening in April 1968, the PUB was able to provide an additional 30 million gallons of treated water a day.

551

552

Electricity consumption almost doubled from 912.5 million units in 1965 to 1,941.6 million units in 1970. To meet the growing demand for energy, the Jurong Power Station (below) was opened in August 1970.

552

553

554

555

557

553
Students at one of the lecture theatres in the National Junior College, Singapore's first. It was opened in May 1970.
554/555
Technical education was geared to train youths in greater numbers to meet the needs of industries, such as these, for skilled workers.

556

556
A BAC Strikemaster jet, one of first three jet aircraft purchased by the Singapore Armed Forces (SAF) in 1969.

As a result of the early British military withdrawal, the build-up of the SAF had to be accelerated.

557
Men of the first Hawker Hunter Squadron of the SAF pose with a Hunter. The Squadron became operational in late 1970 after the officers returned from training in Britain.

558

561
President Yusof bin Ishak died on 23 November 1970. A large number of Singaporeans turned up at the City Hall to pay their last respects before he was buried with full state honours at the Kranji State Cemetery.

558/559
The general election in Britain in June 1970 resulted in a Conservative Government headed by Edward Heath coming to power. The new government revised British defence policy in Southeast Asia and initiated discussions to retain a residual British military presence in Singapore until 1975.

Among those who visited Singapore for defence talks in 1970 were Australia's Defence Minister Malcolm Fraser who came on 19 June 1970 (above) and Britain's Defence Secretary Lord Carrington who came on 27 June 1970 (right).

559

560
An "enemy" is captured and led away by security forces during *Bersatu Padu* (Solid Unity), a five-power defence exercise held in 1970. The land, sea and air defence exercise was launched to demonstrate Britain's capacity for rapid deployment of forces from Britain to Malaysia/Singapore in an emergency and to test the effectiveness of the area's defence capability after the British withdrawal.

The exercise, held in Malaysia, began in April and lasted over two months. Over 27,500 men from Singapore, Malaysia, Britain, New Zealand and Australia took part. Some 900 men of the Fifth Battalion of the Singapore Infantry Regiment were the first national servicemen to participate in war games outside the Republic.

560

President Yusof Dies

561

The Singapore Skyline, 1984

NEW HORIZONS

1971~1984

Singapore entered the 1970s as a politically stable state with a high rate of economic growth. The one-party Parliament that emerged from the 1968 general election became the pattern, with the PAP winning all seats and an average of about 70 percent of the votes cast in the three general elections of 1972, 1976 and 1980. This total dominance of the political scene allowed the PAP Government to deal with the vital tasks of economic development, defence and nation building without distraction. It made considerable progress in winning a popular consensus for a non-communist, multi-racial, multi-lingual, modern society based on the principles of self-reliance and reward for merit.

As part of its policy of self-renewal, the PAP fielded new candidates in each general election and by-election, and this, together with the appointment of younger MPs to ministerial posts, helped to inject new blood into the party and fresh talent into the government. By 1984 a younger team was in charge of most of the ministries and occupied most of the key posts in the party.

A new generation of voters was also joining the electorate, forming more than 50 percent of it in 1984. It had known nothing but progress and stability.

Security remained a key concern for a small country situated in a turbulent part of the world, and in April 1971 Singapore concluded a Five-Power Defence Arrangement with Malaysia, Britain, Australia and

New Zealand. Unlike the Anglo-Malaysian Defence Agreement, which had also covered Singapore, this was devoid of firm commitments to collective defence in the event of external aggression, but it did provide a framework for joint consultations and military cooperation that helped to preserve confidence and stability, especially at a time when Singapore was still in the process of building up its own armed forces. Nevertheless, the defence of Singapore was now the responsibility of Singaporeans. The expansion and qualitative improvement of the Singapore Armed Forces steadily continued, and by 1984 the Republic possessed a significant military capability of its own.

However, in a small country with a compact urban society dependent on economic links with the outside world for its survival, credible deterrence called for more than a military capability. It demanded a clear will on the part of the population to resist any foreign aggression and a demonstrable capacity for civil defence, social cohesion, and economic stability in an

emergency. Thus every citizen was required to make a contribution, either as a member of the citizens' army or the civil defence force, or by helping to keep the economy and social services going.

There were no serious internal security problems. Rapid economic progress and greater social cohesion among a more affluent population had defused the communist and communal threats. Vigilance was nevertheless still needed because stability was a prerequisite for Singapore's progress and could not be allowed to be jeopardised in any way: hence the arrests of four senior staff members of a Chinese language newspaper – the *Nanyang Siang Pau* – in 1971, of Malayan Communist Party agents in 1974, and of members of a clandestine Muslim extremist organisation in 1982.

The main security threats were external. The revival of Malayan Communist Party guerilla bands in the northern states of Peninsular Malaysia and an increase in communist underground activity across the Causeway in the early and mid-1970s were matters of serious concern, following – as they did – serious racial riots in 1969. Singapore could not escape the consequences of communist or communal strife on the neighbouring mainland but fortunately, as the years passed, it became clear that the menace had been contained.

Developments in Indochina were another source of anxiety. South Vietnam, Cambodia and Laos fell to the communists in 1975, and for a time it seemed that there was nothing to stop the Vietnamese from putting pressure on Thailand, the pivotal state in ASEAN, whose security was vital to Malaysia and Singapore. However, the danger receded when Hanoi's moves to convert the other states in Indochina into compliant satellites brought Vietnam into conflict not only with Cambodia (now renamed Kampuchea) under Pol Pot, but with China as well. Vietnam's alliance with the Soviet Union in 1978, its invasion and occupation of Cambodia, and the consequent Chinese punitive invasion of Vietnam's border provinces in February 1979, changed the regional security equation. In Cambodia, Vietnam became bogged down in a struggle against stubborn Khmer nationalist resistance which had the support of Beijing.

This was not an unmixed blessing. Hanoi became increasingly dependent on Moscow for strategic aid, and in return granted the Soviets the use of bases in Vietnam for their warships and aircraft, thus bringing a Russian military presence to Southeast Asia. At a time when the United States was taking a back seat in the region, there developed a long-term threat that ASEAN countries, caught in the middle of a power struggle between China, on the one hand, and the USSR and Vietnam on the other, would be subjected to pressures from all three.

Partly as a consequence of the developments that followed the fall of South Vietnam to the communists in 1975, the ASEAN states drew together. Singapore forged closer ties not only with the Republic's immediate neighbours, Malaysia and Indonesia, but with the other partners in the Association – Thailand, the Philippines and, from 1984, Brunei. This strengthening of bilateral relations was matched by a closer coordination of policies within ASEAN itself. In

response to the occupation of Cambodia, the ASEAN members acted in concert at the United Nations and other international forums to expose Vietnamese expansionism and to bring pressure to bear on Hanoi to withdraw. At the same time they intensified their efforts to find a political solution to the Cambodian problem and to ensure that if the pro-Vietnamese satellite regime in Phnom Penh finally abdicated, it would not simply be replaced by the communist Khmer Rouge.

Relations with countries outside the region were also crucial to Singapore's extensive international economic links. Singapore continued to develop ties with major trading partners and sources of investment, notably the United States, Japan, and the European Community, and with traditional Commonwealth friends. Visits were exchanged with China, and commercial relations expanded, although the Republic's declared policy that it would not establish diplomatic relations until Indonesia had done so remained unchanged. Singapore continued to participate in the Non-Aligned Movement and to foster economic and political relations with countries in West Asia and elsewhere, irrespective of ideology.

The economy made good progress even though the international environment was unfavourable in the 1970s. Oil prices soared, and there were low growth rates, stagflation, protectionism and two recessions in the industrialised countries. Nevertheless, during the period 1971 to 1983, the Singapore economy registered an average annual increase in Gross Domestic Product of 8.8 percent compared with 12.9 percent for the period 1966 to 1970, raising it from $6,279 million to $32,252 million (current prices). Per capita Gross National Product grew from $3,224 in 1971 to $13,783 in 1983. Singapore's official reserves were $19,755

million in 1983, more than six times the figure for 1970. There was full employment from the early 1970s, and relatively low inflation. The Republic emerged as a "global city" closely tied to the international economic system, becoming a base for large multinational corporations and an important financial and communications centre.

With limited manpower and full employment, Singapore could not continue to depend upon traditional labour-intensive industries for its economic growth. Other countries in the region with bigger populations were also industrialising and the island would not be able to compete with them. On the other hand, dependence on migrant workers would bring new social problems and more demands on social services. A programme of economic restructuring to shift to capital-intensive, high technology, high value-added industries therefore began in earnest in 1979 when, for three years in succession, the National Wages Council recommended high wage increases (about 20 percent annually) to induce employers to save on manpower and phase out labour-intensive industries.

The change called for new skills and new attitudes, and the government sought to help achieve the transformation by modifying education policies, expanding technical and computer education, offering financial incentives to industrial enterprises, and launching a productivity campaign.

Meanwhile, the social background was changing. By 1984 the people of Singapore were earning significantly higher incomes, were better educated and were more widely travelled. More and more were English-speaking and bilingual. Nearly four out of five in the population lived in Housing and Development Board (HDB) flats; and 70 percent of the flats were owner-occupied. Better health services had increased the average life expectancy to 71.4 years and in consequence the proportion of old people was mounting. The traditional extended families were breaking up as more married couples set up separate homes. Greater affluence created new demands for recreation and leisure activities, and a desire for a better quality of life.

The problems of the late 1970s and early 1980s were very different from those of the early 1960s. The massive public housing programme and the resettlement of large numbers of people from different parts of the island in new townships of high-rise flats turned strangers with different languages, dialects and backgrounds into instant neighbours. Residents' Committees were established from 1978 to meet the urgent need to help nurture a community spirit among these flat dwellers, and to improve communication between the government and people.

The growing preference for an English education, together with increasing exposure through the mass media and travel to liberal ideas and lifestyles from the West, prompted fears that Singapore would suffer a loss of cultural ballast and a weakening of moral values. More emphasis was therefore placed on a policy of bilingualism, and moral and religious instruction was introduced in schools.

What were the factors behind the success and the impressive progress that Singapore had achieved? One was political stability and racial harmony – if the communist-inspired strikes and violence or the communal tensions and unrest of the early 1960s had continued, foreign investors would not have put their money into Singapore and the economy would not have taken off; the second factor was a political leadership and an administration that provided firm direction and sound policies; and the third was the deter-

mination of the people of Singapore to survive when they were thrown onto their own resources in 1965. They had experienced poverty, unemployment, and political and communal conflicts; they knew that if they did not make every effort to succeed, Singapore would just go under; and they placed their trust in a government which had taken them through turbulent times, responding to its lead with courage and energy.

Trade unions learned to sacrifice short-term sectional interests for the sake of long-term benefits, and the workers gradually came to realise that hostility and confrontation were not the natural order of things between employers and employees — rather it was through cooperation with responsible management that unions could secure their true interests.

Finally, Singapore's progress, especially during the critical years from 1965 to 1970, was assisted by certain favourable regional and international developments. The abortive left-wing coup in Indonesia in September 1965 was followed by the establishment of an anti-communist regime more interested in economic development than foreign adventures, and this was a major blow to the communists seeking to destabilise the region. The massive American military intervention in Vietnam in 1965 meant that communist expansion from the north would be held in check for some time at least. The Vietnam War also yielded profitable spin-offs through a demand for goods and services from Singapore at a time when the economy was feeling the effects of the withdrawal of British forces. The favourable world economic climate in the 1960s enabled Singapore to attract substantial foreign investments, and in the 1970s and early 1980s the economy further benefited from high growth rates in the ASEAN region.

In 1984 Singapore could look forward to a promising future. However, the coming decades would demand all the intelligence, adaptability and energy that had brought Singapore through past difficulties. Although the Republic had made remarkable economic and social progress, there was still much to be done to consolidate its achievements and to ensure prosperity and stability in the 1990s. A sense of a Singaporean identity among a people of diverse races and cultures had emerged, but needed to take firmer root. Some of the crucial intangibles necessary for the sound functioning of a community, such as civic consciousness, concern and care for others, and a spirit of personal self-sacrifice, were still lacking.

Singapore's fundamental vulnerability would remain, given its size, location and the nature of its economy. The Republic would always be affected by the ups and downs of the world economy. If the chronic international debt problem were to result in a serious world recession during the 1980s there could be profound effects on Singapore, with large-scale unemployment and steep falls in incomes. Even if the international economy continued on a relatively even keel, Singapore would have to maintain its edge over others in efficiency to be able to sell its products and services. Complacency, decline in the work ethic, or demands for more benefits for lower productivity would erode the Republic's competitive edge, and thus the basis of its well-being.

The economy would continue to be heavily dependent on the confidence of foreign investors and foreign governments. That confidence rests to an important degree on the quality of administration and the soundness of policies, and could quickly be shaken if a weak or inept government came to power. It could also be shaken if the old problems of communalism and communism surfaced again.

Singapore's security and stability would remain sensitive to adverse developments in Southeast Asia. Although in 1984 there was no immediate threat of an upheaval, the region was known for its turbulent past and was now an arena of competition between rival communist powers. It was not possible to predict what the regional scene would be like in the early 1990s, given the uncertainties of the world economy and of East-West relations, and the complexities of domestic politics in the countries of the region.

The danger could lie in a people, too accustomed to uninterrupted peace and progress over the years,

underestimating Singapore's vulnerability and allowing themselves to be seduced by the more permissive style of politics, economics and social patterns that the West could seemingly afford but Singapore could certainly not. Even in Europe and America, where freedom and democracy were the products of a long period of political evolution and required a sophisticated electorate to sustain, it had not always been possible to balance liberty with responsibility. When this happened social malaise and economic decline set in.

However, the wealth, talent, resources and land area of Western countries permitted a greater margin of error, and major mistakes or irresponsible acts did not necessarily lead to disaster. In developing countries, with vastly different cultures and traditions, Western-style democracy often failed to survive the pressures of ethnic, linguistic, religious, and tribal forces, or the politics of poverty and greed. In Singapore's case, with only 2.5 million people and 618 square kilometres of land area, the permissible margin of error would remain very small. Singapore's survival and progress rest on certain fundamentals which the people and the political parties could not afford to undermine – multi-racialism and racial harmony, equal opportunities, a sound work ethic, a clean and efficient administration, national service and commitment to defence, and a meritocracy tempered by the spread to all of the benefits of economic growth. These would be the prerequisites for sustaining the democratic system.

President Sheares

563

563
Dr Benjamin Henry Sheares is sworn in as the Republic's second President on 2 January 1971 following the death of President Yusof bin Ishak.

Born in Singapore on 12 August 1907, Sheares graduated from the King Edward VII College of Medicine in 1929, and rose to become an eminent gynaecologist.

Politics

In the 1972, 1976 and 1980 general elections, the People's Action Party again won all the seats in Parliament. Although there were 18 to 20 registered political parties in the 1970s and 1980s, no opposition party succeeded in winning any significant following. Many were dormant, or active only at election time.

Only five to seven opposition parties contested each of three general elections between 1972 and 1980. Shown here are rallies of some of these opposition parties.

564

564
Barisan Sosialis
565
The Workers' Party
566
Singapore United Front
567
Pertubohan Kebangsaan Melayu Singapura (PKMS)
568
Justice Party, Singapore

565

566

567

568

569
The People's Front
570
An independent candidate.
571
United National Front
572
United People's Front
573
Singapore Democratic Party

569

571

570

572

573

574

J B Jeyaretnam, secretary-general of the Workers' Party, won the by-election held for Parliament in the Anson constituency on 31 October 1981. He became the first opposition member since the boycott of Parliament by the Barisan Sosialis in 1966.

575

576

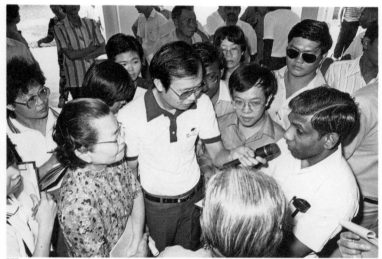

577

578

575/576/577/578/579
Some of the younger ministers at constituency "walkabouts" in 1983 and 1984 to meet the people and hear about their problems.

As part of a self-renewal policy, the ruling People's Action Party fielded young and talented persons as new candidates at each general election and by-election. Some new MPs were appointed to ministerial and senior party posts to prepare a new generation of leaders to take charge when the old guard retire.

579

Defence and Security

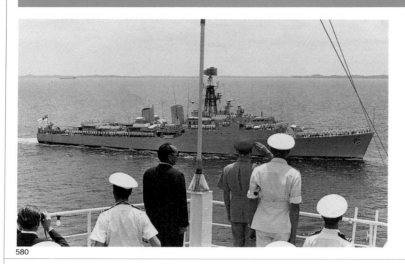

580

582

581

580/581

The end of the British Far East Command on 31 October 1971 is marked by a sea parade of 16 warships escorted by 26 planes and 24 helicopters. The Anglo-Malaysian Defence Agreement, which also covered Singapore, expired on the same day. Singapore thus ceased to be a British military base and Britain was no longer committed to the defence of Singapore.

In a farewell speech to the British Far East Commander-in-Chief, the Prime Minister put on record "the contribution the British forces have made to the stability and security of the Malaysia-Singapore area ... The continued existence, progress and prosperity of Singapore would have never been, but for them (the British, Australians and New Zealanders)."

Earlier, on 16 April 1971, the Five-Power Defence Arrangement was agreed upon. The communique said that the agreement was based "on the need to regard the defence of Malaysia and Singapore as indivisible".

582

The formal signing of documents on 1 December 1971 for the presence of ANZUK (Australia, New Zealand and United Kingdom) forces in Singapore, under the framework of the Five-Power Defence Arrangement. The Arrangement provided for consultations among the five nations in the event of any threat of external aggression against Malaysia and Singapore, and for an integrated air defence system for Malaysia and Singapore.

The ANZUK Command was dissolved in 1975, and by early 1976 the last of the British and Australian forces had left Singapore, leaving the United States with the main strategic responsibility for countering any communist threat in the region.

583

583/584

(Left) A group of Singapore commandos in training and (below) Singapore Armed Forces reservists during an in-camp training session.

By 1983 Singapore could mobilise 200,000 reservists during an emergency, in addition to 50,000 men in active service. Annual training sessions sought to ensure that reservists, who formed the bulk of the armed forces, remained fighting fit and knowledgeable in military skills.

The air force had more than 100 operational aircraft and anti-aircraft defences including batteries of Bloodhound, Improved Hawk, Rapier and RBS-70 surface-to-air missiles.

584

585

585

Every citizen was required to make a contribution to defence, either as a member of the citizens' army or in some other role.

(Left) Residents engaged in civil defence drill. In 1982 a civil defence programme was launched to involve the civilian population in national defence efforts. Volunteers in various constituencies were trained in basic fire-fighting, first-aid and rescue skills.

No. 1834   SUNDAY MAY 23, 1971   20 CENTS   SINGAPORE EDITION

Govt: Detained newsmen 'admit' glamorising Red system

A Nanyang 'confession'

SINGAPORE, Saturday

FOUR detained Nanyang Siang Pau executives have admitted glamorising the communist system and working up communal emotions over Chinese language and culture, the Government announced today.

In a statement, it said: "On May 2, 1971, the Government had in a security action arrested four top executives of the Nanyang Siang Pau, namely Lee Mau Seng, Shamsuddin Tung Tao Chang, Ly Singko and Kerk Loong Sing.

Communal emotions

"Under interrogation, these persons have admitted their responsibility for implementing the Nanyang Siang Pau's policy of glamorising the communist system and also working up communal emotions on issues over Chinese language and culture.

"They have acknowledged

that they knew the launching of this campaign would generate communal strife and lead to political instability in Singapore.

"The Government considers their detention necessary and has, therefore, issued orders of detention under the Internal Security Act."

No comment

Under the Act, the man can be detained without trial for up to 30 days. After that, they can still be held for up to two years under an order from the Minister for Home Affairs.

When contacted tonight, Nanyang's chairman and chief executive, Mr. Lee Eu Seng, elder brother of Mau Seng, declined comment on the Government's statement.

"I would not like to make any statement because a habeas corpus hearing of the four men will be coming up in court on Wednesday," he said.

★ SEE PAGE SEVEN—COL. TWO

LEE EU SENG ...no comment

586
Firm action was taken against any attempt to stir up communist or communal sentiments. When the *Nanyang Siang Pau*, a Chinese daily, ran articles in 1971 playing on the sensitivities of the Chinese-educated and subtly glamourising communism, four members of the paper's senior staff were detained.

587
The main security concerns were external. One concern was the revival in Malaysia of the threat from the Malayan Communist Party (MCP) in the early 1970s. In the late 1960s, after re-building its military strength in the border regions of southern Thailand, the MCP started infiltrating guerillas and agents into the northern states of Peninsular Malaysia to re-establish jungle bases and an insurgency infrastructure. Communist agents in urban areas carried out a spate of assassinations of Malaysian Special Branch officers. There was a step-up of subversion, recruitment of more people into the MCP underground satellite organisations, and a series of violent incidents, culminating in the bombing of the National Monument in Kuala Lumpur on 26 August 1975, and simultaneous rocket attacks on a number of military installations across the Peninsula.

586

A fallen warrior... by its side the head of another warrior

WEDNESDAY, AUGUST 27, 1975   25 CENTS   M.C.(P) 1116/75

Terrorists strike in KL's Lake Gardens

HUNT FOR MONUMENT BOMBERS

KUALA LUMPUR, Tues.

TV MALAYSIA tonight flashed a picture of one of four people believed to be responsible for the bombing of Malaysia's National Monument in the Lake Gardens this morning as police stepped up their hunt for the bombers.

The picture was taken from an identity card dropped by one of the bombers after they blasted and heavily damaged the $1.5 million monument, situated on a hillock near Parliament House.

Chan...picture flashed on TV last night

Police tonight named him as Chan Cheng Yoke, aged about 25. His last known address was 123 Main Road, Kulai, Johore.

An official statement said police could help the in their investigations.

The bombers, one a woman, struck at the bronze monument — a cluster of military figures erected in memory of those who died fighting the communists during the 1948–1960 Malayan emergency — at about 5 a.m.

Shattered

Four bombs were planted. The explosion blew off a warrior holding a Bren gun and the heads of three other soldiers.

It also caused a vertical crack of about a metre long on the marble foundation. Windows of houses in the area were shattered.

A statement by the National Security Council said the bombing was believed to be the work of the communist Malayan National Liberation Front (MNLF).

587

588
This new phase of MCP militancy and subversion was reflected in Singapore in increased communist underground activity. On 20 December 1974, when communist agents were on their way to plant a bomb, the explosives went off prematurely, ripping apart their car.

Lying dead in the front seat is a 23-year-old Malaysian, Lim Chin Huat. One of his accomplices died later in hospital, while a third was injured.

589
Some of the 189 hand grenades seized by the Singapore police in July 1975 following the arrest of several communist agents belonging to underground satellite organisations of the MCP. In the cache were 210 detonators, a .38 revolver, a .24 Colt automatic pistol, 75 bullets, and communist books and documents. Later that month 109 more grenades were seized from the home of another communist agent.

Effective action by the Malaysian security service contained the communist threat. The Singapore security service worked closely with its Malaysian counterpart against the common enemy.

590

590/591
Vietnamese refugees, popularly termed, "the Boat People", awaiting repatriation at a transit camp.

Developments in Indochina were another source of anxiety, especially after the capture of South Vietnam by North Vietnam in 1975 and the step-up in Hanoi's propaganda attacks against Thailand and ASEAN. Thousands of Vietnamese fled the country to escape communist rule, risking their lives in unsafe craft (below). Hundreds perished at sea when their craft sank, or were attacked by pirates.

591

592/593
In October 1978, Vietnamese
Prime Minister Pham Van
Dong visited Singapore as part
of an ASEAN tour. At a press
conference in Singapore he
pledged non-interference in the
internal affairs of Southeast
Asian countries.

592

G.C. DE SILVA (PTE) LTD.
JEWELLERS
G 14, THE GALLERY, STRAITS TRADING BUILDING,
9 BATTERY ROAD, SINGAPORE 1. TEL. 915585

Estd. 1845

TUESDAY, OCTOBER 17, 1978

25 CENTS

M.C.(P) No. 214/1/78

Lee: We must end distrust

'MATCH WORDS WITH DEEDS'

By LESLIE FONG and S.M. MUTHU

SINGAPORE and Vietnam must establish confidence in each other by matching words with deeds, Mr. Lee Kuan Yew said last night.

Speaking at a dinner at the Istana in honour of visiting Vietnamese Premier Pham Van Dong, he said: "If we are to make South-east Asia a region

Quote

Until today, our knowledge of each other was limited to second-hand reports. However accurate and objective, they cannot equal the direct face-to-face encounter.

of peace and prosperity, we must remove distrust and reduce tensions."

The Prime Minister noted that Mr. Dong's statements about Vietnam not supporting subversion, directly and indirectly, made during visits to the other four Asean countries, were not solicited by his hosts — and said this made them all the more significant.

Mr. Lee welcoming Mr. Dong as he descends from the Air Vietnam jetliner.

DONG REPEATS PLEDGE

Vietnam will not support subversion

By LESLIE FONG and S. M. MUTHU

VIETNAMESE Prime Minister Pham Van Dong left yesterday after repeating his point about not supporting subversion —and being told that Asean cooperation is crucial to Singapore's national interests.

He described his two-day official visit as "successful" and expressed satisfaction that agreement was reached with Singapore on taking measures to promote trade and cooperation in economic, scientific and technical fields.

But he pointedly declined to put on record that Hanoi would relinquish hopes of "liberating" the people of South-east Asia and was generally evasive when repeatedly questioned on this at a press conference at the Istana before his departure.

Invitation

He was also vague about Vietnam's preference to talk to the Asean nations on a bilateral basis rather than as a regional group, saying this was a matter needing further discussion.

His talks with Mr. Lee Kuan Yew, who has accepted an invitation to pay an official visit to Vietnam at a time to be fixed later, took place in an atmosphere of "cordiality, friendship and mutual understanding."

Both sides, said a joint

593

594
Soon after this pledge, in November 1978, Vietnam signed a treaty with the Soviet Union which contained mutual security clauses. Then, armed with this insurance from a super-power, in December, Vietnam invaded and occupied Cambodia.

594

595

595/596
Vietnam's moves to control Indochina, especially its invasion of Cambodia in December 1978, brought it into conflict with China. This in turn increased Vietnam's military and economic dependence on the Soviet Union. The use of naval and air facilities in Vietnam by the Soviet military forces in the early 1980s brought a Russian military presence into Southeast Asia.

(Left) A Badger-C in flight. A number of Soviet TU-16

Badger maritime reconnaissance and attack aircraft were reported to be using Cam Ranh Bay, Vietnam, from late 1983. Long-range TU-95 Bear aircraft had been using Cam Ranh Bay from 1979.

(Below) The Soviet aircraft carrier *Minsk*. With a complement of helicopters and Vertical Take-Off and Landing aircraft, the *Minsk* was deployed to the Soviet Pacific Fleet in 1979.

596

597

The occupation of Cambodia by Vietnam put constant pressure on Thailand's military and economic resources.

Periodic Vietnamese offensives against Cambodian nationalists and civilians in the border areas drove many thousands of Cambodians into Thailand with whatever possessions they could carry with them.

598

In September 1981, leaders of three Cambodian resistance groups, Prince Norodom Sihanouk (left), Son Sann (centre) and Khieu Samphan (right) met in Singapore for discussions on the Cambodian problem. The three leaders agreed in principle on the formation of a coalition government to liberate their country from Vietnamese occupation, and signed a declaration of intent to this effect. Singapore and its ASEAN partners welcomed this move and expressed readiness to help the Cambodians realise their aim.

598

Foreign Relations

599

601
(Right) President Suharto of Indonesia during a state visit to Singapore from 29 to 31 August 1974.

602
(Far right) Malaysian Prime Minister, Datuk Seri Dr Mahathir Mohamad on an official visit to Singapore in December 1981.

603
(Bottom right) Sultan Hassanal Bolkiah of Brunei visits Singapore, January 1980.

600

Singapore continued to strengthen its regional and international relations. Special attention was paid to building up close relations with the ASEAN neighbours. In 1972, Prime Minister Lee Kuan Yew visited Malaysia; the following year, Indonesia and Thailand; and in 1974, the Philippines. Following this there were regular exchanges of visits with leaders of these countries. Relations with Malaysia were close, and there were several exchanges of visits between the prime ministers of the two countries. Singapore also had close ties with Brunei.

599
(Top) Prime Minister Lee Kuan Yew and Foreign Minister S Rajaratnam with Field Marshal Thanom Kittikachorn during an official visit to Thailand in January 1973.

600
(Above) Lee Kuan Yew with President Marcos during his visit to the Philippines in January 1974.

604

601

602

603

604

The first ASEAN Heads of Government Meeting held in Bali, Indonesia, on 23 and 24 February 1976.

The Bali Summit symbolised ASEAN's desire and determination to deal with regional developments on a collective basis. A Treaty of Amity and Cooperation and a Declaration of ASEAN Concord were signed at the Summit.

(Left to right): Lee Kuan Yew (Singapore), Datuk Hussein Onn (Malaysia), General Suharto (Indonesia), Ferdinand Marcos (Philippines), and Kukrit Pramoj (Thailand), signing the Declaration.

As a regional organisation, ASEAN also established links with the European Economic Community, the United States, Japan, Australia, New Zealand and Canada, whose foreign ministers had annual meetings with their ASEAN counterparts. ASEAN muted intra-regional differences, provided a framework for cooperation and enabled member countries to draw international attention and support to problems of the region much more effectively than any one member country would have been able to do on its own. ASEAN became a key facet of Singapore's foreign policy.

605/606/607/608
As part of Singapore's policy of friendship towards all, good relations were maintained not only with major trading partners and sources of investments but also with traditional Commonwealth friends, non-aligned countries and communist states.

The Prime Minister in the Soviet Union in 1970 with Premier Kosygin (right); in Egypt in 1975 with President Sadat (below); in Yugoslavia in 1975 with President Tito (below right); and in the People's Republic of China in 1976 with Chairman Mao Zedong (bottom).

605

606

607

608

609/610
Lee Kuan Yew with British
Prime Minister Margaret
Thatcher in 1979 (right); and
with American President
Reagan in 1981 (below).

609

610

611

611
Thirty-two nations participated
in the Commonwealth Heads of
Government Conference held
in Singapore from 14 to
22 January 1971.

612
Foreign ministers of the non-aligned nations meeting at the Bandaranaike Memorial Conference Hall in Colombo, Sri Lanka, on 11 August 1976.

At this conference, and at the summit meeting of non-aligned nations that followed, ASEAN countries played a significant role in exposing Vietnam's intentions in the region.

At the summit, Vietnam and its supporters called on the meeting to adopt a declaration supporting "the legitimate struggle of the peoples of Southeast Asia against neo-colonialism" and made reference to the need for the countries of the region to be "genuinely independent". In communist terminology, this meant asking the meeting to support the armed struggle of the various communist parties of the region against the governments.

612

613
(Right) Japanese Prime Minister Takeo Fukuda visited Singapore in August 1977 as part of his ASEAN tour after meeting ASEAN leaders at their Second Summit Meeting in Kuala Lumpur.

614
The Chinese Senior Vice-Premier Deng Xiaoping visited Singapore in November 1978.

In 1974 and 1975, Malaysia, the Philippines and Thailand established diplomatic relations with China despite reservations about China's support for communist revolutionaries in their countries.

However, Singapore and Indonesia, and later Brunei, did not follow suit. Singapore had publicly stated that it would take the step only after Indonesia had done so. The absence of formal ties, however, did not prevent Singapore and China from developing commercial ties. The two countries exchanged trade offices in 1981, and the Singapore Prime Minister visited China in 1976 and 1980.

615/616
Singapore strengthened its relations with West Asia. Among the West Asian dignitaries to visit Singapore were (below left) the Egyptian Vice-President Hosni Mubarak (May 1979) and (below) the Amir of Bahrain, Shaikh Isa bin Salman Al-Kalifa (June 1979).

Homage to a President

617
People from all walks of life await their turn at the Istana to pay their last respects to the late President Sheares. The President, serving his third four-year term in office, died after a short illness on 12 May 1981.

618
Prime Minister Lee Kuan Yew laying a wreath at the grave of President Sheares soon after the President was laid to rest. Looking on are members of the Cabinet, foreign heads of government and members of the diplomatic corps.

617

618

Economy

619

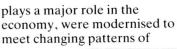

619
The Tanjong Pagar Container Terminal.

Facilities at the port, which plays a major role in the economy, were modernised to meet changing patterns of shipping. In 1979, Singapore overtook Yokohama to become the second busiest port in the world in terms of shipping tonnage.

620
Singapore took advantage of its strategic position to develop marine industries. Shiprepair and shipbuilding industries expanded in the 1970s, and Singapore became a major oil refining centre.

(Below) A typical cantilever jack-up rig built by Singapore yards.

621
Inside the $2,000 million petrochemical complex at Pulau Ayer Merbau.

620

621

A strategic location, judicious planning and investment, and efficient management enabled the Republic to become an important aviation, communications and tourist centre.

622/623
(Above) The Changi International Airport and (left) an interior view of the Passenger Terminal Building.

The airport began operations on 1 July 1981. Built at a cost of $1,500 million, it stretches over 1,663 hectares, part of it on reclaimed land.

624
Tourists in an antique shop. In 1983, 2.85 million tourists visited Singapore, compared to 521,654 in 1970 (not counting those who came by road and rail from Malaysia).

625

625
The earth satellite station at Sentosa.

Commissioned in 1971, the station provides telecommunication links with over 30 countries via the Pacific Ocean and Indian Ocean satellites of INTELSAT.

626

626
An aerial view of the industrial sector of Jurong Town which had 1,400 factories in 1983. Apart from Jurong, 21 smaller industrial estates with another 1,300 factories are situated in various parts of the island.

627

627/628/629
Manufacturing remained a key sector of the economy, accounting for 22.7 percent of the GDP (at current prices) in 1983 and employing 324,000 workers. To remain competitive in world markets, Singapore had to opt for high technology, high value-added industries. Low-skilled labour-intensive industries were being phased out.

High technology industries (left to right): workers at a computer firm; at a precision engineering plant; and at an aerospace firm.

628

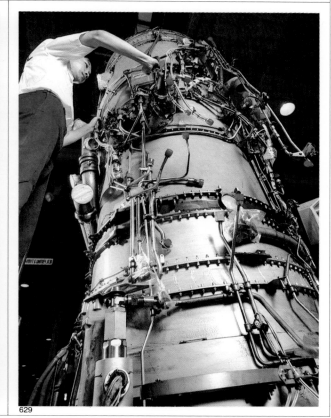

629

630

631

632

630
Shenton Way, the financial hub in the 1970s and early 1980s.

Singapore surged ahead as a financial centre with the expansion of the Asian Dollar and Foreign Exchange markets, the liberalisation of gold market dealings and the establishment of financial futures trading. Financial and business services remained the leading contributors to the overall economic expansion in the early 1980s.

631
Trading at the Singapore Stock Exchange.

632
The economic progress in the 1970s was reflected in the transformation of the physical appearance of Singapore through land reclamation, urban redevelopment, the construction of residential and commercial complexes, and major new highways.

(Right) A stretch of land reclaimed under the East Coast Reclamation Scheme. Between 1966 and 1977, 1,165 hectares were reclaimed from the sea under this scheme. In the foreground is part of the Marina Centre which has integrated hotel, shopping and convention facilities.

633

634

633
(Preceding pages)
The Benjamin Sheares Bridge
leading from the East Coast
Parkway to the city centre.
634
(Above) The East Coast
Parkway.
   High-capacity arterial
highways like these link various
parts of the island and have
reduced traffic congestion. In
1983 an average of $225 million
were spent on the expansion
and maintenance of roads.
   Despite major expansion of
the island's roads, the rapid
increase in the car population
from 1970 onwards placed a
heavy strain on the road
network. Several measures
were introduced to curb the
growth in car-ownership, for
there was a limit to the number
of new roads and expressways
that could be built on an island
with a very small land area.

635

635
The city centre's towering
office and residential blocks
overlooking the Singapore
River.

Social Development

636

With a small population base and no natural resources, Singapore gave priority to developing its human resources and talent. This was essential if the Republic was to make the grade as a centre of brain services and high technology industries. Technical institutions and polytechnics offered a wide range of courses designed to develop the skilled manpower required by industries. University education was expanded to provide the administrators, managers and specialists for a modern industrialised society.

636
(Above) The Singapore Polytechnic campus at Dover Road.

637

637
Final-year apprentices at the Japan-Singapore Technical Institute. The institute is one of several jointly run by the Economic Development Board with either foreign governments or with multinational companies for the transfer of technology to Singapore.

638

639

638/639
The National University of Singapore.

640

641

640
The Nanyang Technological Institute. It trains practice-oriented engineers.

641
Junior college students working with computers.

Computer education was introduced in 1980 in junior colleges, and computer clubs were established in secondary schools to give students a basic knowledge of computers. Computer software institutes were established in 1982 and 1983 to train computer personnel.

642

643

644

642/643
The successful public housing programme resulted in 77 percent of the population living in subsidised Housing and Development Board (HDB) flats by 1983. About 70 percent of the flats were owner-occupied.

Some of the recreational and sports facilities available to residents of public housing estates – playgrounds for children and swimming pools.

644
(Left) Private condominium housing. Apartments like these are sought after by Singaporeans in the higher income group who are not eligible for subsidised housing.

645

645

The availability of better health services increased the Singaporean's average life expectancy to 71.4 years. The proportion of the aged in the population was increasing. Higher standards of education and living resulted in new demands for leisure and recreation.

Under the "Sports for All" programme introduced in 1973, more swimming pools, tennis and squash courts, jogging tracks and fitness parks were constructed in housing estates enabling a wide cross-section of the population to enjoy sports facilities at little or no cost.

(Left) An aerial view of the National Stadium during the 1983 Southeast Asia Games. The stadium was completed in 1973.

646
A cycling track in East Coast Park.

646

647/648/649
National campaigns played an important part in the social development and public education programmes of the government.

647

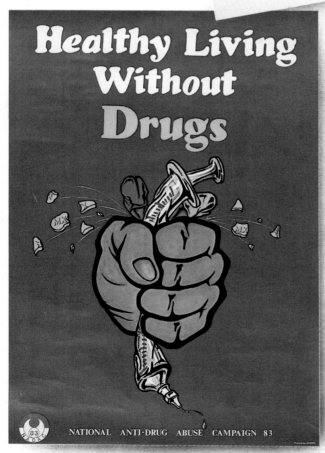

648

649

President Devan Nair

650

650
C V Devan Nair taking the oath as Singapore's third President on 24 October 1981. A former trade union leader, and Member of Parliament, he was born in Malacca on 5 August 1923. As secretary-general and later president of the National Trades Union Congress, he helped to transform the trade union movement so that it could play a participatory role in the social and economic development of Singapore.

The People

651

653

652

651/652/653/654

The government took a lead in promoting cultural activities. The policy was to preserve the vitality of Singapore's ethnic cultures while exposing Singaporeans to the best of music and arts from other countries.

655

The Singapore Symphony Orchestra, established in 1978, at a concert.

654

655

383

656

The Constitution guarantees
freedom of worship. The
preservation of communal and
religious harmony was regarded
as an essential prerequisite to
Singapore's progress.
656/657
Muslims at prayer and (right)
the Sultan Mosque.

657

658

659

658/659
Devotees at a Chinese temple
(above and left).

660

660/661
Christians at a church service.

661

662

663

662/663
Hindu devotees.

664

664
There were ample opportunities and facilities for young people to be involved in healthy and meaningful pastimes. Extra-curricular activities were an integral part of the school curriculum. An annual Youth Festival gave students an opportunity to bring out their talents in sports and the performing arts, and encouraged team work.

(Above) Students at the National Stadium at the start of the Youth Festival.

665
A brass band performance. Almost all schools had brass bands.

666
Students at a march-past.

667
A cultural performance.

665

666

667

INDEX

A

Abdul Rahman, Tunku 122, 124, 147, 189, 227, 230–231, 256–257, 269, 287, 310, 314; Baling Talks 169; proposes formation of Malaysia 190, 215–216; meets Sukarno 250; decision on separation of Singapore 270; letter to Dr Toh Chin Chye 288

Abdul Razak, Tun 269, 276, 312, 321

Adam Malik 311–312

Ahmad Ibrahim (Attorney-General) 143, 145, 195

Ahmad Ibrahim (MP) 149, 154, 193, 239

Aidit 247

Aik Ho Rubber Factory 120, 135

All Malaya Council of Joint Action 90

Aneka Ragam Ra'ayat 187, 196

Anglo-Malaysian Defence Agreement 321, 336, 346

Anti-British League 121

ANZUK – Australian, New Zealand and United Kingdom Forces 346

ASEAN – Association of Southeast Asian Nations 312, 337, 339; formation 295; first Heads of Government meeting in Bali 355

Asian Dollar Market 297

Azahari, A M 225, 247

B

Baharuddin bin Mohamed Ariff 190

Bali Summit (*see ASEAN*)

Baling Talks 169

Bandung Conference (Afro-Asian) 119, 126

Bani, S T 190, 210–211, 259

Bank of China 268

Barisan Sosialis 237, 239, 244–245; formation 191, 217; merger conditions 222; anti-Malaysia campaign 223–226, 240–241, 303–304; connection with Brunei Revolt 225, 247; 1963 election rally 258; boycott of Parliament 293–294, 303–304

Barker, E W 265

Bases Economic Conversion Department 297

Bersatu Padu 332

Black, Sir Robert 152

Black Thursday 151 (*see also Hock Lee Bus riots*)

Bose, Subash Chandra 62–63

Braga, A J 158

British Forces, in Second World War 15–18, 21, 29, 45, 55, 74; against riots 171; during confrontation 226, 255; against Brunei Revolt 247; withdrawal 295–296, 320, 346

British Military Administration 87–89, 106, 114

Brooke-Popham, Sir Robert 23

Brunei Revolt, 225, 247–248

Brunei Sultan 213

Buang Omar Junid 210–211

Bukit Ho Swee Fire (1961) 206–207

Byrne, Kenneth 124, 193, 211, 259

C

Caine, Sir Sydney 130

Cambodia 9, 337, 352

Campaigns 380

Chan Chiaw Thor 157, 185

Chan Choy Siong 154, 173, 193, 259

Chan Say Jame 154

Chan Sun Wing 211

Changi Airport 364

Changi Murals 65

Changi Prison 51, 54, 64, 85, 88, 106, 294

Chen Tien 169

Chew Swee Kee 156, 158

Chin Peng 108, 111, 169

China (*see People's Republic of China*)

Chinese Communist Party 12–13, 225

Chinese education 120, 122–123, 130, 227; first middle school 39; student agitation 118, 140–142, 153, 161, 170, 222, 233–237, 294, 305; All Party Committee 152, 157, 165; examination boycott (1961) 222, 233–235; Wang Gungwu Report 294; Thong Saw Pak Report 294, 305

Chinese High School 120–121, 130, 151, 153, 162, 170, 237

Chung Cheng High School 142, 151, 153, 162, 165, 170, 237

Chung Kuo Council (China National Council) 17, 39

Citizens' Consultative Committee 243, 265

Citizenship 89, 114, 124, 152–153, 157, 177; 1959 election 156; Singapore 188; Registry 203; on merger 221–222

City Council, elections 122, 143, 155–156, 173; strike 168; meetings in four languages 175

City Day 143–144

Civil Defence 15, 137, 337, 347

Civil Service, union 124; Commission on Malayanisation 157; pay cuts 188; Political Study Centre 188, 202, 301

Civilian Memorial 85

Cobbold Commission 221, 228

Commonwealth Heads of Government Conference 314, 358

Communist Party of Malaya (*see Malayan Communist Party*)

Communist united front 88, 110, 121–122, 124, 138, 151–155, 170–172

Community centres 237, 265

Confrontation 225–226, 250, 255, 270, 278–282, 295

Constitution Amendment Bill 293, 300

Constitutional Commission on Minority Rights 293, 300

Constitutional Talks, (1956) 152, 179; (1957) 153, 181; (1958) 154–155, 181; agreement 156

Cooper, Sir Alfred Duff 23

Council of Joint Action, (1946) 90; (1952) 124

Crown colony 89, 114

D

Dalforce (Singapore Chinese Anti-Japanese Volunteer Force) 17–18, 52

de Cruz, Gerald 89, 110, 324

Defence (*see Singapore*)

Democratic Party 123–124, 149

Development Bank of Singapore 297

Dewan Rakyat 269–270

Double Tenth Trial 106

E

East Coast reclamation scheme 368

East India Company 9, 11

Eber, John 110

Economic Development Board 189, 297

Eden Hall 217

Education 11, 124, 338; under Japanese Occupation 69; during British Military Administration 88; under Labour Front Government 157; four language streams 188, 222; under PAP Government 222–223, 233; computer 376; (*see also Chinese education*)

Education Ordinance (1957) 157, 188

Elections, Legislative Council (1948) 91, 117; Municipal Council (1949) 115; Legislative Council (1951) 123, 143; Legislative Assembly (1955) 148–149; City Council 155, 173; General (1959) 156, 182–185; Hong Lim (1961) 190, 214; Anson (1961) 190–191, 215; General (1963) 226, 258–259; Malaysian Parliamentary (1964) 268, 272; Hong Lim (1965) 270, 286; General (1968) 296, 322; Bukit Merah (1966) 303; General (1972, 1976, 1980) 336; Anson (1981) 344

Emergency Regulations 166; (*see also State of Emergency and Singapore*)

Employment Act 296

Employment Exchange 127

F

Fajar 146

Family Planning and

Population Board 328
Family Restaurants 97
Five–Power Defence
  Arrangement 336, 346
Fong Chong Pik, alias "Plen"
  155, 175, 214
Fong Sip Chee 259
Fong Swee Suan 121–122, 124,
  138, 151, 157, 185, 190–191,
  210–211, 225
Force 136 39
Foreign Relations (*see
  Singapore*)

G
General Labour Union 89, 109
Gimson, Sir Franklin 117, 120,
  135, 143
Goh Boon Toh 154
Goh Chew Chua 149, 154
Goh Keng Swee, Dr 123–124,
  189, 193, 208–209, 295,
  318–319, 322
Goho, S C 60, 117
Goode, Sir William 156, 158,
  177, 193–194
Govindasamy, P 259, 276

H
Haji Abdul Hamid bin Haji
  Jumaat 158
Harbour Board Staff
  Association 122
Hertogh, Maria Bertha 119,
  132–133
Ho See Beng 259
Hoalim Sr, Philip 89, 110
Hock Lee Bus Workers' Strike
  161
Hock Lee Riots 150–151,
  162–165, 237
Hoe Puay Choo 173, 193, 223,
  239
Home ownership for the
  people 297, 328
Hon Sui Sen 189, 311
Hong Lim by-election 190,
  214, 270
Housing 102, 119, 127, 188,
  204; Housing and
  Development Board 188,
  263, 297, 377

I
Indian Independence League
  62

Indian National Army 51, 55,
  62–63
Indonesia 125, 225, 254, 268,
  295, 298, 308, 316, 337
Industrial Arbitration Court
  189, 211, 297
Industrial Promotion Board 157
Industrial Relations
  (Amendment) Act 296
Industrial Relations Ordinance
  189, 211
Industrialisation (*see
  Singapore*)
Integrated schools 188
Internal Security Council 153,
  156, 181, 191, 214, 225
Ismail, Dr 256

J
Japan/Japanese, ambitions in
  Asia 12–13; Malayan
  campaign 16–18, 24–49;
  occupation of Singapore
  50–73; surrender 53, 78–79;
  prisoners of war 77, 96, 104;
  war crimes trials 88, 105–107;
  post-war relations with
  Singapore 337, 360
Jek Yeun Thong 190, 214, 238,
  277
Jeyaretnam, J B 344
Jumabhoy, J M 117, 158
Jurong 131, 189, 227; industrial
  estate 208, 296, 366
Jurong Town Corporation 322

K
Kalimantan Utara 225, 247
Kallang Airport 176, 178
Kandasamy, G 210–211
Kempeitai 52, 77, 88, 106–107
King Edward VII College of
  Medicine (*see Medical
  College*)
Konfrontasi (see confrontation)
Kranji War Memorial 84–85
Kuomintang (KMT) 12–13,
  16–17, 60, 76, 119

L
Labour Front 123–124,
  148–149, 151, 155–157, 166,
  170
Labour Party (*see Singapore
  Labour Party*)
Lai Teck 17, 61, 111

Lakshmi, Captain Dr S 63
Laycock, John 91, 117, 143
Lee Khoon Choy 270, 286
Lee Kong Chian 87
Lee Kuan Yew 123–124,
  145–147, 149, 172, 179, 190,
  192–193, 196, 202, 211–213,
  226, 230, 252, 256–257, 259,
  268–269, 285, 287, 301,
  354–361; legal adviser to
  unions 123, 145; formation of
  PAP 123–124, 147; 1955
  election 149; constitutional
  talks for self-government
  152, 179–180; meets the
  "Plen" 155, 175, 214; 1959
  election 156, 184–185; sworn
  in as Prime Minister 157;
  meets Sukarno 189, 213; calls
  vote of confidence 191; radio
  talks 221–222, 232; Afro-
  Asian tours 223, 238, 271;
  constituency tours 224,
  243–246; forums on merger
  240; in Malaysian Parliament
  268, 285; tries to persuade
  Tunku against separation
  270; campaigning in West
  Malaysia 272; on TV, on
  separation 290–291; at the
  Socialist International
  Conference 315; at 150-year
  celebrations 325–327
Lee Siew Choh, Dr 191, 214,
  217, 240, 259
Legislative Assembly 122–124,
  145, 148, 154, 157–159; four
  languages 187, 193; first
  meeting 194; debate on
  merger 223; approves
  Malaysia Agreement 252
Legislative Council 60, 91, 117,
  121–124, 143, 145
Lennox-Boyd, Alan 152, 176
Liberal Socialist Party 155–156,
  173, 183
Lim Bo Seng 39, 83
Lim Boon Keng, Dr 52, 60
Lim Chin Siong 121–122, 138,
  149, 153, 157, 170, 185,
  190–191, 210–211, 225, 247
Lim Guan Hoo 303
Lim Hong Bee 89
Lim Kean Chye 89
Lim Kim San 188, 310
Lim Yew Hock 91, 117, 123,

143, 145, 153; Chief Minister
  153–154, 170; showdown
  with communists 153–154,
  170–172; achievements 155,
  157; opposition leader 194
Lin Yu Tang, Dr 130
Lingam, S V 239
Loyalty Week 186–187, 199

M
MacDonald, Malcolm 129
Mahathir bin Mohamad,
  Datuk Seri Dr 354
Mahmud bin Awang 191, 216
Majid, M A 91
Malam Malaysia 220
Malay Education Advisory
  Committee 188
Malaya, Federation of 90–91,
  129, 156–157, 223, 252
Malaya Tribune, The 25
Malayan Chinese Association
  (MCA) 90, 124, 147, 169,
  226, 258
Malayan Communist Party
  (MCP) 13, 17, 52, 61, 108,
  110, 121, 123, 134, 138, 225,
  267, 337, 340, 349; founded
  12; influence in Chinese
  schools 12, 120–121, 130,
  151, 222–223; strategy of
  "peaceful" struggle 88; in
  trade unions 89–90, 109, 123,
  191, 249; resumption of
  armed struggle 90;
  insurgency 91, 111–113, 120,
  134–136; the 1951 directive
  138; Baling Talks 169 (*see
  also Malayan People's Anti-
  Japanese Army*)
Malayan Democratic Union
  88–91, 110, 124
Malayan Indian Congress 267
Malayan People's Anti-
  Japanese Army (MPAJA)
  17, 39, 52–53, 61, 88–89,
  108–109
Malayan Union 89
Malaysia 266–273, 283–290;
  proposal for 215, 221; White
  Paper on merger 221, 232;
  sharing of revenue 221,
  267–268; promulgation of
  226; Agreement 226, 250,
  252, 267; publicity drive 229,
  240; Malaysia Day

celebrations 256;
proclamation of 257;
common market 267–268;
1964 general election 268,
272
Malaysia Solidarity
Consultative Committee 229
Malaysian Solidarity
Convention 266, 269, 283
Mallal, N A 91, 117, 143, 145
Mao Zedong 119, 126, 356
Maria Hertogh Riots 119–120,
132–133
Marshall, David, forms Labour
Front 123; 1955 election
148–149; as Chief Minister
151–152, 158–160, 166, 169;
City Council elections 155,
175; achievements 157;
Anson by-election 191,
215–216; radio forum 240
Medical College (King Edward
VII) 88, 102, 129
Merdeka Rally 178
Merdeka Talks (see
Constitutional Talks)
Merger 221–225, 228–232, 238,
240–242, 250–253, 256–257;
early reactions to 190, 216;
Council of Joint Action 223;
White Paper 223; options on
223–224; citizenship 224;
referendum on 224, 241–242;
(see also Malaysia)
Mountbatten, Admiral Lord
Louis 53, 78, 81, 108
Municipal Commission 115
Municipal Council 115

N
Nair, C V Devan 121–122, 124,
149, 153, 157, 185, 191, 210,
238, 268, 273, 324, 381
Nair, M P D 143, 177, 303
Nanyang Communist Party 11
Nanyang Girls' High School
120, 130, 151
Nanyang Hua Chiao Middle
School 39
Nanyang Siang Pau 57, 337, 348
Nanyang Technological
Institute 376
Nanyang University 120,
130–131, 177, 227, 258, 260,
294, 305
National Iron and Steel Mills

208, 227
National Junior College 330
National Service 118, 121, 139,
141; during Indonesian
confrontation 278; Bill 294;
Amendment Act 295; first
recruits (1967) 317; send-off
party 318
National Theatre 262
National Trades Union
Congress 191, 219, 296, 324
National University of
Singapore 375
Naval Base 13, 37, 297
Naval Base Labour Union 122
Nehru, Pandit Jawaharlal 119,
125–126, 223, 271
Ngee Ann College 294,
305, 307
Nicoll, Sir John 143, 158
Non-aligned Conference 359

O
Oehlers, Sir George 159,
193, 195
Ong Chye Ann 154
Ong Eng Guan 155, 174, 190,
193, 214, 226–227, 259,
269–270
Ong Pang Boon 193
Onn bin Jafaar, Dato 89
Operation "Cold Store" 225,
249
Operation Pantai Chantek
197
Othman Wok 276, 286
Overseas Chinese Association
52, 60

P
Pan-Malayan Federation of
Trade Unions 89–90
Partai Kommunis Indonesia
223, 225, 247, 294, 308
Partai Ra'ayat Brunei 223,
225, 247
Pasir Panjang Power
Station 263
Paya Lebar Airport 176
Pearl Harbour 16
People's Action Party (PAP),
inauguration 123–124, 147;
1955 election 124, 149;
change in Constitution 154;
communist attempt for
control 154, 172, 175;

Central Executive
Committee 154, 175; and
the communists 154, 187,
189, 191, 237; in the City
Council 155, 173; 1959
election 156, 182–185; first
Cabinet 157, 193; split in
190–191, 214–219; 1963
election 226–227, 258–259;
achievements during first
term 227; as minority
government 239; 1964
Malaysian election 268,
272–273; 1968 election 296,
322; 1972, 1976, 1980
elections 336
People's Association 190–191,
202, 217–218, 265
People's Constitution 90
People's Defence Force
137, 318
People's Kitchens 97
People's Republic of China
9–10, 13, 15–16, 119–120,
125–126, 356
People's Restaurants 87, 96–97
Percival, Lt–Gen Sir Arthur
16, 18, 44–47, 64
Pham Van Dong 351
Pioneer certificates 209
"Plen" (see Fong Chong Pik)
Political Study Centre 188,
202, 301
Preservation of Public Security
Ordinance 152
Prince of Wales 15–16, 24, 31
Progressive Party (see
Singapore Progressive Party)
Public Utilities Board 263
PUTERA – Pusat Tenaga
Rakyat 90
Puthucheary, Dominic 190,
210, 225, 247
Puthucheary, James 121–122,
153, 157, 191, 225

R
Raffles College 51, 88, 129
Raffles, Sir Stamford 9–10
Rahim Ishak 238
Rajah, T T 154
Rajaratnam, Sinnathamby 123,
147, 193, 196–197, 229, 240,
270, 294, 312
Ranee of Jhansi Regiment 63

Rashid Mydin 169
Referendum 222–224, 241–242
Rendel Commission 122–123,
145
Rendel Constitution 123–124,
148, 155, 158
Rendel, Sir George 122, 145
Repulse 15–16, 24, 31
Residents' committees 338
Riots, National Service 118,
121, 140–142; Maria
Hertogh 119–120, 132–133;
Hock Lee 150–151, 161–165;
of (1956) 153, 170–171;
communal 269, 274–277
Rose, Sir Alan 195

S
Sahorah bte Ahmat 193
Said Zahari 225
Samad Ismail 124
School Registration Ordinance
120
Secret societies 102, 157
Selkirk, Lord 191, 217
Sembawang Shipyard Ltd 297,
323
Sheares, Dr Benjamin Henry
341, 361
Shonan Times 57–58
Sihanouk, Norodom 315, 353
Sin Chew Jit Poh 57
Singapore, Pre-World War II
9–13; defence of 14–15,
295–296, 336, 346–347;
Emergency 15, 91, 112–113,
120–121, 123–124, 135–136,
152, 169; surrender of 18, 45;
occupation of 51–73, 81, 85,
87–88; post-war living
conditions 86–87, 92–103; as
Crown Colony 89, 114;
self-government 122, 155,
157; flag 187, 198, 200;
anthem 187, 201; economy
188–189, 205, 208–209, 227,
296–298, 338–340, 362–374;
plans for industrialisation
189, 227, 296; crest 200;
independence 226, 252, 267,
270, 293; separation from
Malaysia 270, 288–290;
proclamation of 289;
admission to UN 295, 299;
foreign and trade relations
298, 310–315, 337–338,

354–360; 150-year celebrations 325–327; factors behind success 339
Singapore Air Defence Command 295
Singapore Airlines 364
Singapore Alliance 226, 258
Singapore Armed Forces 331, 336, 347
Singapore Armed Forces Training Institute 295, 319
Singapore Association of Trade Unions (SATU) 191, 227, 261
Singapore Bus Workers' Union 122, 151, 161
Singapore Chinese Chamber of Commerce 60, 87, 123
Singapore Chinese Middle School Students' Union 152–153
Singapore Factory and Shop Workers' Union 122, 151, 153, 170
Singapore Family Planning and Population Board 297, 328
Singapore Improvement Trust 102, 188, 205
Singapore Infantry Regiment 218, 279, 282, 332
Singapore Labour Party 91, 123, 149
Singapore Maritime Command 295
Singapore People's Alliance 156, 170, 183, 223
Singapore Polytechnic 176, 374
Singapore Progressive Party 91, 115, 117, 123–124, 143, 149
Singapore Town Committee 121
Singapore Volunteer Corps 60, 137
Singh, Jamit 122, 190, 210–211
Sook Ching 52, 56, 88, 107
Soon Kwong 89, 109
"Sports For All" programme 379
Sreenivasan Commission 157
State of Emergency 15, 91, 112–113, 120–121, 123–124, 135–136, 169
Straits Settlements 11, 89, 114
Straits Settlements Volunteer Corps 15, 20, 22

Straits Times, The 24
Strikes 108–109, 123, 151, 161–168, 218–219, 227, 233, 261, 294, 307
Subandrio, Dr 189, 212
Suharto, President 294–295, 354–355
Sukarno, Dr 119, 125–126, 189, 225–226, 250, 278, 294
Syed Jaffar Albar 268–269
Syonan 51, 58, 66, 70, 106–107
Syonan Jit Poh 57
Syonan Shimbun 24, 57, 69

T

Tan, C C 91, 117, 143–145
Tan Cheng Lok 90, 124, 147, 169
Tan Chin Tuan 87, 117, 143–145
Tan Chong Kin 154, 185
Tan Kah Kee 17, 39
Tan Kong Guan 154
Tan Lark Sye 120, 131
Tann Wee Tiong 154
Thio Chan Bee 117, 143
Thomas, Francis 91, 123, 158
Thomas, Sir Shenton 23–24, 42, 64
Thompson, G G 301
Thong Saw Pak Report 294
Toh Chin Chye, Dr 123, 147, 154, 190, 192–194, 229, 259, 270, 282, 289, 299
Trade Union Congress 191, 210–211, 219
Trade Union Ordinance 90, 294

U

UMNO 89–90, 122, 124, 226–227, 258, 267–269
UMNO Alliance 122, 149, 151, 156, 226
Unemployment 119, 127, 188, 205, 296
United Nations 225, 295; receives views on merger 223; survey mission to Borneo 250, 254; admits Singapore 299
United People's Party 190, 214, 226, 239
University of Malaya (in Singapore) 120–121, 129–130
University of Malaya Socialist Club 146

V

Vietnam 9, 337, 350, 352
Vigilante Corps 278–279

W

Wang Gungwu Report 294
War Crimes Trials 88, 105–107
War Memorial 84–85
Wavell, General Archibald 18, 23, 42
Winsemius, Dr Albert 189, 209
Woodhull, S 122, 153, 157, 190–191, 210–211, 225, 240
Work Brigade 190–191, 217
Workers' Party 155–156, 191, 223
Wu Tien Wang 87–88

Y

Ya'acob Mohamed 322
Yamashita, Lt–Gen Tomoyuki 17–18, 45–47, 51, 55, 58, 60, 69, 81, 107
Yang di-Pertuan Agung 252, 257, 269, 284–285
Yang di-Pertuan Negara 193–195, 257
Yong Nyuk Lin 193, 328
Yusof bin Ishak 187, 195, 198–199, 213, 256–257, 300, 310, 333

Z

Zubir Said 201

PHOTO CREDITS

Figures refer to picture numbers

Cover
City Hall and Supreme Court — by Low Chin Hai.

Introduction
The Padang, 1851: An oil painting by J T Thomson — National Museum; Sir Stamford Raffles: An 1817 painting by Joseph — National Museum; Chinese immigrants arriving at Boat Quay — Archives and Oral History Department; The Esplanade, 1905: A painting by A L Watson — National Museum; Empress Place — Archives and Oral History Department.

Chapter 1
44, 45 — Archives and Oral History Department; 19 — Associated Press, New York; 2, 8, 31, 36, 38, 40, 46 — Australian War Memorial; 29, 49, 54 — Collection of T Sato, Tokyo; 3, 4, 5, 6, 9, 10, 11, 12, 13, 14, 23, 24, 25, 28, 32, 33, 34, 35, 41, 42, 55, 58 — Imperial War Museum, London; 57 — Kyodo News Service, Tokyo; 27, 47, 53, 56, 59, 60 — Mainichi Shimbun, Tokyo.

Chapter 2
67, 76 — Archives and Oral History Department; 83, 84, 85 — Australian War Memorial; 66, 87, 88, 95, 103 — Chuang Hui Tsuan Collection; 64, 65, 72, 73, 100 — Collection of T Sato, Tokyo; 74, 75, 79, 80, 105, 106, 107, 108, 109, 110, 111, 112, 113, 114, 115, 116, 117, 118, 119, 122 — Imperial War Museum, London; 61, 81, 82, 98, 99, 101, 102 — Mainichi Shimbun, Tokyo; 86, 93, 120, 123, 124, 125, 126, 127 — Ministry of Culture; 121 — Royal Commonwealth Society, London; 68, 69, 89, 90, 92, 94, 96, 97 — Sentosa Wax Museum.

Chapter 3
171, 184, 186 — Archives and Oral History Department; 128, 129, 130, 131, 133, 134, 137, 138, 140, 141, 146, 147, 148, 149, 150, 151, 155, 156, 157, 158, 159, 160, 161, 162, 164, 183 — Imperial War Museum, London; 132, 139, 152, 153, 154, 175, 176, 177, 178, 180, 181, 185 — Ministry of Culture; 182 — Popperfoto, London; 168, 169, 170 — The Straits Times.

Chapter 4
205, 230 — Archives and Oral History Department; 188, 189, 190, 191 — Associated Press, New York; 211, 212, 213 — Federal Photo Library, Information Department, Kuala Lumpur; 214 — Imperial War Museum, London; 187, 208, 209, 210, 220, 221, 225, 226, 228 — Ministry of Home Affairs; 192, 193, 194, 195, 196, 200, 201, 206, 218, 219, 223, 224, 231, 232, 233, 236, 237, 238, 239, 240, 241, 242, 243, 244, 245 — Ministry of Culture; 198, 199, 235 — National University of Singapore; 202 — Nanyang Girls' High School; 197, 203, 204, 207, 222, 234 — The Straits Times.

Chapter 5
299 — Associated Press, New York; 247, 253, 292, 295 — David Marshall Collection; 246, 254, 255, 256, 257, 258, 259, 260, 263, 264, 265, 267, 269, 270, 274, 275, 276, 277, 278, 286 — Ministry of Home Affairs; 248, 249, 250, 251, 252, 271, 272, 273, 281, 282, 283, 284, 285, 287, 288, 289, 290, 291, 293, 294, 296, 297, 298, 300, 301, 302, 303, 304, 305, 306, 307, 308, 309 — Ministry of Culture; 261, 262, 266, 268 — The Straits Times.

Chapter 6
310, 311, 312, 313, 314, 315, 316, 317, 318, 319, 320, 321, 322, 323, 324, 325, 326, 327, 328, 329, 330, 331, 332, 333, 334, 335, 338, 339, 340, 341, 342, 343, 344, 345, 346, 347, 348, 349, 350, 351, 352, 353, 354, 355, 356, 357, 358, 359, 360, 361, 362, 363, 364, 365, 367, 368, 369, 370, 371, 372, 373, 374 — Ministry of Culture; 337 — Public Utilities Board; 336 — The Straits Times.

Chapter 7
392 — Archives and Oral History Department; 412, 414, 424 — Associated Press, New York; 391 — Ministry of Home Affairs; 375, 376, 377, 378, 379, 380, 381, 382, 383, 384, 385, 389, 390, 393, 394, 396, 397, 398, 399, 400, 401, 402, 403, 406, 407, 417, 418, 421, 422, 423, 428, 429, 430, 432, 433, 434, 436, 437, 438, 439, 441, 442, 443, 444, 445, 446 — Ministry of Culture; 404, 405, 408, 409, 410, 411 — Nan Yang Xing Zhou Lianhe Zaobao; 440 — Public Utilities Board; 386, 387, 388, 413, 431 — The Straits Times; 419, 420 — United Press International, New York.

Chapter 8
465 — Associated Press, New York; 447, 448, 449, 450, 451, 452, 454, 455, 456, 457, 458, 459, 460, 461, 462, 463, 464, 466, 467, 468, 469, 470, 472, 473, 474, 475, 476, 477, 480, 481, 482, 483, 484, 485, 486, 487, 488 — Ministry of Culture; 478, 479 — The New Straits Times, Kuala Lumpur; 471 — The Straits Times.

Chapter 9
508, 510, 533, 535 — Associated Press, New York; 492, 493, 494, 495, 496, 498, 499, 503, 504, 506, 511, 512, 513, 514, 516, 517, 518, 519, 520, 522, 527, 528, 529, 531, 532, 536, 537, 538, 539, 540, 542, 543, 544, 545, 546, 547, 548, 549, 550, 551, 552, 553, 554, 555, 558, 559, 561 — Ministry of Culture; 556, 557, 560 — Ministry of Defence; 524, 525 — P S Raman Collection; 541 — Sembawang Shipyard Ltd; 485, 500, 502, 530 — The Straits Times; 490, 491, 515, 516 — United Press International, New York.

Chapter 10
605 — Alex Josey Collection; 612 — Associated Press, New York; 620 — Far East Levingston Shipbuilding Ltd; 626 — Jurong Town Corporation; 657, 666, 668 — by Lim Seng Tiong; 562, 658, 662 — by Low Chin Hai; 563, 564, 565, 566, 567, 568, 569, 570, 571, 572, 573, 574, 575, 576, 577, 578, 579, 580, 582, 585, 592, 598, 599, 600, 601, 602, 603, 604, 606, 607, 609, 610, 611, 613, 614, 615, 616, 617, 618, 619, 621, 622, 623, 625, 627, 628, 630, 631, 632, 633, 634, 635, 636, 637, 639, 640, 641, 642, 643, 644, 645, 646, 647, 648, 649, 650, 656, 659, 660, 661, 663, 664, 665, 667 — Ministry of Culture; 583, 584 — Ministry of Defence; 629 — Singapore Aero-Engine Overhaul (Pte) Ltd; 624 — Singapore Tourist Promotion Board; 581, 588, 589, 590, 591, 651, 652, 653, 654, 655 — The Straits Times; 638 — by Wong Kwok Kwong; 608 — Xinhua News Agency, Beijing.

ACKNOWLEDGEMENTS

Many people helped to produce this book. It is impossible to individually name all those who have contributed ideas, expertise and photographs.

Mention must however be made of Mr S R Nathan, Dr Yeo Kim Wah, Mr Lee Ting Hui, Dr Edwin Lee, Prof Lee Soo Ann, Assoc Prof Ernest Chew and Prof Edwin Thumboo of the National University of Singapore; and the Curriculum Development Institute of Singapore.

The Ministry of Culture also thanks persons and organisations who willingly provided photographs from their collections. The picture sources are all credited on the photo credits page. Special acknowledgement however, is due to the Imperial War Museum, London; Australian War Memorial; Mainichi Shimbun; Kyodo News Service; T Sato; Information Department, Kuala Lumpur; Sentosa Wax Museum; The Straits Times; the National Library; Archives and Oral History Department; and staff of the photographic section of the Ministry of Culture.

Many individuals, both in the Ministry of Culture and outside, worked with dedication and over long hours. Mr Yeo Siak Goon deserves special mention for his graphic presentation.

Much is also owed to SNPL (Book Publications Dept), who in association with Pica Colour Separation Pte Ltd and Kyodo-Shing Loong Industries, designed and produced the book.